LOVE
IN THE MIDST
OF GRIEF

SATENAM SINGH JOHAL

MEMOIRS
Cirencester

Published by Memoirs

MEMOIRS
P U B L I S H I N G

Memoirs Books

25 Market Place, Cirencester, Gloucestershire, GL7 2NX
info@memoirsbooks.co.uk www.memoirspublishing.com

ISBN 978-1-908223-81-4

Printed in England

IN LOVING MEMORY OF PARMJIT & GURJIT

And within the continued love of family & dear friends

Enabled by the grace of God

Dedicated to my father, the late Mr Sohan Singh Johal,
husband of Mrs Avtar Kaur Johal

LOVE VERSUS PAIN

Pain has an intense and overwhelming impact that tends to affect our emotional, rational, physical and spiritual existence because the event experienced threatens to test the very foundation that is intended to sustain us. Yet the pain reveals something more powerful than itself; love. We have to believe that.

CONTENTS

PREFACE

This book was written in the wake of a devastating double tragedy; the deaths of my two beloved brothers-in-law, Parmjit in 2001 and Gurjit in 2003, though we did not discover that Parmjit had died until after Gurjit's death.

Through reading, studying and talking to my family, close friends and colleagues, I began to consider what we were learning about the trauma of death. Pondering this made me realise that there was so much to say. Yet I knew that I could at least begin to try and express some of my family's experiences of how we responded to death. I say 'some of my family's experiences' because I believed that our feelings, thoughts and views would have to be reviewed with the passing of time.

There was no doubt that this would be a demanding, challenging and difficult task to undertake, because of the emotional pain associated with these personal experiences. They were I knew steeped in a private and internal intimacy and needed time to be unravelled and understood, both on an individual basis and within a family unit.

I believe it is difficult to deal with the impact of death within our relationships without developing our awareness of the impact of the loss, and without support which has to be timely, of quantity and durable enough to allow the trauma experienced to be properly explored.

As a family I did not believe that we could simply leave such issues alone in the hope that one day we would automatically explore and then 'recover' from the trauma. Rather it had to be a concerted effort, namely by adults, to ensure that we facilitated an environment of 'enabling'.

In order to facilitate this, for me the most influential factor was knowing, believing and understanding (though in a limited way) that God exists and is foundational to all development. My belief is not based upon seeking comfort but rather on recognising that pain and distress will be present, yet hope and love will triumph.

By writing this book I recognise that having a belief in God for many people is a deep truth which provides refuge in the midst of vulnerability. At the same time I also appreciate that many people may feel more distressed thinking God did not respond in their case, while others may just not believe that He exists.

What I can say, knowing that my knowledge must be limited, is that my learning is personal. For me this has involved recognising that God cannot be known, believed and understood by my comprehension, only through His love, grace, peace, hope and faith.

It is with the above in mind that I will outline the purpose of writing this book, which has been:

- To communicate that there is hope even when someone has died. This is not a blind hope that ignores misery, rather it is a living and active hope which resides within us and is capable of responding to the trauma experienced. To reveal that expression of our experiences is crucial, and this requires love and patience in providing each other with support in order to explore the trauma that has taken place due to a death.

- To introduce a 'Family Development Support Structure' which can be adapted by individuals and families to enable them to begin to explore their personal experiences due to death. (This is not about seeking to bring about resolution, rather identifying ways in which questions can be asked to encourage discussion).

The book is in two sections. Parts 1 and 2 provide a description of how as a family we experienced the death of two family members within the space of 13 months. Part 3 outlines some of the discussions that took place as a family about our experiences and how this affected our development.

I hope this book enables you to have the opportunity to explore the experiences which have affected you and your loved ones. By doing so I further hope you will be able to embrace the support you need to equip yourself for facing the pain that has been endured.

This book does not have the answers to all life's questions, as upon reading it is clear that limitations exist, yet true strength resides in knowing that we will face many challenges, yet can still encounter love. That is my hope for you.

MY FAMILY

I could write a book on my parents' life - and one day I hope to be able to do so, in order to do true justice to what they taught me. However, for the purpose of this book, I will simply provide a very brief snapshot of my family. What I would say is that they are not perfect and certainly our experiences have influenced our responses. Such experiences are unique on one level, yet I believe can be related to by others, simply because we all experience the joys and sorrows of life.

My father left India in 1956 to come to England, leaving my mother behind, along with his parents and five sisters. His hope, along with many people who had migrated from abroad, was to build a future for his family. My mother joined him in 1961.

My parents purchased a home in Wednesbury, West Midlands, while my father worked in a foundry in Oldbury, five miles away. He used to work six days a week, and get up every morning between 2 am and 3 am to walk to the foundry to open up the building, as his boss trusted him to do so. He did this for more than 10 years before he was able to buy a home close to where he worked. My mother worked part-time for an engineering company in Blackheath, West Midlands. I believe that like many parents of their generation they truly understood the meaning of self-sacrifice.

They raised seven children (five daughters and two sons), of which I am the youngest. Diljit was born in 1961, Dilwant in 1964, Gurbakash in 1965, Jai in 1966, Parmjit in 1967, Sarnjit in 1970 and I was born in 1971.

When we were children family life was always fun and exciting and I can recall many memories which bring happiness and tears. Most of all I remember the many stories my parents told me over the years, ranging from their own childhood and life in India to their hopes for us children.

Through listening to their stories I began to realise the difficulties they had endured in coming to live in England, and that many of these difficulties were shared by other migrant workers. However they also spoke positively about many families they had met who had supported them, and vice versa.

It was amazing to hear such stories, and fascinating to recognise how hard they had worked for my siblings and me, and for their wider extended family. I held them in high esteem for the way they had conducted themselves.

Upon reflection I realised that they were teaching me through the demonstration of their own conduct - their actions spoke louder than their words. Such learning entailed always showing love, not living life in anger, taking responsibility for caring for people and importantly having a belief in God.

This brings me on to my two brothers-in-law, Parmjit and Gurjit, about whom this book is written. I always refer to them as my older brothers. My eldest sister Diljit (known as Dee) married Parmjit in 1981 when she was 20. Parmjit came from India to England in the same year, when he was 24 years old. They had two sons, Baljit, born in 1982, and Amarjit, born in 1985.

Parmjit was referred to by my parents as their eldest son, for they saw him as a son and not a son-in-law; hence he was big brother to Jai and me. He was physically strong, yet I knew that emotionally he was at times fragile when it came to his family. Just like my parents, he would tell us stories about his life in India and the many funny incidents he had experienced.

I knew Parmjit was very family orientated and took his responsibilities as a husband and father seriously, as well as the responsibility of being the eldest son to my parents, whom he loved and valued. He was a very hard-working man, very caring, respectful, considerate, yet funny and entertaining.

Thus it was with great heartache that I watched this man, who I knew loved, cared for and respected his family, being consumed by alcohol. It was hard to see how he began to associate with people who did not have his best interests at heart. Seeing him deteriorate was difficult for my family, especially for my sister, who had to watch her husband wither away, and my two nephews who saw their father become more and more distant to the point whereby he was unable to function and engage within the family. A once loving, caring, kind and considerate man, he was no longer able to treasure those whom he had held dear in his heart. Yet we never stopped loving and supporting him in addressing the alcohol addiction which had arrested his development. Such intervention often helped him to address his difficulties, but in the long term he was not able to sustain the changes he made. There was no lack of effort on his part.

I felt he was a good man and that his behaviour was not meant to cause anyone harm, because I remembered the man he was and not what alcohol had done to him. I knew the hours he spent living in deep distress, struggling against what he was doing, and how he had tried so hard to take responsibility. I knew deep down that he was always loved by us and that he loved us in spite of his limitations.

This takes me on to Gurjit, Parmjit's younger brother. Gurjit came to England from India in 1986 when he was 27 years old. He got married in 1986 to my second eldest sister Dilwant, known as Dilly. They had two daughters, Baljinder, born in 1988, and Sukvinder, born in 1993. So two brothers married two sisters.

Gurjit was like Parmjit in many ways. The one difference between them was that Gurjit was a very patient man who always remained calm no matter how much we used to wind him up. In fact I had never heard Gurjit raise his voice against anyone, which was quite amazing and something to learn from. Parmjit on the other hand would get annoyed if he felt anyone was being cheeky to him, or if he felt cheated in a game. This was hilarious, as both of them were the greatest card cheats I had come across, so they did not stand much chance when they tried to argue the point over cheating. Like Parmjit, Gurjit also took his responsibilities towards his family very seriously and always referred to my parents as his father and mother, just as Parmjit did.

Gurjit was loving, very family focused, wise with words, very considerate and loyal to his family. He was such a nice man and was not afraid to show his emotions. His only fault in my eyes was that he supported Manchester United Football Club. This brought many hours of fun just teasing him about it, and I write this with joy in my heart.

I held them in high esteem because I knew they were my brothers, not an addition to my family, and we loved them so much. I believe the love implanted within us sustained us as all a family.

Now to the rest of my family. Gurbakash (known as Patty) moved to Canada in 1989 and got married. She has two children, a daughter Kirin, born in 1990, and a son Arvinder, born in 1993. My sister divorced in 1996 and remained in Canada with her children.

Jai and Mangender got married in 2000. They have one daughter, Sonia, born in 2001. About four months before they got married my mother became ill and remained in hospital for almost a month. As soon as she came home, my father was taken seriously ill. He was diagnosed with cancer, as well as a number of related difficulties.

Parmjit (known as Pars) left the family home in 1994. She decided to leave to achieve her own independence, because of her religious beliefs. It was not what my parents wanted, as due to their cultural and religious beliefs they wanted her to adhere to their own traditions. It was difficult for my parents to accept her decision, but they were not in a position to change her view. This resulted in Parmjit choosing to form her own identity away from the family and associate with people who had the same religious beliefs as herself. This did not stop us from seeking to maintain our relationship with her, but my parents did not as they disagreed with her decision.

Sarnjit, known as Sam, left the family home in 1995 when she met her partner Darren. Like Parmjit my parents had the same expectations of her, yet she choose to make her own life. Again we maintained a relationship with her, and again my parents did not. Sam and Darren have a son named Aaron who was born in 2003.

Despite my Sikh background, I myself chose to adopt the Christian faith from the age of 18. It may help to explain parts of this book to say at this point that I am a social worker. I qualified in 1998 and have worked in local authority, voluntary and private sector organisations, where my experiences have centred on child protection and safeguarding.

Overall I look at the lives of my parents, siblings and nephews and nieces and realise how truly blessed I have been to have walked with them through life, thanks to the love and grace of God.

WHO'S WHO

EXTENDED FAMILY & FRIENDS

Gurdev - Cousin-Sister

Harjinder - Cousin-Brother

Sunny - Niece

Bobby - Nephew

Kiran - Niece

Narinder - Niece

Gugs - Nephew

Chima - Cousin-brother

Laker - Cousin-brother

Ravi - Dear family friend

George - Dear family friend

Carlo - Dear family friend

TITLES AND TERMINOLOGY

Baba - Grandfather

Nan - Grandmother

Titha - Paternal uncle (elder brother)

Chacha - Paternal uncle (younger brother)

Mama - Maternal uncle

Massi - Maternal aunt

Gurdwara - Sikh temple

ACKNOWLEDGEMENTS

Where can I begin to start to acknowledge the dearest people in my life? The truth of the matter is that every family member and friend has enabled purpose in my life in a way that has been beyond imagining, and has enhanced my life in such a blessed and meaningful way, particularly my late father, a man who taught me through example so much about love, commitment, respect, kindness and hope, and my mother, who always encouraged me to focus upon others and always had her children's interests at heart.

My siblings have always played a major role in my life, and them just being there has been a tremendous support and encouragement as many of the challenges faced have been endured together. Yet, and say so with great admiration, the role of my nephews and nieces has been without doubt a central part of my life, because they have truly taught me resilience. Their presence has always brought great joy, peace and hope to my heart, and just as many children and young people have experienced hardships and traumas, they have shown that ultimately they have endured because their deep love for each other is the firm foundation in their life. I could write a book simply about them, as well as the children I have worked with over the years who have shown great determination in the midst of adversity.

Now to my dearest friends, Ravi and Sunita, who have supported and guided my family and me through our experiences. Their loyalty and love have been a great asset and comfort. To Dal, who patiently read the manuscript and offered great insights into my own emotions and thoughts, and encouraged me to complete the book. His objective approach I found useful, as it provided positive challenge in how I began to write down such experiences.

PART 1

GURJIT

My reason for telling this story about what unfolded within my family is to highlight that we all, to varying degrees, battle to explore what we believe and to learn from and understand what our experiences are about. Such story-telling will always be personal and in reality cannot be based upon perfection, because the trauma of death will surface in many different ways to challenge what we do and how we respond.

For me, this and the next chapter and the detail they hold set the scene for what I know was 'therapy' at work. However detailed, they do not present every perspective but offer you, the reader, access to my personal experience with a hope that as you explore a similar experience, that healing will arise within you, because it certainly supported me at the time required.

You may notice repetition in this section. The reason for this is to show that death is not a subject area that can be addressed simply by thinking that once spoken about, there is no further need to explore. The repetition will also show that it is required in attending to the pain caused by death, because the mind will battle with the emotional trauma.

The names of doctors and non-family members have been changed to ensure anonymity.

CHAPTER ONE

A MYSTERIOUS ILLNESS

As I relaxed in the barber's chair and asked him for a number two all-over cut, I could not have imagined that the next phone call I received would have such an impact on the lives of those I love and myself in such a way as it did.

It was Friday 24th January 2003. I was off work that day and at the barber's, and he was working the clipper up the back of my neck when my phone rang – it was my sister Dilly. The time was 9.30 am. It was not unusual for my elder sister to call me early in the morning.

She told me that Gurjit had fallen in the shower. The hairdresser waited patiently to finish my haircut as Dilly continued to tell me that she had managed to get him up and that she thought he was fine. There was a strange note in her voice, but I brushed the thought to one side.

When my haircut was done I went straight to Dilly's to find Gurjit sitting in bed, wearing a T-shirt and pyjamas and appearing fine. He told me that he would be OK as soon as the painkillers he was taking kicked in. I turned to Dilly and told her that Gurjit was fine, but to ring the doctors to tell them that he was still experiencing discomfort.

She looked anxious and concerned. She told me that Gurjit had been unwell for a number of days, and the physical effect on her was obvious to see. I was still unconcerned, believing that Gurjit would be fine, as I had only ever known him to be ill once in sixteen years.

Gurjit was talking normally, and told me he was OK. I saw nothing which caused me to be concerned. Little did I know how such thoughts would come back to torment me.

Chapter One

When I got home my parents asked me how Gurjit was, as my sister had rung to tell them what had happened. Their faces were full of anxiety. I could not understand what they were worried about, but reassured them that although he was in a bit of pain there was nothing to worry about. I thought this was no different from the uncertainty I was used to dealing with in my work, and Gurjit would be fine in a few days. The rest of the day continued as normal, and any thoughts of Gurjit being ill were moved to the back of my mind.

At about 4.30 in the afternoon I received a call from my nephew Bal, who told me he had just seen Gurjit. His eyes were dark and he looked ill and very pale. Bal's voice carried a hint of apprehension. I reassured him that Gurjit would be fine and had a doctor's appointment some time after 6 pm. Without realising it I was playing down another's concerns, not intentionally but through a false sense of security.

At about 6.30 pm Bal called again and told me that Gurjit was being taken to the hospital by ambulance from the doctor's surgery, and he and my niece Baljinder, aged 14, Gurjit's eldest daughter, were going to follow in his car. He sounded very concerned, and I wondered why.

Even so, for some unknown reason I was still not alarmed myself. I told him to bring Baljinder home and said I would go with him to the hospital instead. I thought the doctors must feel Gurjit needed tests and examinations which they could not do themselves. Also, I had been used to going to the hospital over the years when family members were ill as well as through my work.

Within a few moments Bal arrived and I told my parents that Gurjit was being taken to hospital but not to worry about it. Baljinder and her nine-year-old sister Suki stayed at my house when we left for the hospital.

On the way to the hospital Bal said to me 'Mama, you should see Chacha, he looks really bad. His eyes are very dark and his face is very pale. He could hardly walk and breathe. He just does not look good, his eyes are in a daze.' But Gurjit was so rarely ill that I was still not particularly concerned.

Chapter One

When we arrived at the hospital, Gurjit's ambulance had not yet arrived. We could not understand where he was and what could have had happened. It was nearly 7.15 pm and the ambulance should have been there for some time.

I rang my sister Dilly but got no response from her mobile phone. I was now slightly unnerved, because I knew the ambulance only had to travel about six miles, and more than 45 minutes had passed. I started to wonder if something had gone wrong, and if Gurjit was really ill and the ambulance drivers were attending to him. Perhaps they had taken him to a closer hospital without us knowing. Perhaps Gurjit was more ill than I had realised.

My mind was buzzing with these questions, but I had no answers, so I tried to ignore the thoughts that were running through my mind. Instead I tried to focus on a belief that everything was going to be all right. The wait outside became cold and my body was shivering. I was not sure whether this was due to the fresh wind or nervousness, as the ambulance had still not arrived.

While we were waiting I rang to update my older brother Jai. As Jai's daughter was not well I asked him how she had been; he told me she still had a cold and cough. This was to later be a significant factor that would influence how I made some decisions about who went to the hospital.

The ambulance eventually arrived at around 7.30 pm, and I told Jai I would ring him back when we had some information. The ambulance doors opened to show my sister Dilly with Gurjit sitting on the bed. My first impression was that he was fine, as he was clearly conscious and talking as though nothing was wrong. I remember giving a confused look to Bal, as in my mind I was questioning what he had told me about Gurjit being unwell.

We approached the ambulance and I asked Gurjit how he was.

'I'm fine' he said. 'Tell them to take me back home.' We all laughed, and felt slightly more at ease. I turned to Bal and assured him Gurjit would be fine.

As we were being taken to the Emergency Assessment Unit (EAU), I asked Dilly why it had taken so long for the ambulance to arrive. She told me that they had performed various tests in the back of the ambulance before bringing him to the hospital.

At the EAU we gave further details about Gurjit to the nurse after the paramedics left. We waited, and at about 8 pm Dr Allen came to see Gurjit and began to ask questions. She wanted to know how long he had been like this, where exactly he was feeling pain, if he had travelled anywhere recently and if he had coughed up any blood. Dr Allen was intrigued, as Gurjit had returned from India six weeks earlier.

As the doctor's questions became more detailed, I became conscious that something was not right. Had Gurjit had an injury when he was in India, such as a cut? Was he unwell there? When had he first started looking pale? What had he recently drunk and eaten? Had he had a recent operation or blood transfusion? Had he recently suffered from a virus or infection?

Something in my sister's responses was raising alarm bells in me. The doctor's questions and my sister's answers gave me a fuller picture of what had happened to Gurjit. In particular I learned that he had vomited blood in the early hours of Thursday morning (23rd January) and that this information had been relayed to a doctor at Gurjit's surgery, who clearly had not paid full attention to it. Also that while Gurjit had been in India he had cut his foot while working on his father's farm.

Dr Allen's reaction to that was one of great concern. She commented that in view of this information they should have seen Gurjit earlier. The look on her face made me think she was being guarded, as though she did not want to give any information away. When I asked her whether it could have been a stomach ulcer, she ignored me. I repeated my question and she replied 'No, it's something else.' That gave me a sinking feeling in the pit of my stomach. I felt something was happening that we were not aware of.

Dilly's face reflected anxiety and tension as she held on to Gurjit's hand, while Bal looked very concerned about his uncle and his face was worried. Dilly looked into Gurjit's eyes and smiled at him, trying to reassure him that everything was fine, while Bal just stood there motionless, looking at me as though I had the answers. Yet I was none the wiser. I sought to digest the information I had heard and its implications, while at the same time trying to bring some calmness to what was becoming quite a frightening experience.

The craziest thing was that Gurjit was sitting there trying to start a conversation about his car requiring an MOT test within the next few weeks. As he continued to talk about his car, Dr Allen unsuccessfully attempted to get blood from his arms. The expression on her face was full of frustration and concern. It was becoming obvious to us that she knew something was not right. Her body language and nervous energy began to reveal her anxiety, which surprised me because I did not anticipate seeing a medical professional display such emotions.

She was avoiding eye contact, making only passing glances at us. Yet her response was not insensitive. Rather it appeared to indicate that she was beginning to struggle with something that was taking place. Dilly, Bal and I stood there patiently as she continued to try to get blood from Gurjit's arms and then from his legs.

As over half an hour had elapsed and she was still unable to get a blood sample, it was becoming very tense for us watching, especially as Gurjit showed no discomfort as the needles were inserted. He looked up towards the ceiling as if to ignore what was happening. Dilly was becoming nervous and her face began to tremble. Her lips quivered and her cheeks were moving up and down as she held her left hand over her face to somehow stop her reaction from showing. Bal was shaking his head from side to side in puzzlement and his glances towards me showed that something was taking place which was not pleasant. His eyes were tearful. I kept wondering why the doctor could not draw any blood and if she needed help from a colleague.

All we could do was look at each other and try to offer some reassurance by smiling at each other, for we could not talk as we did not want the doctor to be distracted. Amazingly it was Gurjit who began to break some of this tension, as he started to make light of the whole situation. He continued to talk about his car and about how he did not want to miss out on going to the pub at the weekend to meet his friends. The way he said it and the picture he painted brought a momentary softness to the situation as we were drawn into his laughter. He knew that Dilly would not be impressed with him going to the pub if he was not well.

Dr Allen eventually gave up trying to get a sample of blood. 'There's something not right with his veins' she said. 'I'll come back after the ECG has been done to see if I can get some blood samples then.'

At this point a student nurse came in. Initially her response to us standing by the side of the bed was harsh, and she bluntly told us to wait outside the bay. We were taken aback, but we did as instructed. Perhaps she would feel under pressure if the three of us stood and watched her.

We only stood outside for a few minutes when suddenly our concerns were heightened, because the student nurse pulled the bay curtains aside and the look on her face was full of fright and panic. She quickly ran from Gurjit's bedside past us with a paper in her hand.

When I mean she ran, she ran flat out. We went back to Gurjit's bedside to see how he was, and he now had a very distant look in his eyes, a very deep and dark look. When I looked at him I recalled what Bal had said earlier about Gurjit's eyes. Now Bal said 'This was how Chacha was at the doctor's surgery.'

Chapter One

I now realised why Bal had been so anxious when he had seen Gurjit like that. I too was stunned by the quick change in his facial expression. He seemed to have become a different person within the space of a few minutes. This was now becoming frightening, because there was now no doubt that something was not right.

The student nurse returned with Dr Allen and we were again asked to wait outside while they ran further tests. This time we did not go out, as we wanted to know what was happening.

'What's wrong?' I asked.

'The ECG result is indicating that something is very wrong with the way Gurjit's heart is functioning' she said. 'We need to perform the test again to make sure it's not a faulty reading.'

She tried to offer some reassurance and asked us to wait outside, which we did. When the test had been done we went back to Gurjit's bedside, where Dr Allen was again trying to get a blood sample.

The time was now approaching 9 pm, and my earlier perceptions had been turned on their head. I was left pondering the earlier phone calls from Dilly and Bal. I realised I had not fully or accurately assessed the situation.

During this time I was ringing home to reassure my family, which included my dad, mom, sister, brother and nieces, that Gurjit was fine. I was trying to stop them from being worried, even though I was deeply worried myself. Deep down my stomach was churning and there was a massive uncertainty in me which I had never felt before. I was doing my best to ignore it. I felt strange, but could not put my finger on exactly what was causing me to feel that way.

I was thinking 'Hang on, what's happening here? What am I not seeing? Why does the doctor look more worried than me? Why have they struggled so much to get a blood sample? What has caused Gurjit's appearance to change so quickly?' There were no answers - just questions leading to more questions.

Chapter One

After waiting about a further half hour outside the bay, we went back to the bed without waiting for them to call us. As we entered and stood by Gurjit's bedside Dr Allen explained that they would be undertaking a chest x-ray and that she had managed to get some blood from him to test. She also informed us that they would be placing him on a machine to monitor his heart and breathing, because his heart rate was very high.

Dr Allen was unable to respond to questions or maintain eye contact with me. Her words were slow as she attempted to offer some peace by commenting that they were running all tests as quickly as they could. But I could not ignore the thoughts that had run through my mind, so I asked her what had caused the sudden deterioration in Gurjit, and what were the reasons for his heart rate being so high.

'We don't know what has caused such changes' she said. 'We're trying to find out as quickly as we can.' Her honesty was some comfort, as I could see that she was trying everything to establish what was happening and what needed to be done to ensure Gurjit's health improved.

She connected the machine to him and left the bedside. We were left looking at each other and wondering how he could have been breathing well and talking at 9 pm, yet half an hour later he was struggling to breathe and talk and had a monitor regulating his heart rate.

It was not looking good, but I remember smiling at my sister while she was holding Gurjit's hand and nodding as if to indicate that he'd be fine. When I turned to Bal and smiled, the look on his face was different. My reassurance was not enough, because like me he knew something was wrong. The fleeting look that passed between us held a deep understanding, a conversation we could not speak or acknowledge.

I glanced back at Dilly's face, which was covered by a dark shadow of despair. My stomach began to churn again, because Gurjit appeared more and more distant by the passing of every minute.

Gurjit was a good, hard-working man, with a solid and honest personality. He was a loving husband, father, son, brother and uncle whose character had always appeared flawless to me. He was always supportive and caring to all of us and in fact to anyone who knew him. He had a gentle personality, was always softly spoken and would speak to people with the utmost respect, something I had learned from him. To see him enduring such discomfort was unpleasant, but I still convinced myself that as he had only been ill once in sixteen years, he would be fine.

The student nurse came back in to check on Gurjit. Her appearance and approach to us was now calm and caring, as though she had been embarrassed by her earlier behaviour. She looked at Dilly as though trying to convey some message of empathy. She began to prepare to take another ECG.

Then Gurjit spoke to me. I will never forget the words he spoke; I struggle to write them down as I know that people may not believe it. Taking the risk of writing it down in reality is not a risk, rather it is an honour.

In Punjabi, he said: 'There's a horse waiting outside for me.'

Anyone who believes in God and has a religion or belief system will know the significance of this statement. He knew death was approaching.

Though I too knew this deep down, I was certainly not willing to accept such a reality without a spiritual, mental and emotional fight.

His words had gone within seconds, but their significance was highly uncomfortable. A feeling of helplessness came over me like a dark and heavy shroud. There was nothing I could do. My entire body shook with fear, and inside I felt as though my skeleton had been pulled out of me. I looked at Gurjit and could not form the words to speak back, because my mind was battling with what he had said and with my own beliefs about God.

All I could do was hold his hand and shake my head sideways to indicate to him that nothing was going to happen. He held my hand gently and let his fingers slip from me, and as I tried to grab his hand the nurse turned around and smiled at me.

Dilly and Bal also looked at me in a way that indicated that they must have seen from my face that some serious message had been conveyed, but they did not ask me what it was and I was not prepared to share it. How could I, when inwardly I hated what he had said? It symbolised some deep knowledge that he was not going to survive.

Everything within me wanted to ignore this thought, as I wanted it to be a test of faith. I believed that if I stayed true to this line of thought, I would not have to pay attention to the adverse thoughts. I felt that by not giving in to such negativity I would not be affected and my faith would hold true, therefore he would not die.

Yet I could not understand why Gurjit had said those words to me. It certainly hurt, as I failed through ignorance to see that this was his way of telling me to be prepared for what was to come.

As we watched, the nurse placed an oxygen mask over Gurjit's mouth, as his breathing difficulties began to become severe, and his heart rate was going at such a speed that it was hard to believe that he could still sit there. The staff frantically replaced the heart rate monitor machine twice, as they thought it must be faulty. His heart, pulse and breathing rates were all off the scale. They decided to move Gurjit closer to the nursing station to keep an eye on him.

During this time Dilly and Bal had left the bay to go outside and I was left alone with Gurjit. His health was visibly deteriorating before my eyes.

As Gurjit was being moved, Dr Allen came and stood by me. She remained strangely silent, with a blank facial expression. It reminded me how Gurjit had looked; she remained as though in a daze. I asked her if the results of the blood tests had come back. The moment I spoke she reacted as if she had snapped out of a dream and back to reality. She did not answer my question but began talking about the monitoring machines.

Chapter One

'The readings the machine is giving are unreal' she said. 'I've never seen anything like it in my fifteen years' experience.'

'What do you mean?' I asked.

'The readings are indicating that something is seriously wrong with him. In spite of the medication we have given him, nothing is working and the strain on his heart will be problematic.'

Part of my mind was blank, as though I had not registered, or more likely had ignored, what she was saying. Yet the part of my mind which was conscious of what she said heightened my awareness that she was saying there was nothing they could do. This thinking was not a surprise to me at that point, because the feeling of dread had began to surface within me. I was battling against it.

Dr Allen then edged closer to Gurjit's side, held his hand and gently began stroking it. She looked straight into his eyes and said 'Come on Gurjit, fight.' She turned away from Gurjit and her heavy, tear-filled eyes met mine. She tried unconvincingly to reassure me with a smile. Her empathy was incredible, because the humanity of the act ran through me and my body began to shake physically. I could not grasp the reason why she was responding in such a way.

For the first time since being at the hospital my eyes also began to well up with tears, but I refused to let them flow. Instead I fought, trying to breathe slowly while my body began to tighten with tension. I clenched my fists. My breathing got heavier, my chest became tighter and I felt as though someone had just tied a rock around me. Though I wanted to get closer to hold Gurjit's hand, the heaviness was hindering me from doing so. Time appeared to have stood still. My spine felt twisted into knots, and my legs felt incredibly light, which was bizarre, as my upper body felt heavy.

Then Dilly came back and approached Gurjit. She looked so tired and shattered, her face bewildered as though she was a little lost child. I was able to walk to her, disheartened on one level but trying to remain composed, because I knew what was really going on in my own mind. I told her what Dr Allen had told me, and stupidly, once again I tried to reassure her that Gurjit would be fine, in spite of the fact that everything was indicating the opposite.

Dr Allen came back over, placed her hand on Dilly's shoulder and told her that they were not aware of what was causing the difficulties but were trying everything they could. She then went back to the nursing station and I overheard the nurses saying goodnight to her as her shift had ended. She took her white coat off, walked back to us and told us that another doctor who had seen Gurjit earlier would continue to run the tests. She then walked down the ward and left.

Dilly had tears in her eyes, as she must be conscious now that her husband might die. My mind could not even begin to imagine what she was feeling at that stage. To think about the person she loved so dearly experiencing such pain would have been unbearable. She began to wipe the tears from her eyes, knowing that the love of her life was going to die.

Helpless, I stood by her not knowing how deep her hurt might be. A shard of her pain cut me deep and would never heal again. I could do nothing about it; I could not help her by talking it all away. To contemplate the fullness of their relationship made me try to ignore my fear. I tried to focus on it as a sign of hope, hope that Gurjit would pull through, but the dreadful feelings continued.

Then Bal came back, and we told him what Dr Allen had told us. We stayed by the bed and gently continued to offer Gurjit and Dilly hope. Bal just looked drained. His entire body language was oozing out his love for his uncle and aunt.

Though he kept a positive and gentle smile on his face and told them everything would be OK, I saw the hope in him begin to disappear. He was bravely trying to cope for the sake of his aunt.

Dilly's face began to shrink and become pale. I could not bear looking at her, because there was nothing I could do to bring any life back into her eyes. Instead I kept on looking at Gurjit, who had a breathing mask on. I gazed into his eyes as he continued to battle for his life, feeling totally useless, because I knew I had no capacity to respond. I so wanted Gurjit to live, and the more I thought about this the more I began to resent the thought of him dying.

It was now approaching midnight and I knew I had to pick my other nephew Ami up from work as he worked at a restaurant. My sister told me to go; she would stay with her husband and ring us in the morning, unaware that I had every intention of returning.

We went to pick Ami up. I knew that Baljinder and Suki, would be staying at their grandparents. I had not yet thought about what I was going to say to them. I did not want to say anything except that their dad was going to be fine, even though I knew he was not.

When Ami was told about Gurjit being in hospital, his first reaction was to go and see him, but I told him we needed him to go home first to ensure that everyone was OK, and that I would be going back to the hospital. On arriving home I quickly charged my mobile phone and rang my brother Jai to give him an update. He was the first person to whom I expressed the thought that had been circling in my mind. I told him that it did not look good with Gurjit.

Jai wanted to come to the hospital, but his 16-month-old daughter, the joy of the family, was unwell. As it was the middle of the night, I thought it would be more appropriate for him to stay at home. I hated saying that to him, because he was older than me and had an extremely close and positive relationship with Gurjit. My inability to accept the reality of what was happening influenced my conversation with Jai, because even though I expressed the seriousness of Gurjit's condition I was not able to share the thought that he might actually die. To this day I regret not telling Jai. My stomach was churning again, and I knew that this was because I was failing to consider what was happening.

Somehow I moved to a stage where I was preparing to meet the needs that would arise within the family. It was an 'auto-pilot' response that had kicked in without me even knowing. Yet the strangest part was that I was still not accepting that Gurjit would die, and could not understand how I was going to bridge the gap between that and being prepared to support others.

With this battle going on in my mind I arrived back at the hospital in the early hours of Saturday. I went on to the ward and found Dilly standing by Gurjit's bed.

As I approached her she turned. She looked totally exhausted and her eyes were red. Tears had been shed. Her face was swollen with agony and her cheeks were red. She began to wipe the tears from her cheeks.

She asked why I had returned. I was still not able to express to her the dreaded thoughts running through me that Gurjit was going to die. How could I utter such words when one look at her face was enough to make my entire body quake? I tried hard to think of something comforting, but no words could be found. All I could utter was that I wanted to come back to see Gurjit.

She just looked at me, totally frozen, and raised her hands to take her spectacles off to wipe more tears away. Unable to respond, she walked past me and out of the ward. I knew she was going out to cry again; the tears had already begun to fall as she walked past me. I knew my heart would weep, but knew that it could not fathom the depths of my sister's despair. I knew I would weep for her and for Gurjit, but at that time I did not want my own tears to fall as I knew it would be like a dam breaking inside of me.

It felt awful knowing that my sister was in such agony. My words would not bring hope, and there was no immediate remedy. It felt horrible to be caught up in the battle of death's darkness.

Bizarrely, while this was taking place, I spoke to Gurjit, telling him again that he would be fine. However, the look in his eyes mirrored what I was really thinking. He was not going to be fine.

Chapter One

Then, to my surprise he spoke for the first time since the night before. He pushed the mask aside, pointed towards the doors and said, 'There's a horse and chariot waiting for me over there.'

The words provided the confirmation in my heart of what I knew was going to happen. I grabbed him and whispered 'No!', but inwardly I was screaming 'How dare this happen? This is not going to happen!'. He just nodded towards the door. My body went cold.

I realised that this trauma had begun to evolve, and was now challenging me. It was not going to go away. All I could do was hold on to his hand and maintain eye contact with him, hoping and praying desperately that I was only imagining what he had said. But no matter what strategy I adopted, the dreaded and prevailing thought of death remained. It was only over the passage of time that I understood that this was foresight.

It was becoming too difficult to even attempt to contemplate that death was encroaching upon Gurjit and that its effects would cause so much devastation within us. I tried to focus on being positive, in the belief that it would provide a glimmer of hope.

When my sister returned, her eyes were red and her face seemed to have shrunk. The blankness on Gurjit's face was now being reflected by hers. I attempted to keep things as light-hearted as possible, but it was too awkward, as our silence spoke more than any words could.

Inwardly, my battle continued. This time it was questions about belief in God and whether this afforded any hope at this time. My question was not about whether God existed, rather whether He was going to intervene in the way I anticipated. Yet no response came, and all that was residing in me at that point was a terrifying despair.

In fact I failed to realise that the response was there, I just did not see it. Only upon reflection did I understand that Gurjit's words were the evidence that God was in the situation.

A longing and agonising crying at the edge of my throat was

waiting to travel to my voice, but I was not willing to be consumed by it. I began to switch my focus to my sister, knowing that if anyone needed the hope, it was her. Every time I looked at her, she appeared to be going through different levels of torment, increasing as time was passing on. Her face was swollen with the concern for her husband and the dread of such circumstances.

At about 1.30 am we were approached by Dr Benson, a young doctor. He looked very tense. He told us that they would have to place Gurjit on a life support machine as he was struggling to breathe for himself. He tried to maintain eye contact, but I noticed that he kept looking at the clipboard he was holding, as if it was somehow serving as a defence against having to face us with the bleakness of the situation.

As I looked at him I thought that all the pretending, the hope against the inevitable could now stop. He told us that the life support machine could be used to monitor Gurjit over the next 24 hours.

This gave me something to hang on to. Dilly was fighting back the tears and Dr Benson tried his best to repeat his statement, but this time my stomach tightened because I knew nothing was working for him or for us.

The moment he walked away Dilly left the ward, and this time I followed her outside. The walls of the dam came crashing down on her as her tears poured out a torrent of pent-up emotion. The release of such intensity shook her body as she violently sobbed.

I held her and we comforted each other, though there was no real reassurance I could give her. Yet I remember what she said, which was extremely powerful and incredibly brave: 'I've already prayed. I have asked God to take Gurjit, because he's in too much pain and I don't want to see him suffer.'

I knew this revealed her true and deep love for her husband. All I could offer was my understanding that this was all in God's domain and that God was listening to all our prayers. The only peace we had at that point was a strange thought of knowing that we were aware of the magnitude of the pain, yet this did not prevent us from drawing near to each other.

Gathering my thoughts, I phoned my brother Jai and he immediately asked how Gurjit was. When I told him the doctors were going to place him on a life support machine because of his breathing, Jai just asked 'how serious is this?', to which I replied that it was very serious.

The silence that fell was immense as I did not know what else to say to him, but clearly heard the anxiety in his question. This made it even more difficult to advise him to stay at home because his daughter was not well, as I felt I had no right at this critical time. My mind was trying to juggle everything, and not doing a very effective job of it.

When I rang my eldest sister, Dee, my nephew Bal answered the phone. I tried to get him to pass the phone straight to his mother, but the fact that I asked him to do so told him that something was wrong. 'Mama, what's wrong? How's Chacha?' he said. Because my mind was racing at such a speed I knew I did not have the time to explain to him and then to my sister, for it was too intense. I paused, and told him that I needed to speak to his mother first.

'Mom!' he said, his voice choking. As he passed the phone to his mother I heard him beginning to cry. My sister would have seen his distress and she immediately asked me 'How's Gurjit?'

'Listen carefully' I said. 'They are going to put Gurjit on a life support machine, and I need you and the lads at the hospital.'

I tried to reassure her that this was somehow a positive action rather than there being no hope. I asked her to phone Gurjit's parents in India to tell them that Gurjit was seriously ill and what the doctors had told us, and that we were all praying. It was amazing to think how my mind, fully aware of the direness of the situation, still sought to believe otherwise. Even with these thoughts raging I was trying to hide my heart from such an attack, but there was no refuge.

Chapter One

I asked Dee to put Bal back on the phone, because I knew he would be driving to the hospital. I told him what was taking place and could hear him sniffing through his tears. In the background I could hear Ami crying with my sister as she told him what was happening. Several days later I found out that Bal had been in such distress that he kept taking the wrong road to get the hospital, even though he was familiar with the journey.

When I ended the phone call I began preparing myself to go back home to pick up my parents and two nieces, as well as arranging for Jai to be at the hospital knowing that Gurjit was going to die. This was a journey I did not want to undertake, but I had to do it for them.

At the hospital, Dilly and I went back to Gurjit's side. As I slowly followed her my legs felt light again and my feet very heavy. It was as though I did not want to go to Gurjit's bedside, and the more I moved my legs the heavier the burden I was feeling about his imminent death. Dilly's footsteps would have been even more tormenting, as she was going to lose the love of her life.

As we stood by Gurjit's bedside it was shocking to see how fast he was deteriorating. I turned to my right to see Dr Allen walking towards us, now without her white coat. It was a surprise to see her as only a few hours earlier her shift had ended, but for some reason she had returned. When she came to the bed the look on her face was frightening to me because I could not understand why a professional like her was showing such emotion. She held both Gurjit's and Dilly's hands and said that she knew that Gurjit was being placed on a life support machine and that the test results were indicating that he had a serious viral infection which was affecting his major organs. When I looked at Dilly, all I could see was her reaching out with longing to have her fear of love turned into hope.

'I'm really sorry' said Dr Allen. Any lingering hope was now totally dashed. On reflection, her truthful comments gave me the permission

Chapter One

I needed to acknowledge that Gurjit was going to die.

Yet I still ignored the dreaded thought as I moved to another level of belief, the belief that the whole dreaded experience was a lie. For I knew that if it was a lie I would not have to think about Gurjit lying there dying or dead. It sounds ridiculous, considering that only minutes before I had been dreading the journey home, and now all of a sudden I believed that no matter what the doctors said or what I feared, Gurjit was going to pull through, because everything had been a test of faith.

My mind pushed and challenged all the thoughts that were present. I knew that the fear had created certain vulnerabilities - eg, was there any point in ignoring what was taking place?

I went off to make three phone calls to friends who were so close that they were practically part of our family. I relayed the circumstances that were unfolding and asked them to pray. At this stage I had a renewed hope, a hope of a miracle, which meant that no matter what happened it could change.

As I finished making the calls, my nephews Bal and Ami arrived along with my sister Dee. The look on their faces was full of gloom. We made only eye contact, because at first none of us were able to utter a word. Our silence spoke the inner agony we felt. The fearful look in each other's eyes was signalling that we would have to face a lot more pain, while knowing it would be a hundred times more intense for Dilly and the girls.

As I was thinking about this, my body began to shiver again, even though it was not cold. I tried to ensure this was not projected in my voice, as I still attempted to install a glimmer of hope and faith that in spite of the bleakness of the circumstances there would be a way out.

We all went to Gurjit and I looked at Ami's face etched with bewilderment and disbelief. He was unable to form any words when he saw his uncle lying down with all the monitors and tubes attached to his body.

Chapter One

Bal just held Gurjit's hand tight, while Dee offered Dilly the best moral support she could. I just stood back, as the closeness was again shielding me from accepting the reality that was unfolding before my eyes.

It was not clear how at one stage I could have hope and at another I could be in a vacuum of such uncertainty when seeing how those dear to me were so shaken at Gurjit's bedside. The image was a horrendous haunting as my tears began to slowly creep up on me like a cloud of dense fog, moving slowly as not to get my attention. Gurjit was not the only one who was motionless; we all were, because the sense of life leaving him was so horrible.

No words were spoken as we all looked at each other feeling so dejected. Dee was holding Dilly gently with her arm around her shoulder as Dilly leaned into her, shedding tears on them both. Bal with his cap on kept shaking his head sideways, glancing at his uncle lying there. Gurjit's eyes were locked on to Dilly.

Ami was beside himself. The disbelief in what he was seeing began to immediately provoke tears as he gently spoke to his uncle. 'Chacha, you're going to be OK, don't worry' he said. My heart, if not already broken, was slowly disintegrating as his words pierced me like a thousand splinters.

Within moments Dr Benson and a nurse came towards us and informed us that they would now be placing Gurjit on the life support machine. They gave us some time to be with Gurjit before we needed to go to another room.

To this day I cannot recall what any of us said to Gurjit then; we just stood there as if in a silent movie. The numbness that engulfed me, I can imagine engulfed us all and the feeling of helplessness was disabling.

Then my sisters and Ami walked away, while Bal and I stayed for about a minute longer, facing each other on opposite sides of Gurjit's bed. As we went to walk away, Gurjit grabbed my left arm and Bal's arm and pulled us both back towards himself. For the life of me I could not understand where he found the strength to pull us both back. While he pulled us back, Bal looked at me and with his face contorted with severe distress said 'Mama, Chacha.'

We suddenly stopped. Gurjit just looked at us, moved his head sideway and then nodded. The gaze in his eyes was not of giving in, but of giving himself up. All I could do was look at him and nod back as a sign of acknowledging that we both knew that this was the last contact we would have. I held his hand and then gently our fingers began to slip away, and there was nothing I could do to hold on any more.

It was the most horrible feeling, so indescribable, words could not fathom or explain what this separation was like. It hurt more that many of my family members did not have that opportunity to at least say something to him, and the haunting, lingering look in his eyes remained with me.

Bal continued to look over his shoulder at his uncle lying there, but I could not look back. I walked straight as if somehow trying to focus, but I was not sure what exactly I was to focus upon. We then made our way to the little room that the hospital staff asked us to wait in.

At about 2 am Dr Benson walked in with a nurse, and his expression said it all. He looked uncertain as to what to say, and for a few seconds he did not say anything at all. The thought that went through my mind was 'don't you even dare tell us that he has died! Don't you even dare utter those words.'

He just looked at us all and I remember Dee holding Dilly, while Bal, Ami and I stood. We were feeling totally numb, not knowing what the doctor was going to say. As he opened his mouth the initial silence was so crystalline that time appeared frozen, which would have been a welcome and preferable state to the words that might shatter the heart into infinite pieces.

'Gurjit is on the life support machine' he said. 'We have had to resuscitate him as he had a heart attack, but we did manage to revive him.'

It took seconds for my mind to process this information, which I quickly interpreted as hope; he was not yet dead. Maybe the test was over.

He then told us that they would be monitoring Gurjit for the next 24 hours. I hung on to these words as evidence against adverse thoughts of the imminence of death. The burden I was feeling felt lighter, because I now thought Gurjit could pull through in those 24 hours. I was grateful for the injection of what I thought was new hope. The fortress I had built in my mind appeared to have stood firm. Fear I thought could no longer have an influence, and the torment momentarily appeared to have subsided.

We quickly discussed what we needed to do, which was to make arrangements to get the rest of the family members to the hospital, now that Gurjit was on the life support machine. It was agreed that Dee, Ami and I would go back home and tell the rest of the family - Jai, my parents and Gurjit's two daughters, as well as phone our immediate extended family. We knew that Gurjit's survival was on the line, yet there was the slightest, very slightest chance that there was going to be light at the end of this tunnel that we were all trapped in.

Leaving the hospital, the next mission was focusing on how to tell my parents and nieces of the seriousness of Gurjit's condition. The silence in the car as we travelled back allowed us just enough time to briefly think about this and about how we were going to support and comfort each other.

Then the moment of truth arrived as we pulled up on to the drive around 2.30 am and I realised I had gone into the autopilot role again, no doubt influenced by my training and knowledge of trauma, even though it had been challenging me all night.

I opened the door knowing that my parents and nieces would be asleep. Dee and Ami went to the lounge while I walked up the stairs. Each step felt like climbing a steep hill, and I tiptoed, trying not to create too much noise, and went to my mother and gently woke her up. She asked me what was wrong, to which I told her that she needed to go downstairs and I would tell her there with Dad. She immediately uttered 'Gurjit'. I nodded and placed my finger on my lips to indicate the need for her to remain silent for a moment while I woke my father up.

The look on her face was agonising. I knew she had seen straight through me and there was nothing I could have done to prevent it. Even though I thought I had found renewed hope, one look at my mother's face began to dissolve that hope. For the frightening thought of telling her that Gurjit was going to die was the message I had been trying to keep locked up like a genie in a bottle.

My father was already awake. I put the bedroom light on and he looked at me and said 'Where's Gurjit?' I looked straight at him and said I needed him to go downstairs with Mom and I would tell him there, as the girls were asleep upstairs. The look on his face was the same as my mother's, total agony, because I knew that he also saw straight through me. Gurjit was his son. I quickly left the room, because I could not contemplate their pain at that stage.

We went downstairs and my mother was already crying, Dee sitting next to her, telling her in further detail what was taking place. Meanwhile Ami was pacing up and down in the kitchen. My father followed downstairs and burst into tears as soon as he saw the distress on Ami's face. He knew something terrible had happened; it was terrible because I would try to give some hope when there was very little to give.

'Where is Gurjit?' asked my father. 'Has he gone?'

It was a blow that my dad thought Gurjit had already died. I sat him down and told my parents that Gurjit was on a life support machine and that it was very serious because he had a viral infection which the doctors were trying to identify. This was the first time besides speaking to my brother Jai that I had half acknowledged in a subtle way that Gurjit was going to die.

Chapter One

They looked at me with intense shock. Horror registered on their faces with the realisation that the son-in-law who they had lovingly embraced as a son was going to be no more.

The sense of powerlessness I felt was great, as I knew that Gurjit's life was not in anyone's hands and we had no control. At that point I did not want to focus on who had the power and control; I needed to focus on communicating as sensitively as I could with my nieces and gently awakening them to the realisation that their father was going to die.

Their experience of their father was positive, and the close relationship they had was now at serious risk of disappearing forever. The thought of the hurt this trauma was going to cause them was beyond comprehension.

I left my parents downstairs to be comforted by Dee and Ami, and went back upstairs to wake my eldest niece Baljinder. She asked how her dad was. When I told her how ill he was, I purposely maintained a steady eye contact. I could not bring myself to tell her he was not going to survive.

She looked at me in total bewilderment and I imagined that fear crept into her heart at that moment. I tried to smile at her, but all I saw was a young person in a state of overwhelming dread. Her face was sapped of energy as she sat up and looked around silently, mulling over what I had told her.

She looked at me again and asked 'What's happening to my dad?' I sat on the side of the bed and told her that the doctors were trying everything to find out what had caused the infection. 'I want to see him' she said. 'I want to go to the hospital.' I told her that we would all be going back soon.

I then went to wake my youngest niece, Suki, who woke up before I could even speak. 'How's my dad?' she asked. I told her that her dad was very ill and had been placed on a life support machine. She sat up at this point and her words ripped through me like a jet of icy water. 'But he only had a cold and a headache!' she said.

Chapter One

I told her that the doctors were trying everything they could to help her father and that I needed to go back to the hospital, and would come back to take her and her sister there. Her inner longing for her father could not be hidden as she caught the significance of what it all meant. Her eyes revealed a truth to me; I knew that she somehow knew her father was going to die.

I thought I had experienced enough shivers in my body, but none matched the one that came then. It was like a bolt of lightning ferociously ripping me apart. 'How could she possibly know this?' I thought. I tried to offer her some reassurance by telling her we would all be going to the hospital.

When I went back downstairs, my parents and Dee were still crying and Ami was fighting the tears that had welled up in his eyes as if he was afraid that they would be betraying his uncle by acknowledging that he was about to die. I knew this because I had been doing the same.

As I sat opposite my mother and sought to offer as much reassurance as I could, she held her head in her hands shaking from side to side. 'It can't happen to my son!' she said. She was asking God to take her instead of him. My father was just crying and kept asking how Gurjit was. It was clear that he was not accepting what I had said to him. This was not a surprise, as I too had fought against accepting that all this was happening.

All around me tears were continuing to fall, yet I had not still shed a single tear. I suppose I was still trying to convey a faltering message of hope. The battle being fought inside me was desperate for a resolution to all of this. The truth of the matter was that no matter what I hoped for, Gurjit was deteriorating, and there was no sign of progress.

The deadliest silence fell. All I could do was sit there and watch my parent's emotional torment. The thought that ran through me was 'We are going to lose a family member.' The coldness I felt was such that I would rather have been left at the North Pole.

Then Bal rang me on my mobile. He told me that Gurjit had been moved to the Intensive Care Unit on the same floor. I said we would be there soon and told him not to worry. What nonsense, because the reality was that we were all distraught and nothing else was going through my mind besides 'what are we going to do now?'

I went back to the hospital with Ami at about 3.30 am and we spoke in the car. Though our words were few they were significant, as we began to acknowledge the pain this was causing us.

Ami told me how it was hurting him so much. Knowing that Gurjit might die was even more painful for him, as his own father Parmjit had left home in the past (Parmjit was Gurjit's elder brother and my eldest brother-in-law). Ami expressed the hurt of knowing that his father was not there when he was needed and said he felt angry about this. He told me that he could not think too much about his father at that moment because he needed to focus on the pain of his aunt and cousin-sisters.

I remember telling Ami that whatever happened it was not the fault of anyone in the family, as we both knew that Dilly was already feeling emotionally hurt, because she thought she should have taken him to the hospital earlier.

When Ami and I went to the Intensive Care Unit, Dilly and Bal were sitting outside with the main doors to the unit shut. (As it dealt with serious incidents they were keeping us out at that moment). We told Dilly and Bal that everyone at home was aware of what was happening. Dilly just remained silent as Bal held her hand and looked totally dejected. While we were talking, two doctors, Dr Clarke and Dr Dennison, came out to speak to us. They took Dilly and me into the family room.

I knew this meant things were very serious. The room was very small, and Dilly and I sat down while the doctors sat to the left of us. They began by telling us that they knew this was a difficult time for the family. The look on their faces was very empathic and genuine as they expressed their concern about Gurjit and acknowledged that this was heavily affecting us as a family.

Chapter One

They told us that Gurjit's condition was extremely serious and that it was highly unlikely that he would survive, because of the viral infection that was destroying the major organs of his body. They were truthful, direct and caring, but it did not make it any easier to accept what they told us.

When they left the room, I comforted Dilly as best I could. She was devastated by the information. Her entire body shook at the news and tears rolled down her cheeks. This began to shake me inside more than anything I had ever seen or experienced before.

My heart broke, seeing Dilly being taken apart little by little by the torment of losing her husband. The doctor's words appeared absolute and her despair and grief had flowed freely, harsh, uncontrollable emotions of hurt, loss and pain. Every sob appeared to ask 'God, why him? Why me? Why not me? What about the children?'

As she wept all I could say was that all our prayers had been said and it was now in God's hands. Then I said that not even death would have victory over Gurjit's soul. The moment I said that I stopped myself and realised what I had said. Those words came from the deepest part of me, the part I had tried so hard to push away.

I remained still for a few seconds grasping the significance of what was going to take place, and that to many people such a deep religious belief may appear a step too far and the words considered inappropriate to express at that time. However, when all things had been stripped to the bare bones, it was this that carried us through at that time because we believed in God. In spite of the difficulties of the situation we still believed and understood that it was an unshakeable truth for us. Yet this held a real dilemma and for us was the real pain.

The raw emotions were being shaped by our faith. Dilly's faith was pulling her through and she told me that part of her already knew that Gurjit was going to die and that she did not want him to suffer. Rather she wanted God to take Gurjit away to where he would be free, at peace and without pain.

Chapter One

We left the room and went to the waiting area where Bal and Ami were. As soon as they saw their aunt's face and the agony and pain she was experiencing, they came over and hugged her. I approached them and told them what the doctors had said, and explained that as a result I needed to go back home and fetch everyone else.

I left the hospital and rang my brother Jai to tell him what the doctors had said and say I needed him to meet up at Dad and Mom's. I also asked him to ring Dee to ensure that the girls were woken up and told. We also made arrangements for a dear family friend George, who is practically a brother, to assist in taking family members to the hospital.

Sprinting out of the hospital to make a quick dash to my car, I was inwardly kneeling in prayer to God knowing that death was becoming tangible and preparing to take Gurjit from us. The thought of being without him began to rip my heart out and to scar my mind with turmoil.

The drive back home was a sombre one, as I knew that my prayer was no longer to be of physical healing but rather of spiritual healing. I realised that the hours that had been given were for us as a family to gather and be at Gurjit's side to say our goodbyes.

I arrived home about 4 am to find everyone waiting anxiously. My parents were crying and my nieces began to cry too. I reached out to my nieces and hugged them and told them that it was OK to cry because they loved their dad and that this was hurting us all, but we were all here to support each other.

I spoke to Jai and George, but the expression on my face said it all to them as they looked at me and said 'let's get to the hospital.' I was grateful that I did not have to explain, as they knew what we as a family were going to have to face for the first time - the death of a loving caring husband, father, son, uncle and brother.

Looking into Jai's eyes I saw the challenge - where do we turn to now? This was the difficulty, as we could not rise above the event. We just lacked the capacity to fully engage, or at least that is what I thought.

Chapter One

Even having to acknowledge that death was pending, the despair was shaking my reality. Hiding seemed to be an easier option than facing it, but somehow I knew that if we all did that we would actually be withholding our feelings from each other and our inner isolation would be further compounded.

As we were about to leave I received a phone call from Bal. He was shouting down the phone in a frantic state and telling me to hurry up back to the hospital as numerous doctors and nurses had rushed into the room. Gurjit's heart had stopped and they had only just managed to resuscitate him.

I got my mother and father, as well as my sister-in-law Mangender into my car. George drove Jai and my nieces in his car while Dee stayed behind to look after Sonia.

Mangender spoke about the time of her own father's death and the effect this had upon her family, saying that she could recall how her father had died. She told us that she knew what Dilly and the girls were feeling and hoped that Gurjit would pull through. She attempted to provide reassurance to my parents through her own experience.

In the car my mother continued to pray, asking for God to take her life and spare Gurjit's, while my father was resigned to the inevitable, saying 'Gurjit's life is in God's hands and it's God's decision, a decision which we can do nothing but accept.' My father's powerful words revealed his mechanism for responding to the trauma that was about to hit our family.

As we rushed to the hospital, an overwhelming thought began to emerge in me and a prayer formed of its own accord, holding all the tension contained in me. 'We are experiencing the depths of despair' I prayed. 'How do we look to you from such loss? We are longing, but the pain and torment is questioning where the hope is and we need the direction of your care. Please hear our cry and reconcile the way you know best.'

Chapter One

Upon arriving at the hospital we made our way hurriedly to the unit and into the family room. My parents began to weep loudly as they held on to Dilly, and my nieces were crying loudly too as we all tried to give and receive comfort to and from one another. I did not stay in the room long as I needed to know what was happening to Gurjit, even though I knew the answer. I still hoped that somehow it was the worst nightmare I had ever had and that somehow I would awake from it. It did not happen.

I wearily walked to where Gurjit lay, knowing that Bal and Ami would be there.

Yet before Jai, George and I could get near the ward, Bal and Ami came out. They told us that they had been standing outside the unit when the doors had sprung open and they saw at least five doctors and as many nurses running down the corridor, and within a few seconds another set of doors opened and they saw at least another six other people running towards them. They told us they had been prevented from going in because the doctors were working on Gurjit. After all that happened a doctor had come out to tell them that Gurjit's heart had stopped again and they had managed to restart it.

A few of us remained in the family room, while the rest of us stood in a reception area outside the intensive care unit. We all sought to console one another. That was all that we could do. I remember how Bal and Ami were holding on to Baljinder and Suki and their tears were falling as they began to mourn. Their misery shouted out to me. It was a great burden for them to carry.

At this point none of us had gone into the unit because the doctors were still attending to Gurjit. When we were allowed to, Jai was the first one in. As he moved the curtain aside and saw Gurjit lying on the bed with even more tubes than when we had seen him before, Jai broke down. He placed his hand over his eyes as though he was trying to push the tears back. I placed my hand on Jai's shoulder from behind as we gently moved towards Gurjit.

Chapter One

Jai's anguish at seeing our brother in such a state was intolerable, for his face was tortured. He stood by Gurjit sobbing, saying 'Gurjit please get up, Gurjit fight this, don't go.' This was Jai's way of expressing his love for Gurjit. Jai began to gather his thoughts and compose himself, and then my parents came in with Bal and Ami and I could see Jai's fragile composure dissolve.

My mother began screaming and banging her hands against her head, pleading with God not to take Gurjit. My father, supported by Ami, just said 'son, we are here, now you can get up, listen son, get up!' I felt tears trickle down my face for the first time. My father's words were like a runaway train powering through my body, and I tried to wipe them quickly to the side, but to no avail. Though the tears were falling my mouth remained closed; there was no outward cry, just heavy breathing. These few minutes were so tough that being in a raging furnace would have been insignificant.

I walked away from my family as their tears and cries continued behind me. I needed to gather what was left of my shredded thoughts as my emotions temporarily took control and washed over me, covering me like a shroud. I needed them to burst out and release all the unbearable distress that had built up inside me.

As I rushed out of the unit another dear friend, Ravi, who we regarded as a brother, came to the hospital. His timely presence checked my emotions, as I had someone I could share them with and gain practical support in an impractical situation. Jai and I spoke to Ravi about the gravity of the situation. The emotions had already begun to create havoc in Ravi as he began to weep and his body language was tense. He stood motionless, holding his hands over his eyes and muttering a prayer of compassion. He looked at us with eyes full of tears and his face contorted so that he was unrecognisable. Unable at first to say anything, he finally began to ask where Dilly and the girls were.

Chapter One

We looked at each other with a deep sense of fear, knowing that death was going to take place and that it was unimaginable even to contemplate. There was nothing we could do for Gurjit. Knowing how hard his death would hit us all, the thought of what Gurjit had been thinking and feeling about death was more terrifying.

We tried to provide Dilly and the girls with all the emotional support we could muster. We talked about Gurjit, about how much he meant to them and to us all, allowing us to start talking about the void that was going to appear in all our lives.

Previously time appeared to have slowed down, but now for some unknown reason, it speeded up. The minutes flew past as we all moved to and fro from the family room, speaking words of comfort and love to one another.

At 6 am the intensive care unit doors opened and Drs Clarke and Dennison came out of the unit toward the family room. Jai and I were directly in front of them, thinking, but not conveying to each other, that Gurjit had died. Before they could say another word or step any further towards the family room we simultaneously said 'You are not going in there to tell our family that he has died, his daughters are in there and we will tell them.'

Both doctors stood still and paid attention. They approached closer and informed us that Gurjit was dying and that there was nothing more they could do. All his major organs were closing down and it was only a matter of time before he died.

Jai immediately asked them whether there was any possibility that the organs could begin to function again. One of the doctors shook her head sideways and the other said 'I've never seen it happen before.' Jai continued to ask the doctors if there were specific medications that could assist in reducing the pressure on Gurjit's heart. The doctors informed him that they had tried every known medication and nothing could reverse the damage the viral infection had caused.

Chapter One

We thanked them for being truthful and direct and told them that we would tell the rest of the family. They in turn thanked us. As soon as they turned away Jai and I embraced, desperately crying, knowing now that Gurjit was going to die.

The knowledge that had been tormenting me now strangely allowed me to express the pain. I could feel our bodies trembling with this knowledge and our tears falling on each other.

The sound of Jai's distress was something I had never heard before. It was like a spiral of screams filling the air, growing louder and appearing to pull us closer together. It was as though our pain had merged into one. We tried to compose ourselves and attempted to muster up some strength so that we could face our loved ones, whose faces were already so dejected and inflicted with torment.

The thought that ran through my mind was - what support could be provided to my family at this time to cope with the enormity of the loss of life and the ending of a relationship? For no more could I turn away from the reality that we were about to share the most wounding happening in our immediate family's life. The looks in our eyes revealed that there was still love for each other, though love that had been wounded.

George moved towards Jai and me, crying his eyes out. He knew our actions were the signal that Gurjit's life was at its end. We embraced and he told us that this was too painful for him. We asked him to come into the family room as he was like family, but George told us he was unable to as he could not face seeing the girls knowing Gurjit was dying. He asked us to forgive him. There was nothing to forgive, as his pain and sincerity was unquestionable.

We went into the room. Jai sat by my mom and I sat next to Suki. I remember that Dilly and Baljinder were next to each other and that Bal and Ami were by my father with Ravi next to them. Jai and I spoke simultaneously and told everyone that Gurjit was not going to survive.

Chapter One

An eruption of tears arose, the mourning started and intensified further as I held on to Suki. Her entire body seemed to have caved in. The trauma had begun to invade her fragile mind. Everyone's tears fell, speaking volumes, and we choked as we tried to speak words of support, which were barely recognisable amid the crying.

It was now a matter of either accepting or continuing to reject what we had been told, and even at that point my heart still sought to reject it for the sake of my nieces. Yet it was futile.

Now the next challenge presented itself, with my nieces wanting to see their dad. Jai and I knew that the quantities of drugs circulating in Gurjit's body had begun to cause physical changes which would not be pleasant for anyone to see. A hard decision was made - that we could not let Suki see her father like that, even though she was so desperate to see him. This was not an easy decision, but we came to realise there were no easy decisions. There was nothing easy about any of this.

Baljinder was adamant that she wanted to see her father, to say goodbye. Yet if Suki could not see him, how could Baljinder? We were trying to protect them, even though we know that at times people need to learn through experience; however this was not an experience that any of us wanted for them. We told Baljinder that it was going to be incredibly painful for her to see her father, yet we would support her in doing so. We spent some time trying to prepare her for it. Deep down we knew that no matter what we said it could not prepare her for what she was about to see, because we ourselves could not be prepared. It was difficult knowing that it was going to hurt her, yet we could not protect her from death. Thus we supported Baljinder's request to see her father.

Jai and I went in with Baljinder, Bal and Ami gently holding her. With her hands raised to her face her lips began to quiver, and the destitution in her eyes could not be measured. She began to curl up and burst with deep pangs of wanting her father.

A few moments were enough, before she wanted to leave, and we supported her as she left the bedside where her dad lay so still. Immediately she told me that she wished she had listened to us. She did not want Suki to experience what she had. She told her 'Suki, I don't want you to see Dad like that, please don't see Dad like that, I wish I had listened.' Suki appeared to accept her sister's statement in a subdued and compliant way. They were both severely traumatised and exhausted by the torrents of emotion that had been sweeping over them.

We all continued to provide the best emotional support that we could. Time again appeared to have slowed down to enable us as a family to gather our thoughts and begin to prepare our minds for the inevitable. The waiting was agonising as each minute presented some hope of recovery amid the apprehension. This inner battle kept on as I questioned our beliefs and how they were holding us, considering everything appeared confusing.

Standing by Gurjit's bed in the intensive care unit was painful for us all. We tried offering more words of comfort to one another, but the rawness of the pain was overpowering. Thus we gently began to talk about our relationship with Gurjit and how it had been forged with love and commitment.

This brief reflection enabled us to see that such intense love in our midst gave us hope as a family to understand that we could respond to the burdens that would arise due to his death. It amazed me to think that even then with death approaching, we had began to use the time available to prepare for it in a way that both recognised the pain it was causing and would cause and the impact it would have. The unity and strength that was at the root of our relationships was keeping us steady through our love for each other at a time when individually we felt little hope and were shaken to the core.

It was after 8 am when Ami came to us and told us that two doctors needed to speak to Dilly, so we left Gurjit's bedside. We approached the family room where Dr Allen and another doctor, Dr Edwards, who we had not seen before, were waiting outside. We decided to ask all other family members to vacate the room and many of them went back to Gurjit's side.

Dr Edwards introduced himself as the Senior Consultant looking after Gurjit and told us that Gurjit had contracted a viral infection which had caused a multiple-organ failure. He told us there was nothing they could do to keep him alive as the drugs they had prescribed to combat the viral infection were having no effect. Unfortunately Gurjit was going to die.

He said they would need to begin to reduce the drugs, otherwise Gurjit would experience another cardiac arrest which would cause him more pain. Also, the drugs in his body were causing his body to swell and would have no beneficial effect if continued. He explained that the Coroner's office would have to be notified as a matter of procedure, due to the fact that Gurjit's admission to the hospital had been less than 24 hours previously.

Those words were the final release, not from hope that a miracle might yet happen, but from the hidden acceptance of what would happen as I saw Dilly's entire body, mind and soul taking such an emotional onslaught as she wept tears of deep heartache.

Jai and I stood numbed as if our breath had been frozen and our tongues stilled. Unable to form the words we needed, we watched our sister's grief pour out on to and over us all, covering us like a dark and draining blanket. Her wound lay bare and we lacked the balm with which to ease her pain.

Yet while this was taking place a part of my mind was challenging my understanding of God, for there was belief mingled with despair, and peace tainted with fear. Lingering thoughts of hope continued to persuade me that this was all still a test, and to dismiss the perceived reality and to look beyond this in faith. Yet I began to be pulled back into reality and realise that there was going to be no redress to our plight. Under the circumstance all we could do was demonstrate our love and care for one another, which was our faith.

Dr Allen's head went down and when she lifted it again there were tears in her eyes, which showed me how desperately she and all the staff had cared and had tried everything in their power to ensure Gurjit's survival. Her words were genuine and she showed a clear practised approach in giving bad news, yet there were tremors in her voice.

The empathy they displayed showed me that it was a painful situation for them too. Their thoughts, no doubt, would be tinged with introspection and self-evaluation of what they might or might not have done differently. Yet for us it was clear that in the short time that Gurjit was in hospital the doctors had responded with great speed and efficiency. We knew they had tried everything and their hopelessness was obvious. Their discomfort was plain to see.

When the doctors left we knew Gurjit's medication would be stopped and we would not have to make a difficult decision about switching the life-support machine off. Though not an immediate thought, it was there nevertheless, and only after they had left did the enormity of knowing this sink in.

Knowing that it would only be a matter of hours before Gurjit passed away we decided that Baljinder and Suki should be taken home and other close family members should be contacted. Jai and I explained to the girls what the doctors had told us and said we would need to take them home. Baljinder accepted this, stating 'I don't want to be here when Dad dies'. But Suki still clung to the hope that her father would pull through. 'I want to be here when he wakes up' she said.

Suki required comforting, and time was spent talking to her with sensitivity to again explain that her belief showed how much she loved and cared for her father. Baljinder spoke to her and supported her in accepting that their dad was going to die and that there was nothing they could do about it.

Chapter One

Jai went on to explain to the rest of the family what was taking place as I prepared to transport the girls back home. They had to be protected from the full enormity of the pain that was going to be released at the hospital. We left the hospital and they sat at the back of the car to provide each other emotional support.

We talked all the way home. The conversation was very open at this stage about death taking place and the fact that it was important to maintain focus upon their father's life. The sisters both began talking about how their father used to talk to them about loss and about supporting the family, and they both recalled his sayings. 'Dad always told us that if anything happened to him we needed to look after each other and listen to the family' said Baljinder. This was heartrending, as it was very relevant and prophetic to what they were now experiencing.

I was not going to stay long at home as I needed to get back to the hospital. I told Dee that it would only be a matter of hours before Gurjit died, and that we would phone her. I gave Baljinder and Suki a hug and told them that the most important thing for them to remember at present was the fact that they had loved their father and that he had loved them. I talked in the past tense to them as a way to begin the process of mourning and acknowledge and accept what was happening. Acceptance I knew would be a hurdle that would have to be navigated later for us all. I gave them, Dee and my 16-month-old niece Sonia a hug and left home to head back to Gurjit.

Before going back to the hospital I went to my parents' next-door neighbours, whom we had known for over 25 years. They knew Gurjit as he used to do part of their shopping. I knocked on their door and Auntie Edna (as we called her) answered, smiling in her usual pleasant manner, and asked me to come in.

She had no idea what I was going to tell her and her husband, Uncle Bill. Bill greeted me as I went into their lounge and asked what they could do for me, thinking I had perhaps come to ask to borrow a garden tool as I had done many times in the past.

Chapter One

I asked them to please sit down as I needed to tell them something. They both looked worried and Auntie Edna immediately asked 'has anything happened to your Mom or Dad?' I said no, and an expression of relief came on their faces as they had thought I was going to tell them something serious. But of course I was. I looked at them and told them that Gurjit was extremely ill in hospital and was on a life support machine with only a few hours to live.

They both slumped back in their chairs and Auntie Edna immediately began to cry and say 'but he is my son as well!' Uncle Bill began shaking his head sideways saying 'why, why does this have to happen?' I went on to briefly explain what had been taking place and where the rest of the family were. They were in shock and inconsolable.

The few minutes with them was important, as they had a very close relationship with my family and to sit and observe their reaction and their tears reinforced how much they cared for us and how much we meant to them. In their sincerity they told me to hurry up and go back to the hospital and support the family. It was painful to have left them looking weary and burdened with the news that I had shared with them. I thanked them and told them that Gurjit thought of them highly, as I knew they did of him.

Returning to the hospital I knew that before I got there Gurjit might well be gone; I had fully accepted at this point that he was going to die. I carried on praying and realised that I had been praying in my heart ever since I knew he was going to die, twelve hours earlier. My prayers acknowledged, painful as this was, that my trust and belief remained in God's existence. What would be needed was for the emotional healing to commence.

I realised that there was nothing wrong with knowing that circumstances do not always turn out the way people want them to. At this time the knowledge provided little comfort. However a great strength remained in knowing that as a family and with people all around us to provide support, our broken hearts would be restored.

Arriving back at the hospital, I ran quickly up the stairs to the intensive care unit and into the family room, which was empty. The whole family were around Gurjit's side. The curtains had remained closed around the bed and when I walked in my mother was hugging Gurjit and my father was holding his hand. Everyone was crying.

Jai's tears were rolling down his cheeks, displaying his tormented face as he said to Gurjit 'We all love you and care for you! Please Gurjit, get up.' Dilly was pleading in her agony for Gurjit, gently saying 'Gurjit, please pull through this for me.'

Bal, even in his distress, was supporting his aunt, holding her with all the strength he had in his body and mind. I went to my mother and gently held her, telling her it was OK to let him go. My mother's crying was high-pitched and her wailing could be heard throughout the ward, yet the hospital staff kept a sensitive distance.

I looked at my mother, whose tears had filled and blurred her vision. I said to her 'It's OK to let him go.' She continued shaking her head from side to side, unable to contain her grief and accept the cruelty that had unfolded. She continued shaking her head as if to shake the moment away.

As Jai gently held my father their faces were in total eclipse, and I saw the utmost despondency falling on them both. This was so painful to watch, knowing we could see each other's turmoil. The sadness that I saw fall upon them was so intense that it rattled my innermost being.

As Jai and my father sought to embrace each other, it felt as though they were capturing their love for Gurjit and were longing to transfer it to him so that he would get up as an act of faith. Their brokenness was so touching, and so heartbreaking.

My mother was hanging on to me, with her head sunk down on my chest and my shirt was soaked with the deluge of her tears. She could not utter a word, her lips shaking like leaves hit by a gale-force wind. Her fingers were tightly woven in prayer as she cried so loudly.

Chapter One

Seeing them like that, I felt that the crushing truth was that hopelessness needed the restoration of hope, for everything appeared null and blank. The sense of shame and misery was as if a tornado had left a path of destruction. I could look no further into myself as the emptiness was too deep to embrace. The same emptiness was in us all.

We all moved back to the family room, where the crying and wailing continued and the room seemed to get smaller and tighter. It was just too difficult to breathe in the midst of such heavy distress, and I came away to try to assemble my disjointed thoughts.

Watching everyone so lost and knowing I was also at a loss was unbearable, because each tear revealed deep pangs of longing that Gurjit would live and that Dilly and the girls would be spared this tragedy that was falling upon us.

At this point Jai went back home to drop off his mother and sister-in-law, and Amarjit went with him. As he was en route to the hospital our cousin-sister Gurdev and her husband Harjinder had arrived at my parents' home in a distressed state. I asked Jai if he could return and bring them to the hospital, which he did.

I did not know that within minutes of talking to Jai, reality was about to stare us squarely in the face; Gurjit was about to die.

CHAPTER TWO

FACING THE UNTHINKABLE

SATURDAY 25TH JANUARY 2003

I walked back to the intensive care unit at about 11.20 am. As I got close to the door Baljit came out. His entire body was stooping and he was crying deeply. When he looked up and saw me, he said 'Chacha's gone, Chacha's gone! This is hurting so much, he's gone!'

I felt as if I were falling into an abyss, for there was no stopping the increasing, terrifying pain. Bal's legs were barely moving as he stood with his head sunk in his hands and the tears crept through his fingers. The noise was so indescribable that the screeching sound numbed me. His agony could not be contained. As he looked up, his eyes searching, longing for a miracle, screaming and shouting for a change, the gaze was of utter and total longing for Gurjit's life to be restored.

We stood there and embraced for a few moments, as we knew we would have to tell my parents as well as other relatives who had arrived. Instead of going into the intensive care unit, where I knew Dilly was alone with Gurjit, I just stood still and wondered what had actually just happened. I heard Bal open the family room door and say to everyone who was in there 'we need to go and say goodbye, Chacha's gone.'

The wave of tears began to beat against everyone in the family room as relatives were trying quickly to get out. Yet Baljit came out first with my father, who looked at me and said 'I am going to say goodbye to my son, your brother, God has taken him.'

My father's words were true. His face showed how much he believed what he said and how much he longed to be with his son. I felt my father knew that this was the end of a journey and that there was no return to what had been. My father stood broken, his body shaking with the reality of the loss of a child.

Everyone else came quickly out of the room, and I stood watching each pass me, still waiting for everyone to go to Gurjit's side. I did not follow them. Rather, silence surrounded me as I fell to my knees and cried out for Gurjit, knowing that part of my family's life had ceased. All that was left were tears that tore me apart, and untold words of love. I felt that time was not standing still but ending, for us as a family. I felt sick, knowing that the pain would now burst out, uncontrollable and with immense impact. I fought so hard to resist this reality, but within a split second I knew it would have to be acknowledged. I knew how much my family and I needed God's grace.

Once I had gathered myself I tried to get hold of Jai, but was unsuccessful, so I walked into the intensive care unit, where there were about 20 family members all squeezed into the side unit where Gurjit was. The noise was heart-shattering, for there was nothing we could do but cry. I saw my mother in a frenzy, banging her hands against her head and shouting at the top of the voice 'Why God have you taken my son and not me?' It was as though all I could do at that time was watch everyone screaming and crying, as no words at that time would bring any deliverance or meaning.

As I continued to look at everyone crying, I could not see Gurjit lying there because Dilly and a number of relatives had covered him. The doctors and nurses stood at a distance with their heads bowed, paying respect to the knowledge that our mourning was given the appropriate space.

My mother became more and more distressed as she held on to me, for I tried to shield her from the torrid waves of pain that were hitting her. It felt as though we had been shipwrecked. As my mother clung on to me, shouting and screaming in desperation, her body began to collapse and her legs could no longer support her. Yet she refused to crumble as she turned towards where Gurjit was lying and then began to move towards him. Relatives moved out of the way for her and she collapsed on to Gurjit, grabbing him and pleading, with Dilly, for him to get up.

At this point I had to leave, because all I could think about was getting hold of Jai, knowing that he was going to be totally shattered, broken into infinite pieces, the moment he heard the words 'Gurjit has died'. I walked out the intensive care unit, trying again to ring him. As I was walking towards the main doors Jai opened them. As soon as he saw the tears running off my face he ran towards me. I grabbed him and told him that Gurjit had gone and he shouted at the top of his voice 'No, he can't have, he can't go!'

Jai tried to run while we were still embracing each other. I looked at him again and said 'Gurjit's gone and there's nothing we can do.' The blankness on his face was like looking into a bottomless pit, total pain yet incredible love was also there and I knew it was extremely deep within him. I looked again, believing I had failed him, then let him go. He ran to the intensive care unit.

I felt I had failed, because he should have been there when Gurjit died. The feeling of knowing Jai's pain began to slice me even more.

My cousin-sister Gurdev immediately broke down in tears and looked at me, shaking her head vigorously sideways and grabbing Ami. The fear on Ami's face was so tormenting. His aunt's arms were glued to him and her cries were so loud while I could hear his muffled pain as his head was to the side of her shoulders.

He looked up as I walked towards them, and his eyes were like a little lost puppy, wondering where he was and what had happened to him. We embraced and our tears were rolling on to each other. As we cried, I could not think. My mind went totally blank for a few seconds, hoping that any minute now someone was going to throw a jug of cold water over me and I would wake up from this nightmare. But the cold water never came.

Gurdev frantically began to run away from the intensive care unit in search of Gurjit. I had to hold her still for a few more seconds as her body was violently shaking. Ami then took her towards the unit.

Harjinder just stood motionless. He leaned back against the wall and stared upwards, his eyes welling up. As I walked towards him he told me to go back to the family, but I knew I couldn't without embracing first, which we did. He was in total shock, as we all were. His eyes were glazed in bewilderment. He did not want anyone to see him in that state, and kept urging me to leave him and go to the rest of the family.

Even before getting to the main doors I heard the intense crying, and it continued to be an unbearable sound to hear. It seared through me. The rawness of our loss filled the ward and the sound, the terrible and dreadful sound, was lingering. I knew that such sounds would echo for days even in our quiet moments and that they would not leave us, because they were the innermost deepness of our love screaming out.

The crying intensified as I drew the curtains back to get near to Gurjit's bedside. I was unable to do so because of the number of relatives already present, so I stood back. Everyone's faces were full of anguish, hurt, agony, turmoil, torment, distress, disbelief, bewilderment, shock, horror, fear, anxiety. I knew that I had displayed all such emotions that were raging within my heart. All I could do was watch. The pain of seeing everyone else's pain was shaking whatever capacity there was left in me to stand and respond.

As relatives began to move around Gurjit I noticed that there were two staff members also standing at the top of the bed. They were sensitively offering words of comfort to Dilly and my mother. They looked towards me, as they must have noticed that I was staring at them, surprised that they were actually seeking to emotionally support my family at such a distressing time. Their presence was welcome.

My mother was clinging on to Gurjit for dear life and would not let him go. We had held her as she was ready to collapse and I cried with her, saying this has always been in God's hands. It was difficult to take her away from her son, yet it was becoming clear that through her pain and exhaustion she was not going to be able to stand for much longer.

She came with me and we walked towards the family room, her fragile state increasingly obvious. Her body was trembling with shock, and I felt every particle pulsating in her body as she clung on to me. I knew it would only be a matter of seconds before she collapsed. The only 'safe' place was together.

The moment we entered the family room a nurse came in behind us. He had seen the condition my mother was in and would have known what was about to take place - as soon as we entered the family room, my mother collapsed like a demolished building. There was nothing I could do to hold her up. It was as though I held on to her body but her entire skeleton had left her. The nurse immediately stepped in and we managed to pick her off the floor and place her on a sofa in the room. He told me that he would be back. We had to clear the room as the same nurse and a doctor entered to treat her, which they did with great attention and care.

I stayed with my mother and my sister Gurdev came into the room totally drained. When she saw my mother she began to cry loudly, struggling to breathe and shaking her head sideways while banging her hands against her head. It was awful to see her in such a distressed state. I held on to her as her body was still shaking and her tears were falling on to my shoulder. When she looked at me, the dejection in her eyes was untouchable. Then suddenly, and from nowhere, she looked up at me and mustered words which touched me deeply, considering that she was in so much emotional pain. 'Go to Gurjit' she said. 'I'll stay here with Mom.'

Chapter Two

As I was ready to leave my father entered the room, aided by Bal. He collapsed into the chair and burst into a river of tears, wailing and praying for Gurjit to return. Bal attended to him, holding him and preventing him from falling out of the chair as his entire body began to curl into a ball. He was inconsolable in his grief.

The sight of my parent's distress was overwhelming, and my stomach and chest tightened to such an extent that I thought I was going to explode. I felt so tense outwardly, yet crazily felt an inner peace. I could not fathom where it came from or understand its relevance in the midst of such total despair.

Watching everyone's plight, including my own, showed that there was no hiding place from what was unfolding before us. There was great pain in the fact that we would not be able to show Gurjit our love and care. The questions would continue to rage for a long time ahead as I could see how downcast we all were. Our words could not accurately reflect what had happened.

I phoned home and Dee answered. As soon as I said her name she began to cry. 'Gurjit's just died.' Her crying became louder and I then heard Baljinder and Suki in the background crying too as they realised what the phone call meant. Dee placed the phone down on the table and I heard her go over to the girls and knew she was embracing them, as the crying became muffled. Shortly she came back to the phone and I told her that we would be home soon and that I knew that she would be able to provide as much comfort as possible to the girls, whom she loved dearly.

'I miss him' she said. 'Why has this happened? Tell Dilly I love her and that I'm here for the girls.' Her words sent shivers down my spine, as her love was seeking to pierce the agony and pain we had begun to experience. The tremble in her voice expressed her desire to be at the hospital, yet her role of being with the girls was something that could not be forgotten, because I knew when she embraced them that she covered them with pure love, and her support enabled the girls to commence mourning.

I told her we would be home as soon as we can, but deep down I did not even know what that meant. Upon ending the call I could still hear the girl's utter devastation ringing through my ears.

When I went back to the unit Jai was clinging to Gurjit so intensely that we left him to hold on. The release of emotions from Jai was like a raging fire, and the best thing was to stand back and allow it to burn. I went up to Jai, who was telling Gurjit 'You can't go, because you have to be here when your daughters get married and when my daughter gets married.' His words expressed a desire to wash away everyone's pain.

I held on to Jai to express my emotions in feeling his pain and told him that it was all right, because Gurjit knew Jai's love for him. Jai just held on to Gurjit and the anguish was indescribable.

Jai's tears were falling like a tropical rainstorm and could be heard striking Gurjit's body and bouncing on to the floor. His entire body was trembling as he held on to Gurjit, and his face was contorted and gripped with pain. As he moved his head slowly close to Gurjit's face, the brotherly intimate love was self-evident to all who knew him. Jai's grip further revealed all our vulnerability, because the desire visible in his eyes was for life to be restored.

In Jai's own time he finally let go of Gurjit, and we all went back to the family room. The floor was wet with all the tears that had fallen. My mother was lying down, but still conscious at that point with tears running down her face so fast I could not see her eyes.

Everyone was consoling each other in the best way they could. The fear of knowing the separation had come spread into knowing there was no direction to go. The fact that we had each other to hold was the only comfort. It was very difficult even to try to remain focused, because everyone around me was in shock. It was so numb, raw and frightening. Not knowing what to do next and wondering how anything could ever be done was dreadful.

Chapter Two

As I continued to look around at all those in the room, the realisation of what had happened took a further hold on my emotions as I knew this was irreversible. Such reality was so hard-hitting because there was no immediate comfort to fall upon. It became even more painful when I saw Dilly beside herself with grief. Bal and Ami were trying so hard to offer their aunt comfort, while in total agony themselves and wanting their uncle back.

My parents' heightened distress was unbearable. It was a terrible sight to behold, and no words could seek to offer an explanation. Thus, as I embraced my mother in silence, I heard her innermost, boundless love for her son and her daughter.

A male nurse came into the family room and asked if a few of us wanted to come back to Gurjit's bed to say a final goodbye before they began to remove all the equipment. Dilly, Jai, Baljit, Ami, Laker (Gurjit's cousin brother), and I went back to find another male nurse waiting. He explained that they would remove the equipment and begin to wash Gurjit's body. They explained that he would be kept in the hospital mortuary.

As we walked back to Gurjit's bedside, I had never hoped so much for him to be alive, somehow pulling through the bleakest experience against all odds. Yet as the curtain was opened for the final time, there was no hope of that. We all looked at each other in silence, as words appeared insufficient. As we stood around Gurjit's bed side, stripped of strength, I saw an inner resolve in Bal and Ami, for they stood either side of their aunt acting as pillars of immense strength. They were holding her sensitively, caringly, lovingly and sympathetically, with deep sorrow for her loss. They moved slowly with her step by step as Dilly approached her loving husband and her face reflected the pain of separation, with the knowledge of the tragedy of what death would now mean for her and her daughters.

'Massi, Chacha's still in our hearts' said Bal. His words were a reminder of what our relationships were all about – love. This could not be taken away.

Gurjit's lifeless body lay there, his eyes wide open. Jai gracefully placed his hands on them to close them, and as he did so the tears ran wild. Such an act was so respectful and bound by love, the love of a brother. 'Gurjit, we love you, please come back, please come back!' said Jai. His heart seemed broken into pieces, and he appeared to go into a trance as he looked at Gurjit, his body still violently shaking. Very few thoughts were going through my mind besides pondering upon the severe and intense pain that had arisen for my family. I was becoming more and more broken, and as I looked at everyone even more pieces of me were becoming shattered.

Dilly slowly bent forward and kissed her husband on his lips with such tender love that nothing could separate her from Gurjit at that moment. Her love, so deep and personal, touched a chord in my heart as her tears fell on to Gurjit. She gently rubbed the tears into his cheeks as though it was her final gift to the love of her life. Laker, out of all of us, tried to remain composed, but the moment he saw Dilly doing this he completely broke down.

Each of us then held on to Gurjit's hand and one by one we kissed him on the forehead as our final farewell. We thanked the male nurses for their support as they stood respectfully and sensitively to allow us this brief and personal time. Their words of condolence were so gracious and meant so much. 'We are so sorry for your loss and our thoughts are with you' they said.

We all looked at each other and knew it was time to leave. It was dreadful, because we all wanted to stay. The slow, agonising steps as we walked back to the family room seemed never ending. As the door slowly opened, we could not all go in because there were so many present, so Jai went in as we stood outside. We heard him tell everyone that the equipment was now being removed and a male nurse was washing Gurjit's body.

Chapter Two

When my parents came out of the room and saw Dilly, they clung on to her and their muffled cries expressed their intimate love for her. My mother looked at Dilly and kept shaking her head sideways and repeating 'No, no, where is Gurjit, where has Gurjit gone? He's not gone, he's at home, he's not gone.' The devastation revealed by her words of deep love could not provide her, or any of us, with any reassurance, for we knew this could not be obtained at that moment.

I approached my parents and Dilly, gently held them and said 'it's time for us all to leave to go home.' They were words which I wished did not have to be conveyed without injecting that I wanted Gurjit to be with us. The look in my mother's eyes when I said that was so crystal clear, yet her face darkened like a cloud ready to burst as her tears continued to trickle down her face.

All she could do was to look at me. She could not speak; all her energy had been sapped. My father was totally lost. His eyes revealed an intense shock, and he was unable to move as he stood looking at Dilly's agony. I could only imagine what he felt as a father who was not in a position to provide safety to his daughter.

Dilly was so overwhelmed that she began to keel over and had to be held by my cousin sister Gurdev. We could not see her eyes for tears. I gently held her again and tried to offer some comfort, knowing it was truly difficult to convey any such message because everything seemed as though this was not really taking place.

As we all began slowly making our way out of the hospital my mind was going blank again, unable to register fully what had occurred, yet strangely knowing we would have to do something about it. It took forever to leave the hospital, as heavy footed we started heading out towards the car park. Every yard seemed a million miles.

Of the twenty or so people there I had my parents, Dilly and Gurdev in my car. In the car, Gurdev rang her daughter (my niece Sunny) and told her that Gurjit had died and for her to get to the house. I could hear Sunny shouting down the phone 'Mom don't joke with me, please don't tell me that!' My cousin-sister repeated what she had said and I could hear the panic in her voice. This was compounded by Sunny's screams rattling down the phone louder and louder. It was hurtful knowing that no one was with my niece to give support as she received such devastating news about her uncle's death.

I felt so sorry for Sunny. I only wished that someone could have been with her, as I knew she would be travelling on her own to get to her grandparents' home while having to comprehend the enormity of what she had been told. I knew this would be tearing her apart, but there was nothing I could do to offer her any support at such a crucial time.

Gurdev then ended the call by saying 'Hurry up and get to your grandparents' home.' After this she was trying her best to console Dilly. All I could think of at that moment was getting home quickly to see Baljinder and Suki, who I knew would be totally distraught about their father's death.

Then my father began talking about how he had woken up in the early hours of the morning knowing that Gurjit was dying. He went on to say that on the Wednesday, when Gurjit had come over to the house as he did every dinner time after finishing work, for the first time ever he had left without saying goodbye. This was the last time he had seen Gurjit alive. He said that when Gurjit had left that day he had known something was not right and felt that something was on his mind. He wished he had said something to him. He continued to sob and express his sorrow to Dilly by telling her we had all been robbed of Gurjit.

Listening to my father was painful, because I knew that what he said was so true to him. He had the capacity (as most parents do) of knowing something was not right. It was quite clear that for Gurjit this was true, because none of us had known that he had a viral infection. It hurt, knowing that he was so ill but that it had not revealed until it was too late for medical intervention.

Chapter Two

My father continued to cry and to question why this had happened. His expression of love was revealed through a selfless question and desire for his son to have life. 'Why, death, did you not come to me?' he said. 'Why have you taken my son and not me? God please give him back, he is needed, take me!' His heartfelt plea revealed the bottomless pain in his heart, mind and soul.

My mother said the same thing and began to pray, asking God why he had taken Gurjit rather than her. Dilly was crying and was being comforted by Gurdev, and I told them all that we should remember the truth of our love for Gurjit and his love for us, and that death was not in our control.

As Jai, Ravi and I had spent time with Dilly at the hospital talking about Gurjit's death before him dying, Dilly, even though hurt and in pain, understood that there was nothing anyone could have done. I slowly began to understand that our prayers for healing and restoration to take place for Gurjit were in fact being answered, not in the way anticipated but in God's way, which was not our perceived ideal way.

There was still no doubt that it was very raw and hurting so badly, because no amount of preparation could deal with the level and intensity of anguish that had arisen in our hearts. Dilly was unable to speak, understandably so, as she remained slumped on Gurdev's shoulders crying loudly. As I glanced in my rear-view mirror I saw a woman who had been wrecked by tragedy. She had taken the most severe assault to her entire being - the loss of her beloved husband. She looked so exhausted, and every time I glanced back I saw her lift her head towards the back of the car, as though she was searching for Gurjit and wanting him back.

Pulling on to the drive was completely different, because this time there could be no way my mind could even seek to explore a delayed hope. I could not offer this to anyone. Getting out of the car seemed to take an eternity, as my parents' own physical frailties were compounded by the intense shock they had experienced. Dilly's tragedy had completely immobilised her and she remained in the car crying. 'What am I going to say to the girls?' she said. 'What can I tell them? How can I look into their eyes and tell them?'

Slowly she began to get out of the car, but the few steps to the front door seemed like running the 100-metre hurdles. As we stood outside I was ready to open the door, and as I turned towards my parents and Dilly and Gurdev, the expression on their faces was the same. Total fear had gripped them as I knew it had taken a hold of me. They did not want to enter the house.

They all stood their shaking their heads and remained rooted to the ground. The few moments of silence I felt were sufficient for us to then enter. The moment we stepped into the house, intense crying could be heard from relatives who had arrived. Not even the sounds of a billion seagulls could have compared with the cries that were being uttered.

My priority was to see Baljinder and Suki, who were upstairs. Yet as I made my way upstairs Dee was walking down the stairs with Sonia in her arms. Even at 16 months, she knew something was amiss. I saw her little lips drop and was shocked by what she did. She pointed towards the light bulb and said 'bub.' The significance of this was remarkable, as she had a fascination for the light when it came on and Gurjit was the only one who used to pick her up and show her the light bulb - he nicknamed her 'bub'. This was terrifying, because nothing could compare with this experience for us as a family.

I looked into Dee's eyes. She tried to remain brave as she held Sonia, but tears were streaming down her face. Sonia gently began to touch them, and in her own little way wiped them away. It was an amazing sight to behold. She said 'the girls are there' and pointed upstairs, and her jaw began to drop, for no more words came forth.

We embraced for a few seconds and her tears began to soak my shirt even further. As I continued upstairs each step seemed to be heavier than the last. The burden of knowing I was going to see my nieces totally broken and crushed inside was too much to bear, yet I needed to be with them.

Baljinder and Suki were crying. I went up to them and said 'We are all so sorry that your dad has died,' and then we just held on to each other. Their strong grip was welcome, as I did not want to let them go any more than they did me. Their faces were contorted and tortured with intense despair. It was so unfair to see, so cruel. The shock had begun to set in and they were struggling to breathe. It looked as though life had left them.

As Dilly entered the bedroom with Jai and Mangender, the girls let go of me and she called to them with a desperate cry. They went to her immediately with arms open. The screams echoed the pain and panic and each scream continued to become more heart-shattering and then earth-shattering, for our entire world had been shaken. Jai and Mangender huddled around the girls and they all continued to cry, as well as me. The intimacy was so strong as Jai's arms sought to provide a shelter to weather the deep, agonising pain the girls and Dilly were feeling.

It was clear that Dilly, Baljinder and Suki were our priority and needed the space to mourn before cultural expectations took over. Although I knew relatives would all want to see them to offer their condolences and support, the girls had already asked that they be left alone with immediate family only, and they were supported in this. Jai and Mangender remained with them, followed shortly by Bal and Ami, whose cries began to pierce me even more. They were so intense that there was no limit to the inner turmoil and torment of the pain we were all experiencing.

I went next door to see Uncle Bill and Auntie Edna and told them that Gurjit had died. Edna hugged me, sobbing 'I'm ever so sorry, I don't want to believe that this has happened!' Uncle Bill sat down with his head in his hands and said 'it's not fair that good people die.' He kept shaking his head sideways while Auntie Edna cried. I embraced her and told her that I knew it was hurting them because they were practically part of our family. They asked me to go and be with my family.

After returning Jai had begun to make the difficult calls to immediate relatives and friends. He handled each call with great courage and clarity, knowing that the relative or friend on the other end of the phone would be distressed at both hearing the information and wanting to hurry up and visit.

There was just no way I could have made any of those calls. I was so grateful that he was able to do that, because at that point it felt as though everything within me had just fallen out. As he made the calls the tears were flowing down his cheeks and he tried to wipe them as they moved to his lips.

The two most difficult calls were to Gurjit's parents in India and to my sister Patty in Canada. Considering the time difference between the countries, the call to India was made first. The love flowing from Jai over the phone to Gurjit's father was soothing to hear. He told how Gurjit had lived his life with a great ability to show respect to people. Jai sensitively handled the call by reassuring Gurjit's father that we all knew how much they loved Gurjit and how much he loved them all.

After the call had finished he turned around and his body trembled with the knowledge of Gurjit's death. At first all I could do was look at him. Then gently we embraced, as we knew the next phone call was going to be just as difficult because of the emotional ties involved - it was to our sister.

When Jai made the phone call to Patty the first thing he said to her was 'Patty, I've got something to tell you which is going to hurt.' I immediately heard her begin to cry, as she clearly would have realised that something must have happened to a family member. Jai went on to say 'Patty, Gurjit has died.'

Chapter Two

The moment the words were uttered Jai broke down. I could hear the screaming coming from Patty and heard her say 'No, no, it's not true, please tell me it's not true.' Jai went on to relay the sequence of the night's events and how it had all culminated in the tragic death of Gurjit. Jai oozed sensitivity and support over the phone by reminding Patty of Gurjit's love for us all and our love for him. I admired Jai's ability to provide such support to Patty, knowing that at that stage she was all alone, thousands of miles away, with no immediate option of being with us as a family.

Jai then said to her, 'Patty, we all love you, and we know this is very difficult and we are all thinking about you, please, please try not to worry about us, please, because we want you here and know that you are hurt.' He continued after wiping his tears, 'we know you loved him.' Again all I could do was to stand and watch as Jai continued to provide emotional support to her over the phone.

While he was still talking to her, Gurjit's uncle had fainted in the lounge and I was called by my father to attend to him. He was due to go back to India the next day. When he recovered he said he did not want to go back to India, but my father spoke to him about the importance of ensuring that Gurjit's parents were supported while funeral arrangements were made. I wondered what he could be feeling.

Gurjit's uncle cried and cried as my father put his arms around him; they were both inconsolable, yet trying to console each other. I sat with them, wondering how Gurjit's uncle was going to face the journey back to India. What a heavy burden he had to relay to Gurjit's family.

My father continued to offer words of comfort to Gurjit's uncle. I could see that he was consumed with sorrow and helplessness. 'You tell Gurjit's father and mother that he was my son too and that we loved him so much' he said. 'You tell them that my heart has gone with their son as well, because this day too I have died. You tell them he was my son and I love him.'

Then my father began to shatter into pieces and I embraced him and Gurjit's uncle, trying to offer them support. Holding my father's hand I said 'I already know your heart has broken and that he was your son, my heart has also gone today.' We sat there with deep tears of mourning.

More relatives arrived, and each time Jai or I ended up explaining what had happened to Gurjit. The continual reliving of the event was agony, as it gave no respite to actually think, so the fact that we took this in turn was the only way we could get some time away from the despair. I knew they were all hurting and all needed time to express their pain, but I felt that part of my mind was closing to the severity and complexity of the pain as this was the only way I could focus on what needed to be done for my family.

As Jai and I continued to take it in turns, we would go upstairs to spend time with Dilly and the girls and Bal and Ami, who had remained together since we had returned from the hospital. Yet it was very difficult to actually commence any conversation because the emotions were raging in all of us.

This exchange between Jai and me went on until some close family members from Huddersfield arrived. We both had to be present to provide them with as much support as we could gather, knowing we were also in total agony ourselves. Our relatives were beside themselves the moment they entered the house. Trembling and in disarray, they were shedding tears fast and their faces were swollen with the torment in our midst.

No words were spoken at first . They just grabbed us and released a torrent of screams and tears. My body was physically shaking as I tried to stop my cousin from collapsing. My older niece, Narinder, was jumping up and down and screaming out so loud 'No! No! This can't be happening. No! No! This isn't true. It's not true, it can't be true!' She then ran to my mother and grabbed her so tightly that the crying could not be heard, but the moment she let my mother go, the screaming was unreal.

It took a while before any words could be offered, as no words could even remotely plug the hole that had been created in our lives. Slowly Jai began to tell them what had happened, but each sentence was met with high-pitched screams. They had to be left for a while longer before anyone could seek to provide them with a rational explanation as to how Gurjit had died, because everything seemed totally irrational.

At this time I left the room, as I just wanted to be close to Dilly and the girls. As I went back upstairs to them, they were all asleep. They were overcome by the physical and psychological exhaustion that death had wrought.

When I saw them, how deeply I wished that when they woke up somehow I would be able to tell them that Gurjit was alive and there was no need for their tears of mourning, but there could be joy that he had returned and the pain they were feeling could now disappear. How I longed to be able to deliver such a message of hope, peace and love, but despairingly I knew this would never be a conversation that would take place. All I could do was stand in the room and watch them, knowing that their minds had been severely affected and their emotions would have been raging like a furnace within them, totally uncontrollable.

Meanwhile relatives continued to arrive. Though they wanted to see Dilly and the girls, they respected her request to be left alone for the moment. Every relative and friend expressed his or her condolences and wanted to provide as much support as they could, for they knew that Gurjit's death was incredibly shocking and had created a mortal wound to us as a family.

We kept having to repeat what had happened, which continued to create feelings of insecurity. All Jai and I could do was focus on supporting Dilly and the girls as priority and then attend to every other immediate family member. Hence we took this time to begin to make some tentative plans to ensure someone remained with Dilly and the girls at all times on a rota basis to support them.

Chapter Two

When Dilly, the girls and the lads woke up at about 9 pm they all said that they felt it had been a dream and that Gurjit was alive. The thing that made them realise that it was not a dream was the realisation that they had not woken up in their own beds, and they could still hear people crying downstairs.

We sat together and began talking. Bal and Ami were telling us that they were finding it difficult to believe Gurjit had died and did not know how to accept it. 'This is too strange' said Bal. 'We think any moment now he is going to walk through the door.'

Their exhaustion was still evident, yet they were trying to offer their aunt and cousin-sisters comfort and their eyes were full of compassion. Their faces said it all, they wanted to take their pain away. Yet the dejection that was also present on their faces meant they would have known this was not going to be possible.

Bal's and Ami's tears continued to trickle down their faces as they embraced Dilly, saying 'we're so sorry that Chacha's gone, we're so sorry'. The tears interrupted them as they struggled in expressing the tragedy that had brutally wounded them. 'We love him and we want him back!' they said.

The girls were in bits, holding on to each other so tightly with tears bursting out like a broken water pipe. Though it was distressing to hear, they had to continue to cry to begin to let the inner turmoil and pain surface.

Dilly said 'Though I don't want to accept that Gurjit has died, I know that he is not coming back.' Her tears rose again and overflowed, as she continued 'I love him so much, I want him back, I'd do anything to get him back.' Her body slumped on to Bal's shoulders and her weeping continued. Ami tried to offer emotional support to her by saying 'Massi, we all know how much you loved each other and that this hurts so much. Massi, we all want him back, I want this all to be a dream, I want someone to tell me that Chacha's alive.' His tears fell upon her as she kept nodding in agreement with his tender and kind words of love.

I held the girls as they clung to each other. Baljinder said 'I know my dad was not there when I saw him in the hospital, I miss him, he is my dad and I love him, I just want him to come back to us.' Suki said 'How can I have a life without my dad?'

Listening to them was important, yet it hurt, because I felt as though I was trapped in a cage and unable to fully respond to them. Their pain was staring right at me. Their words rang a deep chord. The reality of their father's death was slowly unfolding as their relationship with him had suddenly ended and life for them without him was tragic.

We spoke openly about how this reality was difficult and troublesome and that it would be some time before we would understand what to do. We were just trying to express that we would remain close and that we were seeking to give and receive comfort to each other from the hurt that we had experienced.

We talked about Gurjit's life and reflected on his personality and character. Dilly said: 'I know he loved us all and that he was a very good husband and father. I can't think what my life is going to be like without him now, I just can't even think about this, I want him to walk through the door and tell me that the doctors got it all wrong. I want him back.'

Baljinder said 'I want to bring my dad back. I don't want to believe he has gone. I can't believe this has happened to us. He was here and now his gone.'

Suki was too distressed to speak and was comforted with being told how much we knew she loved her father and how much he had meant to her and how much he had loved her. Upon hearing this her tears continued to pour down as her lips quivered from the profound and irreversible loss that she and the entire family had just been dealt.

To think that we could already begin to have such conversations was unreal. Yet when they were taking place it became apparent that we had just started to begin to recognise the impact death had begun to have upon us.

My thoughts centred upon how to do things, in other words, how were we going to support each other? How were we going to protect each other and from exactly what did we need protection? How could this wound in our hearts be removed?

Upon looking at that for a brief moment I realised that the fullness of the pain needed to be felt before those questions could even be looked at.

After spending this time together talking, it was important for them all to eat and drink, even though I imagined that they had no desire to, because only death being reversed would bring us any fulfilment and that was impossible.

The night was drawing to an end, though there was no end in sight in what death had created. Rather I felt there would be a constant battle over the weeks and months ahead to express our pain from loss.

CHAPTER 3

THE AFTERMATH

SUNDAY 26TH JANUARY 2003

It was the early hours of Sunday morning before I went to sleep. My mind did not want my eyes to close, but my body had been awake for almost two days and had to get some rest, physical rest at least. However, the sleep was only for a few hours and I woke up around 6 am with my whole body shaking uncontrollably and floods of tears rolling down my face.

The strange thing about the crying was that I could not actually recall any thoughts running through my mind to explain the reason for it. It took a few moments to realise what had happened, that Gurjit had died.

I began to pray to God, because I knew I had no strength left to respond to the days, weeks and months ahead. I asked God for us all to be strengthened and for us all to provide support to each other, because the heartache was the heaviest burden we had ever experienced. The moment that thought became embedded, tears gushed out, and it was so impossible to contemplate what I could do to even bring about some level of comfort.

I was no longer able to sleep. I sat up on the sofa bed on which I had been sleeping downstairs alone. I kept my eyes shut and could feel that the tears were still gently trickling down. As I sat there my mind strangely began to seek to order various tasks that had to be done in the next few days. My mind prioritised the tasks. First I had to ensure that Dilly and the girls were comforted. Second I had to see my parents to ensure that they were physically coping, despite their ill health. Third, I had to clear out Gurjit's bedroom in preparation for a Sikh religious ceremony. Fourth, I must touch base with Jai, Bal, Ami and Dilly and have a family discussion. Fifth, I should prepare for more arrivals of relatives and friends. Finally, sixth, I had to prepare tasks for the Monday, which included contacting the funeral directors, Gurjit's employers and his doctor.

Then my thoughts became still as doubts arose over whether we as a family would be able to respond to each other and be able to give each other emotional support. This suffering would continue as the tragedy was already ripping deep within and howling for release. I knew that trying to embrace the significance of this would be a constant struggle.

When the first sounds in the house were heard I slowly moved to see who was up, as quite a few of us had slept over. There was a cold sensation in opening the door, as though someone was ready to jump out at me, and I hoped somehow it would be Gurjit, telling me that he had pulled through. How much I hoped that this was all still a nightmare. I had never hoped so much in my entire life for something to change.

Any hopes that what had taken place was a dream were dashed at the sight of Dilly's tortured face. She stood shattered and destroyed, all levels of functioning on hold. Her weeping in itself could have reaped a harvest of love. As she saw me she said 'It is too painful to know that Gurjit will not be with me and this hurts so badly, but I do believe he is with God.' Her expression of love revealed the harrowing horror that Gurjit's death had created for her.

I held her as her weeping became louder and I could hear her heart beating frantically for her lost love. The tears were in my eyes too. I was thinking that this was too much to endure, yet knew there was no alternative.

Dilly said 'I know the girls need me, I know everything else needs to be done, but I keep thinking about Gurjit, I want him to be with me. I don't know what to do.' We spoke about how her involvement was important in making decisions and I said Jai and I would support her in this, as we all knew that she and the girls needed the time together to provide each other support.

At this stage the girls awoke and the first thing Suki uttered was 'where's my dad, is this a dream?' When they saw their mother's tears they began to break down and their bodies curled into balls as they embraced each other. 'We want our dad to walk through the door and tell us that it was all a joke' said Baljinder.

We spoke about how we all wanted that to happen and for all these thoughts to go away. It was so painful to know that deep down their father was not coming back. 'We don't know why Dad's not coming back and we don't like it' said Suki.

Knowing that life's turmoil was in their midst, and that they were subdued with absolute despair, the reality could not be dismissed. Their needs were insurmountable. Our challenge was to see what we could achieve with all our care.

It was like being on a ledge, facing down and seeing nothing but darkness, yet when looking at each other there was some hope to be imparted. However it was difficult to see beyond what was present, and this was especially true when I saw my parents, who were distraught, finding it difficult to accept that they had spoken to Gurjit for the last time.

My parents began to question the events before Gurjit's death. 'He should not have gone before us, it's not right' said my father. My mother said 'this pain has torn me apart. My heart cannot cope with it. Why has God done this to us? How did we not know how ill he was?'

They began to crumble through the onslaught of emotions and questions that began to surface. My father said 'Gurjit must have known this was going to happen. I never got to tell him how much he meant to me.'

Chapter Three

As my parents' crying became louder, physical pain had begun to set in, and they continued to say 'we wish he had not gone and hope God will give him back to us.'

Their faces painted a picture of their perfect love for their son, and this could not be taken away even though their lifeless eyes were full of gloom. We spoke about how the questions that we all had would not be answered, if at all, at the moment.

They sat there destroyed, and I wondered what they could do to reduce the pain their daughter and grandchildren were experiencing. The rug had been pulled right out from underneath us and it felt as though there was no safety net to fall upon.

After leaving them (which was difficult, because I knew they would be wrestling with unresolved emotions and thoughts for a long time), Bal, Ami and I went to Gurjit's house. We needed to prepare his bedroom for a Sikh religious ritual for the funeral. As the front door opened I had a strange feeling that somehow Gurjit was there, because everything was the same. All his pictures with Dilly, the girls and the family were on the walls in the lounge and leading upstairs. In each picture he was smiling and so full of life, with so much to give and live for. I wished I could have got him out of one of the photos and make him alive again.

It was too painful, because it felt as though from every picture he was watching us and that his smile was trying to offer us some reassurance that we would be able to respond, even though that was not my primary wish – what I wanted was to get him back, for my entire family.

We stood for a while and looked at each other and we began to cry, knowing Gurjit would never be here again when we visited. Bal and Ami stood broken and Ami remained glued to the front door. He was unable to step forward, caught in an understandable fright of the knowledge and reality of death. Bal, with tears of sadness, moved towards him, and as he did so Ami began to bend over and a deep well of tears sprung out of him in absolute grief. Bal gently embraced his younger brother and managed to prevent him from collapsing to the floor. Their tears felt as though the ground around me had been shaken by such brokenness.

Ami began to mutter, 'I can't do this, I just can't believe Chacha's not here.' It was as though he knew that to take part in preparing the house was further acknowledgement that Gurjit had died, and this was too traumatic to embrace. Bal responded to him, 'I feel the same, but we have to do it for Chacha.' Such words began to give Ami the strength to move forward.

The few moments allowed them the space to steady themselves before we went upstairs. On the stairs, each photo of Gurjit told its own story, and we would pause to reflect upon them. But it was very difficult, because seeing each picture was like an obstacle stopping us from reaching his bedroom. We crept up the stairs, thinking that we knew this man, his life, his love and care, and what a privilege it was to have had an experience with him.

As we approached his bedroom, Bal wanted to open the door. As we entered I felt as though my breath was going to be taken away. The glass of water he had been using was still on the bedside cabinet, and his towel was still on his pillow. Inwardly I screamed, 'how has this happened? Can anything be done to change this dread we have experienced? '

I recalled how less than two days before Gurjit had been sitting in his bed talking to me and I hadn't realised how seriously ill he was. It was very hard to contain this along with remembering what he had said. Ami said, 'what is Massi Dilly thinking? What's going through her mind knowing that Chacha will never be in that bed again?'

We glanced at each other, realising that we could not even begin to comprehend what that meant for her. Ami's question made me think even more about what Dilly was feeling, and what she would feel knowing the next time she walked into her bedroom that Gurjit would never be there again. We were totally lost, and we would have to somehow find each other through this disastrous experience.

There was very little we could say, because the numbness was monstrous. We delicately began moving each item out of the bedroom and placing it elsewhere, as the room would be used as part of the religious ceremony and a place for family and friends to sit to reflect upon his life and death, and more importantly upon the gift of life given by God.

Our own silence was a reminder of our ever-present pain. Though we took time to undertake this troubling task, I knew we all wanted to leave as soon as possible.

As we began to rearrange furniture downstairs in the back lounge, the phone rang and a man spoke in Punjabi, asking hesitantly to speak to Gurjit. I asked him who he was and the man told me that he was Gurjit's friend from work. I informed him that I had some difficult news to tell him, that Gurjit had died in hospital yesterday. The man again asked to speak to Gurjit; I again told him that Gurjit had died. I realised he was finding it difficult to accept what I was saying, for I could relate to this. I told him that I knew it was hard to believe. When I rephrased the words from 'Gurjit has died' to 'Gurjit is no longer here', the man began to sob on the phone and apologised for crying. I told him there was no need to apologise. He went on to tell me that the reason he had rung was that another friend of Gurjit's had seen the family at the hospital. He had not wanted to believe it when he had been told in the pub what had happened, so he had rung, but no one had answered. He told me that when Gurjit did not visit the pub he feared the worst.

I explained to him what had happened. The man kept crying and saying that he was so sorry and that he did not want to believe Gurjit was no longer here. I reassured him, saying it was fine to cry and it was difficult for everyone to believe what had happened. As a family we knew Gurjit was an extremely good person and would be missed by all who knew him.

I did not know how the conversation could be ended as I had never told anyone such daunting news over the phone, and I believed the man sensed this, as he told me that he would let us go because he knew what we needed to do. It felt very strange having to tell someone such distressing information over the phone, because I was always used to attending to distressing events in person.

Once we had finished rearranging everything, we again stood still for a few moments to ponder about Gurjit. The deep sorrow in our hearts resembled a raging herd stampeding out of control.

We looked at each other again and knew it was now time to leave and prepare ourselves the best way we could for another day of having to relive the tragedy that had undone our lives. 'Guys, it's time to go' I said, and Bal replied 'It's so quiet here, I think any minute now Chacha's going to open the front door.' Ami began to squeal in discomfort. His cries got louder as though outraged at the ending of the life of his uncle.

As we quietly left his house, Bal was shocked to see my great aunt walking up the road. He turned to me and said 'Mamma, look.' Bal immediately went to her and embraced her, while I was wondering how she had got here considering she lived in London and was a frail woman. She was in despair, crying her eyes out and as we embraced she kept on repeating 'why has this happened to my family?' All I could say was that only God has the answer to that question.

The walk back to the house, though a short distance, was like a long voyage interrupted by repeated hurdles that sought to stop us reaching out to each other. I tried to comfort my great aunt by saying it was OK to feel what she was feeling and that we all knew how much she loved Gurjit and how much he meant to her. Her teardrops fell into the palm of my hand as she clung on to me with Bal and Ami close behind. When she went inside my parent's house she immediately collapsed into my mother's open arms, and their crying was stifled by the fact that they were embracing so closely. All that could be done was to stand back, for it was their time to express the devouring effect Gurjit's death had upon them.

Jai, Dilly, Bal, Ami and I spoke frankly about the reality of the situation and the knowledge that Gurjit was never going to return. We discussed the fact that Dilly and the girls would need safeguarding appropriately, in terms of the level, nature and intensity of support they required at this time. The next few days would be made more difficult by the fact that funeral arrangements would have to be made and we began to delegate tasks, knowing that Dilly and the girls would be involved in this process.

With such a trauma in our midst there was a powerful dynamic also taking place at the same time, as my sister Sarnjit (Sam) was expecting her first child. He was born that afternoon at 3.11 pm. There were so many emotions experienced, ranging from joy to sorrow. It was very difficult to grasp life and death events that had taken place, let alone understand the thoughts that were invading our minds.

On the one hand we were happy for Sam and Darren, yet we were unable to express this because our minds were numb. Much as I knew we wanted to see them all, we just were not in a position to do so.

Even trying to focus was extremely difficult, because all that could be felt was the emotional pain. It was too overwhelming and could not be ignored, and it certainly could not be dealt with in an instant as I hoped it would. There was too much to respond to at once. Even trying to think about it was unbearable.

This I knew would also affect Sam. I felt for her, as she was so distraught at Gurjit's death. I can only imagine that she had similar feelings and thoughts about wanting to be with Dilly and the girls. It was a traumatic wound for her to bear and very little comfort could be provided to her at that time. All we could do was hope that our wounded hearts and minds would have the space to think about them in the midst of such loss and to be there for them when we could.

Even with the knowledge of the birth of our nephew, Jai and I had to continue to make time for the arrival of many relatives and friends, and again we rotated this because it provided us individually with some personal space to reflect privately. Yet every time relatives arrived it felt as though we were being battered from pillar to post by the range and intensity of thoughts and emotions that rose every time we needed to explain to relatives what had taken place. This was not their fault; rather they also needed comfort for their distress.

Periodically we would get together during the day. We needed to ensure that everyone was getting some rest, though it was difficult to sleep with the knowledge of Gurjit's death.

We needed to do something, even though everything appeared to be falling apart. No one was going to be left alone, and the heightened sensitivity to this made us more aware of supporting each other in talking about our feelings and the pain this caused, even though the pain was too difficult to understand at that time.

We spent time sensitively talking about how hurtful this was and how Gurjit was sadly missed and how we knew that a part of our lives had also died, for the wound of death is permanent. It was important to have these discussions, because we knew we were not alone, even though I knew we felt loneliness without Gurjit.

By evening we were all physically tired, as the day in many ways had gone fast. As I was preparing to go to sleep at 11 pm I was interrupted by knocking on the porch. At first I wondered who this could be, as well as thinking something else might have happened to someone we knew. I did not know what to expect. So we were very surprised to see Gugs, my nephew, at the door, knowing that he had travelled from Scotland as he was studying to be a doctor at Edinburgh University and was about to sit his finals.

Chapter Three

He stood there with blood-shot eyes, his face so still and bewildered. When he entered he began to cry quietly and kept shaking his head. 'I can't believe that this had happened' he said. He was physically shaking and dazed, and could not stand still, for he did not know which direction to go. I sat him down, but all he wanted to do was to see his grandparents and aunt. The tears were flowing freely.

Gugs' eyes began to fade and he was descending quickly into a state of total despair, from which there appeared no escape from the reality that he knew had taken place. We did our best to try and calm him down, while giving him the space and time to express his pain. Bal and Ami approached him and embraced and helped him to sit down. He looked at them as their tears began to surface and they sat huddled together crying as quietly as they could. None of them were able to speak.

After a few moments he gathered himself and we went to the other room, where he immediately went to his grandmother and cried, while telling her not to cry. He turned to his grandfather and held on to him while they both cried.

After a while they asked him about coming all the way from Scotland, knowing that he had an important exam the next day, to which he responded that he could not stay there knowing that Gurjit had died.

We spoke to Gugs and told him that Gurjit would not have wanted him to miss such an important exam, which he needed to take as part of his assessment for being a doctor. Gugs responded by telling us that he would pass the exam anyway and just wanted to be with us, to which we fully understood.

His position about his exams was a confident one in the midst of an event that did not inspire any confidence. As the crying intensified Gugs was empathetically consoling my parents, and they way he held on to them it was as though he was seeking to swallow their pain and make it his own. This was a task that none of us could do, for the pain was not going to go away. As Gugs tried to comfort them, his tears were rolling down fast. Bal and Ami went to him as the overwhelming and profound loss began to cover his face. It was as though he was crying out to also be rescued from the captivity that death had brought to us all.

When Dilly walked into the room, Gugs looked as though a ton of bricks had landed on him. When she approached him he latched on to her and held her extremely tight, as though he did not want to show his pain to her, rather to feel her pain. 'This is not real, how could he die so young?' he said. 'This isn't happening, it can't be happening!' 'I know' whispered Dilly.

They sat together and he held her hands tight, looking at her with his entire face contorted in agony. It was as though he was inviting her to shift all the burden of her pain to him. It was reminiscent of Bal's and Ami's desire to take the pain of their cousin-sisters.

He began to ask questions based on his medical training, and found it difficult to understand how Gurjit had died as he began to question the actions of the general practitioner. He was angry because he wanted to know why the doctors who had seen Gurjit earlier had not run various tests. 'This is wrong, it's just wrong, he's too young to die' he said. He sat there inconsolable, yet trying to console us all. We were all attempting to do that.

Though it was getting late, I knew Gugs had not eaten and so I encouraged him to eat something light to at least give him some strength. After he had eaten he told me that his train back to Scotland was at 5.30 am. So getting some sleep was important before he took his exams. However he just wanted to talk, though it was already the early hours of the morning. I spoke with him in more detail simply because he wanted to, and I felt that our time was going to be short. I gave him further information about what had happened and what the doctors and nurses had done to try to save Gurjit. We began to speak about the effects this was having on everyone within the family and how we were supporting each other.

Chapter Three

He broke down in floods of tears when he thought about his cousin-sisters. 'What are Baljinder and Suki feeling?' he said. 'How can this be fair to them?' His words were interrupted as he grabbed a pillow to try to muffle the sound. 'How is this fair? What can I say to them? What are we going to do? How can I help them now?'

I reassured him the best way I knew, by reminding him of his close relationship with them and the love and care they had for each other. His sobbing continued and then there was a silence which lasted a while. Then he began to tell me about a friend named James. He told me that when he had found out about Gurjit late the previous night he had just sat on the sofa crying, and when James had come into the flat and seen him he had told him 'My uncle has died and I don't know what to do.' James had sat by him and said 'I don't know what to say but I will sit here with you.'

'You've got a very good friend there, someone who clearly cares for you' I said. 'Now you need to get some rest. You've only got a couple of hours and I'll take you to the station.' He replied that he would get a taxi, but I responded that if I drove him there we could talk on the way.

As Gugs fell asleep, I stayed awake for a little longer to think about his bewilderment. It reminded me even more of the importance for my family of continuing to talk and be there for each other, even though it would be distressing at times. I thought about my family's love and how this, I hoped, would act as a shield against death.

CHAPTER 4

PICKING UP THE PIECES

MONDAY 27TH JANUARY 2003

After Gugs and I had had a few hours' sleep I woke him to take him to the station. He was saying 'I still can't believe this, it's a bad dream, I want it to go away.' I told him his pain was understandable, but it would not go away. He went on to say 'But what about the girls? They are so young to have this happen to them, this is so hard.'

He fought so vigorously to hold back the tears, yet his love meant that his eyes opened in a deluge. It was as though he wanted his tears to dissolve his aunts' and cousin-sisters' pain, and the awareness of his razor-sharp affliction was battering against my soul.

As I drove we spoke about the importance of his work as a doctor. He acknowledged the reality of having to face and respond to death, and said he needed to look at this experience as a way of beginning to understand the impact death would have on him and those he sought to support.

Arriving at the train station he began to compose himself, and as we embraced I felt his heart racing. I told him how proud Gurjit would be of him, knowing that he has almost qualified as a doctor. 'I know, I wish he was here to see it' he said.

The tears resurfaced and I told him that under the circumstances he might need to consider whether to seek a deferment of his exam, to which he said 'I'm going to pass this one for him.'

I then did something which I had not done for the past few days – I somehow smiled. We embraced again, and he said 'Tell my aunt and the girls that I'm thinking about them,' and walked away to get his train. As he began to disappear he kept looking back, waving at every turn until my eyes could no longer see him.

As I left I could not imagine how he would be able to focus on such an important exam, and I felt a heart-wrenching sorrow thinking about how he would cope. It was so hard to see my nephew having to be alone at this time, yet I knew Gurjit would not have wanted this to have hindered Gugs' final exams. It sounded crazy to embrace such thoughts, but it was the only way I could make sense of what was happening.

Strangely, as I drove back home, it was probably the first time that I did not really think. It was as though my thoughts had run away. It was such a bizarre feeling to have experienced, because before that my mind had so many scrambling thoughts.

I began to realise that this 'strangeness' was going to linger for a while, and part of this involved knowing that my emotions would always wish for Gurjit to be alive, while my mind would always reveal the truth - that there was no return. I knew that every member of my family would be having a similar experience and it was one which we did not need to fear.

Arriving home, I remembered that everyone was still asleep, so I sat alone in the lounge knowing this was the day to begin to make contact with many people from various organisations about Gurjit's death. While I was doing this I was drifting in and out of sleep and waking in a state of hyper-alertness, thinking time had passed. When I heard the noise of footsteps around the house I knew it was day.

Again Dilly, the girls, Dee and the lads and I spoke about what we knew would be happening. Their faces were incredibly weary; the darkness that surrounded their eyes spoke volumes. Dilly asked how Gugs was, and I relayed his message to them, at which point they all smiled about Gugs saying he would pass his exams for Gurjit. Again their smile was the first for days. It was an amazing sight, as it was clear that Gugs' words had touched us all in a graceful way.

The morning began to pass as we waited in apprehension for the Coroner's Office to contact the family. At about 10 am the phone rang and my stomach churned, as I thought they would be informing us that they would be undertaking a post mortem on Gurjit. The thought of knowing Gurjit had died was immensely painful and difficult for the family, yet to think about a post mortem was alarming, as in the back of our minds was the knowledge that we would also be preparing Gurjit's body for the funeral. I took a few deep breaths as I moved towards the phone. The weight of the phone was like lead as I picked it up. A gentleman with a distinct accent introduced himself as Mr Harris, the Coroner's Assistant. He asked to speak to Dilly, and when it was explained that Dilly did not want to engage in any conversations at that time, he said 'I fully understand and respect her decision. Before I go any further, on the Coroners behalf as well as on my behalf I express my condolences to Mr Gurjit Singh's family and would like you to know that we will seek to offer any support required at such a difficult time.'

These words from a total stranger conveyed a deep respect for life and empathy for the family, which was touching and compassionate. I thanked him for his sincerity.

He went on to explain that the Coroner had agreed with the hospital consultant's diagnosis of the cause of death being a multiple-organ failure due to a viral infection. As a result they would not perform a post mortem unless we as a family felt that it was necessary. I informed him that this was a decision for my sister to make and that I would contact him back.

What a decision for my sister to consider, so intimate and sensitive for her. As I approached her I could tell that she knew who the call had been from. When I told her what the Coroner's Assistant had said she said 'I don't really want Gurjit's body to be touched by them,' and began to cry again. Her tears could have filled a swimming pool. She was not going to be rushed into making a decision. After she had had time to think she said 'I believe what the hospital have said as to the cause of death, even though I don't know how it happened. I don't want anyone to see Gurjit's body hurt.' Her sobbing became louder as the thought of what a post-mortem could do to her beloved husband's body. It was incredibly difficult to grasp.

After taking advice from a family member who was a doctor, Dilly didn't consider a post mortem would be beneficial. She said 'I'll still get to see him knowing no one's touched his body. I was so scared that they were going to do that to Gurjit.'

With her hands held firmly together, she wrapped them around her face as her tears gathered like a wellspring. The coroner's office, once informed about Dilly's decision, appeared released from the burden of having to perform the post mortem.

After such an intense morning, there again appeared to be a temporary state of limbo as we continued through the day responding to the influx of relatives and friends. This continued until the time Dilly, Bal and I had to go to the Coroner's Office to collect all relevant documents needed to register Gurjit's death. We had spoken about this and Dilly, even though in total bewilderment, wanted to be present. I told her, 'You've been a tremendous support to the girls under the most extreme level of pain and distress.' She began to cry. 'I don't think I can be here for the girls, but I know they need me' she said.

Bal and I sought to comfort her by reminding her that she and Gurjit had always been there for the girls and that Gurjit's strength in her as well as her own love would support her, even though we knew it was very, very difficult at this time.

Dilly remained distressed, and understandably so, as she knew the insurmountable task ahead of her, the registering of her beloved, caring, committed, faithful, considerate and loving husband's death.

Having arrived at the Coroner's office we slowly made our way to the lifts. As we walked, Dilly's eyes were red from crying and her shoulders seemed burdened with the weight of the world. Bal had his arm around her, gently supporting her every step of the way as he offered comfort by saying 'this is about Chacha, we need to do this for him.'

The lift doors opened and I felt that entering meant that there was no escape from death. It was a frightening feeling to have, that the process of now registering Gurjit's death had started and there was no going back.

The silence in the lift was short-lived, as we only had to go to the third floor. After stepping out of the lift and introducing ourselves at the reception we now had to wait to be seen. The wait was very brief, as the Coroner's Assistant attended to us very quickly. He explained to us what needed to take place and gave all the appropriate documents required to register Gurjit's death. He gave these to Dilly, who remained silent, but with tears still rolling down her face, to which the man said 'We are very sorry for your deep loss as a family', to which Dilly replied 'Thank you.' A few seconds elapsed as Dilly began to look intently at the documents in her had. She was distraught, because the papers signified the ending of life.

The Coroner's Assistant gave Dilly time and waited patiently before going on to say 'you will need to go to the hospital to collect the consultant's report, as this is also required to register your husband's death.' Once he had said that he saw how Dilly became more distraught as she began to cry and lean on Bal. He then said 'I'm sorry if this had not been explained earlier and I know it will be painful to go back to the hospital, but you do not have to go in person.'

It was clear that the thought of returning to the hospital only days after her husband's death was traumatic. He once again offered his condolences to us as a family and we then left. The stay had fortunately been very brief.

Chapter Four

Knowing that Dilly was shaken by the thought of going back to the hospital, we spoke about this. I said to her 'Dilly, do you want to go to the hospital or would you prefer to go home? Bal and I can go back to collect the report.'

She looked at me, and with tears that had never really stopped flowing since Gurjit's death she nodded to indicate 'yes'. I was uncertain what she meant, yes to go the hospital or yes to go home. I sought to clarify, and she said yes, she would go to the hospital. Her words revealed a tremendous resolve in the midst of formidable pain that she was experiencing.

As the Coroner's office was only about a mile from the hospital we arrived there in a matter of minutes. Getting out of the car and looking at the Main Entrance sign of the hospital and knowing that this was the place where Gurjit died sent a spine-chilling dread and a desire to get away as quickly as we could. I could only begin to imagine what Dilly was experiencing, and when I saw Bal, his face was squashed and in his eyes was a desire to protect his aunt from further agony.

Walking through the main entrance I thought about all the times Gurjit had walked through those doors when he used to visit my parents in hospital. He always walked slowly and never looked rushed, and would walk with his hand stroking his beard. We waited patiently to be seen and when we were seen by an Asian woman, she looked very surprised when she realised Dilly was also present. It was clear from her face that she did not expect Dilly to be there, however her eyes did express sympathy as well as respect for Dilly's courage in being present at such a time.

She explained, as the Coroner's Assistant had, the process for registering Gurjit's death, yet she was unable to maintain eye contact with us, in particular Dilly who sat silently. Then suddenly I saw this woman's eyes begin to well up. I thought she was about to burst into tears when she touched Dilly's hand and gave her the consultant's report and said, with a gentle smile, 'this is for you.' We thanked her and left the small office quickly.

Once we left the hospital, we spoke about how strange it felt being there. It was as though we were stuck in an illusion, some kind of trick, as though Gurjit was really still there, yet could not be found. But the paperwork in Dilly's hand confirming Gurjit's death was the stark reminder of the very harsh truth of his death. There was no escape from the heartache of our love towards Gurjit and the loneliness of not being with him. As I drove home, we remained quiet as the magnitude of Gurjit's death began to sink even further into our minds.

When we arrived home the day went very slowly, and everything remained in a time warp. We continued to receive relatives and friends throughout the day; however our focus was upon Dilly and the girls who had their private space to continue to mourn.

In the evening I went with my cousin Chima to the Gurdwara (Sikh temple) to speak to the elders in relation to making arrangements for the religious service to be performed at Gurjit's house and at the temple on the day of the funeral. I was so glad that Chima was with me, because he knew what to say and do and I stood and listened and felt a little part of the burden had lifted from me.

I spent the night alone at Gurjit's house sleeping downstairs. The atmosphere within the house was odd as I began to realise that the deep desperation of wanting Gurjit's to be there was not going to suddenly go away.

I knew that as a family we were aggrieved by the knowledge that his death was irreversible. I constantly kept waking up; hoping and longing that any moment someone was going to shake me and tell me that everything was going to be OK and death was going to be reversed and that all the pain would be a distant memory. However no-one woke me up and there was no shaking off the pain, because the effects of death had begun to become entrenched in my mind.

Chapter Four

I stayed awake as much as I could because part of me was afraid to go to sleep, as every little sound in the house caused apprehension and every thought was 'could it be Gurjit?'. But every emotion of sadness dismantled that thought.

As the hours passed, I sat pondering on Gurjit's life. The room I was in began to feel as though it was getting smaller and smaller and my eyes became blurred, and then I realised that the tears had crept up again and welled inside of me and then burst out unstoppable, as I sat sobbing with my head in my hands thinking about Dilly and the girls and Gurjit.

CHAPTER 5

A SAD BIRTHDAY

TUESDAY 28TH JANUARY 2003

The next thing I recall was being woken up by the phone at about 8 am. It was Jai asking me 'How are you?' as he knew I had spent the night alone at Gurjit's house. I replied 'It's very weird, knowing that Gurjit will never be here again when we visit.'

I appreciated his sensitive call, which echoed his love, and thanked him for it. We then spoke briefly about the significance of the day, as it was Dilly's 39th birthday and it was also going to be the day for registering Gurjit's death. This was the date we had been given by the Registry Office for an appointment.

After saying goodbye to Jai, I got myself ready and went to my parents' home, where Dilly and the girls had remained. Everyone was awake when I entered and there was a strange calmness in the house, as though somehow more and more of the reality of Gurjit's death was sinking in. Dilly asked me how I was, to which I smiled to indicate that I was doing the best I could.

Dilly, knowing the magnitude of the day, said 'At least I'll know he was with me.' At these words, she stood shattered and torn in pieces. Her desperate loneliness was like the ocean's depths, immeasurable and gloomy. It was like trying to hold oil in one's hands, knowing that no matter what force was applied the oil would eventually slip through. For no capability could withstand the experience of separation.

Knowing it was her birthday, my mind struggled with how we as a family could begin to say to her 'happy birthday' when her husband had just died. Yet it was said, because she needed to hear the expression of our care. Watching her brave smile light across her face was as though she still knew that purpose existed, even though everything inside and surrounding her appeared bleak. Standing with such a painful separation could not be fully understood, and in itself caused all of us additional pain. It felt as though we had been left wandering, as we recognised that these were dark times which reinforced the need for us all to know how unbearable it was and do the best we could to support each other.

When Baljinder and Suki came downstairs and saw their mother they immediately said 'Happy birthday Mom,' and went and hugged her. She smiled at them and then burst into tears. Their words carried their love, said with such conviction and care during the most agonising time of their lives. Their embrace was so tight that even air could not get in between them. Baljinder told us that her father had already brought their mother a birthday card and present.

I could only have a glimmer of the thoughts running through Dilly's mind. How on earth can you even begin to contemplate the power of such an act? For Dilly knowing that Gurjit had left behind a present was an incredible act of his love and consideration for her.

After gathering our thoughts the best we could, Dilly and I went to the Registry Office. On the way, Dilly said 'the happiest day of my life was when I got married to Gurjit. His death has been the saddest and most difficult day of my life, but registering his death means that I am the one who does this.'

We then spoke about how if we remained silent about the pain it would leave us locked away from each other and the inner conflict would be too great to even begin to manage on our own. We spoke about how she felt and knew that Gurjit was so caring and thoughtful, putting others' needs before himself. Reflecting upon his character and personality provided an opportunity to feel the warmth he demonstrated. It also gave us some time to begin to focus upon what was going to take place - the registering of his death.

Upon arriving at the registry office we did not have to wait long. A gentleman walked into the reception and showed us to his office. As he did so he smiled gently, as though trying to convey some reassurance to us at this most uncomfortable time in our lives.

As we sat in his office, he came across as focused and methodical in what he needed to do. Thus he appeared to keep his distance from what was taking place for Dilly and me. However his calm demeanour suddenly changed when he asked Dilly her date of birth and she said '28th January 1964.' He raised his eyebrows as the significance of this struck him, and his hands shook as he typed. He looked at Dilly and his words were few yet sincere, as he told her that he was truly sorry for her loss.

He then gave Dilly the copies requested signed with the date of 28th January 2003, and he said to her 'no matter what, keep the original. It's got your birthday on it.' His comment was not interpreted as insensitive, and Dilly's loving smile for Gurjit was evident when she said to him 'Thank you for that.'

Then she erupted like a volcano, clinging on to Gurjit's death certificate as if she was embracing him. I gently supported her out of the office and said to her 'Dilly, you were remarkable in there, and your love for Gurjit will never disappear.' She continued to cry as I placed my arm around her and walked her towards the car.

On the way back I remained silent, as those few moments of Dilly holding the most heart-wrenching papers in her hands were so intimate.

Our stay at home was short as Dilly, Jai and I were preparing to go to the Asian funeral directors. On seeing holding Gurjit's death certificate, Jai hugged her and said 'I know this is hard, happy birthday Dilly.' They began to cry. We then left and remained quiet throughout the journey. Upon arrival at the funeral directors a religious song was being played which was so tranquil (it was actually chosen by Dilly to be played at Gurjit's funeral).

We were then greeted by a young Asian lady, who introduced herself as Rajinder.

At this point I felt a build up of tension in my body and a tightening as though it was ready to collapse. In contrast, when I looked at Dilly she was frozen. It was understandable. Jai looked like jelly without a bowl. His inner turmoil was evident, as his body was shaking and I could see that he was desperately trying not to allow it to get to him.

Rajinder started by expressing her condolences to the family, and thanking Dilly for attending in these difficult times. She made an interesting statement which turned into a question before she began to speak about the funeral process. She said that she wanted to know about Gurjit and the family.

This enabled Dilly to tell her story of her life with Gurjit. Rajinder went on to sensitively ask, holding Dilly's hand, how Gurjit had died. Dilly at this stage became understandably stirred with her longing for the love of her life and the awareness of the daunting truth that he would be with her no more. She began to weep silently, trying not to let her mouth open to release the grief contained.

Reaching out to Dilly, I watched feeling helpless, yet thinking that she needed every opportunity for the release of such intense emotions that were threatening to run riot within her heart, mind and soul. Such a sight showed that her emotions needed to be 'felt' and there could not be any immediate understanding of what reasons existed for Gurjit's death having taken place.

Rajinder quietly said to Dilly that she understood that this was an incredibly difficult time for the family, and asked her to take her time, to which Dilly shook her head as a sign of her desperation not to let Gurjit go.

Chapter Five

Jai held Dilly's hand and said 'Do you want to carry on and tell Rajinder?' to which Dilly responded by shaking her head again. Jai then said 'Do you want me to tell her?' to which she quickly nodded. Jai then explained to Rajinder the circumstances of Gurjit's death and talked about Gurjit's life, and how hard it was to begin to even believe that he would never return. Jai was in anguish as he reflected upon the events leading to Gurjit's death and his tears slowly fell from his face.

Rajinder thanked Jai for sharing such personal and tragic details and shared her personal experiences of loss, acknowledging that it was a distressing time. She began to explain the funeral process and the types of arrangements that could be undertaken.

After completing the appropriate paperwork, she said something which stuck in my mind like a thorn; it was not something that I would have considered. She said 'the funeral is not about Gurjit's death, but about demonstrating an acknowledgement and respect for his life and relationships. I know how difficult this is for you as a family. I know because it hurts so much when someone you love so much dies. I remember when my father died and how I thought I would never live and how painful it was. But I know my memories of my father are always in my heart.'

Listening to this young woman was quite remarkable, because her level of awareness and sensitivity provided comfort to me, and I felt for Dilly and Jai as well. A strange peace arose in an experience where everything had been turned upside down and I thought even my feet did not have any co-ordination.

Rajinder's words about her own personal loss were very timely, as she tried to offer us some hope, and this was further reinforced when she said to us 'You did not just have a relationship with Gurjit, you also had a shared life with him.'

Dilly began to slowly smile when Rajinder said that, as clearly she realised that she had been living that shared life with Gurjit since marriage, and that their bond had grown stronger over their sixteen years together.

Rajinder began to show Dilly a 'catalogue' of caskets and flower arrangements that could be chosen. She did this with great sensitivity and care for Dilly, holding her hand throughout and taking the time to speak about each picture.

Dilly chose the type of casket on the basis of how light it was, as she said 'Gurjit brought so much light into my life and I'll never forget him.' Dilly then told Rajinder that she wanted the girls to choose the flower arrangements. At that point Rajinder suggested that the girls visit and choose the flowers they wanted. Dilly was initially hesitant at the thought of the girls attending, but felt reassured by Rajinder, who said 'I understand it is difficult and your daughters will be hurting so much, yet they are so much part of this and it would be nice to see them.' Her words were not insensitive or inconsiderate, rather affirming that as a family we were in this together.

Upon agreeing this between Dilly and Jai, I said to Rajinder 'I'll contact you to arrange for the girls to visit you, if they want to.' In response she gave Dilly a catalogue to take home for the girls to choose the flowers, should they decide not to visit.

Rajinder made me recognise even more about how as a family we would need to embrace the reality and not avoid it, because although our physical relationship with Gurjit had ended, the emotional part was still alive within us and would give us strength and hope. She came across as someone who had an amazing understanding of the respect of life and the impact of death.

We thanked her for her kind words and support and on the way back we did not stop talking. We spoke about how this was timely input, as strangely, under the circumstances, we felt uplifted, which we had not thought could occur in such an environment. We spoke about how Rajinder clearly knew what death meant and had a deep cultural and spiritual understanding of this, which was reassuring to know.

Chapter Five

Dilly said 'Rajinder was so warm and really wanted to know about Gurjit, the girls and me and she showed so much respect. I feel that she has given me a little more strength.'

It was strength that she certainly needed on her 39th birthday, to contend with two extremely distressing events; registering Gurjit's death, and then making the funeral arrangements. This was not something that could be done without her being reminded of the intense pain in her heart as Jai and I looked on, knowing she was mortally wounded.

We explained to everyone at home what the funeral arrangements were and the girls were shown the catalogue for flower arrangements. They chose flowers which symbolised their love, affection and respect for their father.

The rest of the day passed by with everyone checking up on each other by ensuring we all got rest, physical at least, as the emotions were switching on and off. It felt as though time had deliberately speeded up so that we did not have to be caught up in constant despair and dismay. It was strange to experience this because it brought some relief while knowing that the next day would still have to be faced, and the day after and so on, when it was something that in all truth would surface more emotional turbulence and pain.

CHAPTER 6

PAIN REVISITED

THURSDAY 30TH JANUARY 2003

While the funeral arrangements were being made, we had another shock. Dee phoned me and told me that our nephew, Gugs' friend James, had died.

My mind went blank as I tried to register what she said, and I realised this when I asked her what she meant. She told me that Gugs' sister (our niece) had just contacted her to say that Gugs was in a state of breakdown. I thought that this surely could not be the same young man who was Gugs' best friend and flatmate, yet it was. What an affliction of sadness for Gugs and his friend's family. It was difficult to even begin to imagine what he was feeling and thinking at this time, so brutal was the loss and so persistent was the pain.

Immediately I told Jai what had happened and said that once I had spoken to Gugs I would get back to him. When I rang Gugs with thoughts of praying for him, knowing that this would be beyond belief, he was already crying loudly and was apologising to me as he was unable to utter any words. I could not even contemplate what he had begun to endure within the space of a few days, and told him to take his time.

His crying continued as he kept saying 'I can't believe this is happening, I just can't believe this is happening, it's unreal.' I replied 'This is very, very difficult and we are very sorry to know that your best friend has also died, it's so terrible and we wish we were with you at this moment. Everyone here is hurt knowing your friend has died.'

He somehow composed himself enough to tell me what had happened. After taking his exam on Monday he had left to go home, as he wanted to get back to see us with his parents. This was the last time he saw James. He knew he was not feeling well, so he asked a few other friends to keep an eye on him.

After several attempts to get hold of James he became concerned, because no one else had seen him either. As a result he phoned the police and asked them to go to the flat. The police began to look for him as a missing person and found his body in a canal. At that stage the cause of death was unknown.

Gugs began to cry loudly on the phone, and then remarkably asked how his aunt and cousin-sisters were, to which I told him 'it's still very shocking to know Gurjit's died and it is incredibly hard to understand.'

I tried to pause and consider what a traumatic experience this would be for James' family and friends, including Gugs himself. For what comfort could be provided under these circumstances, and how could this bring any value, with Gugs so distraught at having to contend with the death of his uncle and best friend within the space of five days?

I kept thinking about the onslaught his mind would have taken and how deep this tragedy was. How could he be sustained at this time, knowing that everything he was holding on to was being dismantled - something which I knew we all had been contending with over the past few days?

He began to blow his nose and then said 'If I had stayed in Scotland, James would still be alive, I feel bad that I left to go home.' The sound of the never-ending tears hitting the phone interrupted his thoughts. 'I want this to be all a dream; I want someone to tell me that this is all a dream. I just can't believe that all of this is happening.'

I could understand how he could think this, because I already knew that Dilly had similar thoughts that she should have done something more for Gurjit. Such thoughts would certainly challenge anyone and make them feel intense guilt.

Chapter Six

I said to him 'What you have said shows how much you truly were his best friend. I know this is difficult, but you could not have possibly have known this was going to take place. Gugs, you're not responsible for any of this.'

'I know, but I feel it so badly' he replied. I responded, 'This shows how loving and caring you are and how hurt you are. We are all thinking about you at this time.'

'I know, but it's hard to take all of this in, first my uncle and now James, it's all so mad' he responded. He continued to cry, saying 'I've got no more words in my mind to explain what has taken place.' I responded to this by telling him this was fully understandable and as he had already realised, it was going to take a while to get to grips with. I continued to tell him that the incredible pain he was feeling, which we were all feeling, was the expression of our deepest love, care and consideration, because there was no doubt that even though everything appeared illusionary and evasive, we still had to be steadfast in the most testing of times.

Gugs again asked how Dilly and the girls were, which was a reflection of his character, being so compassionate. I tried to reassure him that as difficult as it was, as a family we would respond to each other's brokenness through our love.

It was as though already our longing for security, even though distant, would reappear like a ray of shining hope, providing a banner which would give an encompassing message that the wilderness has not prevailed.

Thinking about the few days in which Gugs had experienced such significant losses without having any time to even think was heartbreaking, as he appeared to try to ensure that his friend's death did not distract him from grieving about his uncle and the loss this meant for us as a family.

It was certainly a lot for anyone to take. I gently spoke to him about this and tried to reduce the feelings of conflict that I imagined he was feeling about mourning by reassuring him that everyone fully understood his love for his uncle and that he needed time to look at the death of his friend as well, which we also fully understood and would support him in, and that he should not feel that he was letting anyone down. He began to sob.

I continued to talk about how painful this was for him and how the way he spoke to me about his friend James showed how close and positive their friendship had been. I reminded him that being together was about us all knowing that we are in this together and that when one of us hurts we all hurt, to which his cries continued to echo down the phone.

I asked him how he would feel if his aunt was told about his best friend, as I felt it was appropriate to ascertain his view. He told me 'I wish I could change all this and take all the hurt away, but I can't and that's what hurts the most.'

After further discussion he told me that he wanted his aunt to know, as he knew she would feel hurt even more if it was kept away from her, even though she was contending with the death of her husband.

Listening to Gugs was like being in the middle of two planets set on a course to collide, so complex to even begin to think and feel and to know how support could truly be given. Nothing appeared clear, for the very foundations under us began to move and stability could not be held. Being sustained seemed millions of miles away.

It was difficult to say goodbye to Gugs under such shocking circumstances, as I felt that we were both being pulled apart in wanting to end the call. There was so much uncertainty I felt about how to handle this, yet somehow we managed to say goodbye.

After speaking to Gugs, I went to see Dilly. Dee had already told her about Gugs' friend. Dilly was in tears, along with Dee and the lads who knew the distress Gugs was under. Baljinder and Suki were also present and were aware of what had taken place.

Chapter Six

Dilly's cries became louder and then she collapsed her head into her hands and said 'he's only just lost his uncle and now his best friend, this is not fair.' I sought to offer some reassurance that even though it was harrowing for Gugs, we would all support each other over the coming days and Gugs would be in our thoughts. I went on to tell them what had happened and what Gugs was feeling and how this was the same as what we were feeling and that we would take time out to see him soon.

I told Dilly and the girls that we could sit down later and talk about the funeral arrangements. This was going to be difficult, as everything had been since Gurjit had died. We began to talk about Gurjit's death, his loss as a husband and father. This further revealed that it could not be removed or taken away from our hearts, mind, soul and life.

As they spoke, an incredible and unbearable torment was echoing and there was no shield to be able to resist this. Their mourning, though it showed the relentlessness of death, also importantly continued to reveal the expression of their love. For we spoke about what it meant to not have Gurjit present and that the only way forward was to know deep down that the pain and sorrow would be matched by the love Gurjit left within us all. Dilly said 'I couldn't have asked for a better husband and father for our girls, he was so good, we miss him so much, I just want to hold him again.'

Her run-down body trembled as though being hit by a bolt of lightning, and her tears flowed freely. It was extremely difficult to even seek an explanation of what we had all experienced. The girls shedding tears and in devotion said 'we know Dad loved us, and no one can ever take that away from us, and he knows we loved him so much. We just want this pain to go away.'

Looking at them, knowing that death had brought about an ending of a relationship which had previously captured their hearts, to then see their heart being abruptly pierced because of separation, caused a consuming longing for what could no longer be. Being still in the midst of their tears conveyed our awareness that we needed to continue to express the depth of our grief.

They all remained together as I went to phone Jai to inform him of my conversation with Gugs. Upon hearing what I told him, Jai said 'how on earth is he coping with all of this? This is so tragic.' I said to Jai that this thought was shared. We then spoke about the funeral arrangements in that the girls would be spoken to later on in the day, which he would also be involved in.

On talking to the girls later in the afternoon about the funeral arrangements, they said they wanted to visit the funeral directors' and crematorium. Baljinder and Suki talked about how everything to them was very strange and knowing that their dad had died was not something that they had expected while they were so young, which made it even harder for them to accept.

The weight of such disappointment in knowing he would no longer be there for them was certainly creating a deep despondency as their bewildered eyes revealed that they would have moved heaven and earth to have their father back.

As they reflected upon the last time they saw him alive they smiled compassionately and recalled what they had said to him. Baljinder told us that she had said 'Dad, you're going to be fine,' and Suki recalled that she did not know why she had said to him 'Dad I love you.'

Their uncontrollable agony revealed so much pain as Baljinder said 'I wish I had never said to him that he was going to be fine, I feel bad saying that when I didn't know how ill he was.' Her tears rolled together. She was broken as she attempted to wipe her eyes. With Suki's head resting on my shoulder and her tears falling on to me, her body quivered with the knowledge of her father's death as she said 'I wish I could have made him better.'

In response I said, 'Everything you've said shows again how much you loved him and this is the little treasure that will remain in you. It will always remind you how much you cared for him, because you know he loved you so much.'

They cried. Yet I believed this also gave them impetus for hope to surface in the midst of the dark despair that had descended. Even in such a short space of time they were seeking to make sense of what was happening and were holding tightly to the positive impact their father had had within their lives, in order to respond to the excruciating reality of his death.

Suki at that point mentioned to me a 'memory box' and I sought her views on this. She told me that it was to keep whatever a person wanted to remind them of someone or something; she had learned this at school. She said, 'I want a memory box so that I can keep things to do with Dad, so that when I grow up I will not forget about him. I'm afraid that I'm going to forget about him. I'm worried, because I don't have a dad and I don't know what it means for my mom and Baljinder; I'm going to be different from my friends.'

I offered as much reassurance as possible, knowing that even though it might bring some comfort it would also bring a constant reminder of loss. I told her that as a family we were all here to support her, Baljinder and their mom and that we knew how scary this was for them. 'None of us are ever going to forget your dad because he meant so much to us all' I said. She nodded and cried out loudly.

We remained silent for at least five minutes as they continued to cry, revealing more of the deep suffering that they had experienced. Difficult as it was to hear this torment, fear, pain and desolation combined with their deep longing for their father, it was their way to express such an outrage against loss.

We spent more time sitting there in silence as their tears could not and should not be stopped. After a while, Baljinder said 'I feel so numb and I'm worried because I do not know what to feel and how I will react at the funeral.'

Chapter Six

We spoke about how her feeling numb was not about her not caring, but rather about the fact that she cared and loved her dad so much that it was hard to begin to think and feel what his loss meant. I told Baljinder 'none of us at this moment know what to feel, but we are feeling the pain of knowing your dad is not going to be here any more. Yet we are feeling each other's pain and we will be here to support each other.'

They were reassured that as the funeral was about honouring their father's life, however they responded they would be supported, because he would always be their father. They expressed their fear of being approached by many people at the funeral and were anxious about how they would cope with that. However, they were reassured that extended family members would be sensitive to the space they needed and a few of us would be with them at all times.

Inwardly I felt it was dreadful to try to hold everything together, because it could not be done. We stood a better chance preventing two horses pulling us in opposite directions. Dilly, listening to her daughter's pain, was overwhelmed as she hugged them tightly and expressed her love and comfort to them, saying 'I know how much you loved your dad and how much he meant to you and that you are going to miss him so much. I want you to know how much I love you, and this will never change.'

Bal and Ami then appeared, a timely arrival, and spent time with Baljinder and Suki while Jai and I spoke with Dilly. Privately she told us 'I don't really want to live, and it is only because of the girls that I know I have to be strong even though I don't feel it.'

We spoke to her about how her thoughts and feelings were understandable, and that the comfort we had was the fact that we all had a relationship with Gurjit, hers being the closest. She replied 'the thought of living without Gurjit is unbearable, it is difficult to live.' Jai said 'We know, because we know how hurt you are. We all miss him so much and would do anything to get him back, but Gurjit's not coming back and that hurts even more. We will be strong together.'

Chapter Six

I said to Dilly 'It's OK to feel what you are feeling; I need you to know that Gurjit's life within you will give you the strength to move forward even though at the moment everything seems so difficult.' She began to cry, saying 'I know he's still in my heart, but I wish he was here.'

We confirmed that her views were valid and a sincere expression of her love for her Gurjit, and the mark Gurjit had left within her and us all, as well as our own relationships and belief in God which would sustain us through such a difficult and unknown experience.

To think that the day had started with the knowledge that Gugs' friend had died was painful, and then in talking with Dilly and the girls such pain became even more unbearable. On top of this, we still had to prepare our minds for the Sikh religious ceremony in Gurjit's house. This would be the first time Dilly and the girls had returned home after Gurjit's death, so it was going to be extremely difficult for them.

On arrival at Gurjit's house Dilly and the girls were already in dismay as their eyes reflected so much pain. Jai, his wife Mangender, Dee and my parents were already there. On entering the hallway Dilly and the girls began looking at the photos on the wall leading to the staircase. Bal and Ami were comforting them by placing their arms around them, seeking to shield them from further emotional turmoil. This sent shivers down my spine as I saw how much agony this was causing all of them, as well as myself.

When we went upstairs and into Gurjit's bedroom, Dilly paused, tears trickling down her face. She was supported by Dee and Mangender in slowly walking into the bedroom where the Sikh priest was present. Everyone remained silent as the ceremony started with an opening prayer and then a reading service.

The ceremony would take place over an entire week, culminating with the funeral. After a while the girls wanted to leave the service and were supported in doing so by Bal and Ami. My parents sat there with their eyes closed but with tears running down their faces, my mother offering a quiet prayer.

Chapter Six

After a while I left the room to see how the girls were, while Dee and Jai remained with my parents and Dilly. On seeing the girls were being comforted by Bal and Ami, Baljinder said 'It's so strange knowing Dad's not here. That's his bedroom and he's not there. He's not going to be there again!' I hugged her and said 'I know, but at least he is in our hearts and minds.'

The rest of the day was taken up with the arrival of more relatives and Gurjit's colleagues and friends. The day was very significant and upon reflection of all that happened I began to try and seek some understanding. I focused specifically on relationships, because my family had experienced so much distress within a few days.

It felt as though we had been entangled in a web which sought to hinder us from moving towards each other and remain attached. There was no doubt, rather a constant reminder that this pain was very harrowing, along with a hope that with love and commitment we would be able to support each other in expressing the deepest and despairing thoughts and feelings, even though we might not understand them. For it was clear that this was not going to disappear and I knew that it was going to be difficult to fully embrace each other's pain in one go, yet I believed there was hope within us that we could draw near to each other, knowing we were all vulnerable. There were no exceptions.

CHAPTER 7

SIGNIFICANT ARRIVALS

MONDAY 3RD FEBRUARY 2003

Dilly, Dee, Jai and I had spoken about the arrivals of Gurjit's father and our sister Patty's arrival from India and Canada respectively. We knew that Gurjit's father would be traumatised by his son's death and that this would also be compounded by the disappearance of his eldest son, Parmjit.

Unfortunately Gurjit's mother was too ill to travel to England. I could only imagine how desperately her heart was crying out for her beloved son.

We also knew that the news of Gurjit's death would hit Parmjit very hard because in spite of his personal difficulties related to alcohol misuse, he did respect and love Gurjit as well as all of us. Dee said to Dilly 'I feel so sorry for you that you have lost Gurjit, I know you loved him so much and that he loved you so much. Much as it hurts to say this, Parmjit should be here to support you, and it hurts to know that he is not.'

Her tears of regret seeped through her hands as Dilly hugged her and said 'thank you. I know Parmjit loved Gurjit and that it's going to hurt him very hard when he finds out that Gurjit has died.'

Their tears and cries merged as Jai and I looked at each other. The expression on his face was probably the same as mine, knowing that everything at that moment remained unbearable. Jai then said to them 'Much as we all want Parmjit to be here, we have to focus on Gurjit, and still hope that someone can find Parmjit before the funeral takes place.'

Dee and Dilly were left to continue to mourn Jai, Bal, Ami, our dear friend George and I began to speak about the continual support for everyone, and in particular Gurjit's father and our sister Patty. Jai and Ami would be picking Gurjit's father up from Birmingham Airport while George and Bal would be picking my sister Patty up from Heathrow. We spoke about how all that we could do was to offer all the comfort we could to them and explain in further detail the circumstances surrounding Gurjit's death and importantly how Dilly and the girls were at the present moment.

George and Bal then set off to London. The rest of the day continued with more relatives visiting the home to express their condolences and mourn with us as a family.

Before I knew it my sister was only minutes away from home, and at that time it was strange because it was the only time during the day that only immediate family were present. It seemed as though space had been created to provide some privacy for her arrival.

Her arrival brought the first of the day's reminders of pain. The moment she walked through the front door it was as though the life had been completely drained from her. She was so downcast, bursting with tears as she held on to Jai and the sound of their synchronised crying was like a high fever, totally uncontrollable.

Her body was trembling so much, that her legs began to buckle as she slipped to the floor and had to be prevented from falling by Bal, Ami and Jai. Her face was striving to find relief as well as give it, and she looked as though she was pleading for Gurjit's return as she cried out loudly to us all 'No, this can't be happening! I want to see Gurjit, I need to see him, where is he, has he really gone?'

Her lips were trembling as she grabbed Jai, who said to her 'I also want him to be here so much, but Patty, he's gone.'

Once she was able to let go of Jai she launched herself at me and we were crying and she was choking under the downpour of her tears so much that she could hardly catch her breath. Through what I imagined was exhaustion she was not able to say anything. Her tears soaked my shirt with a fragrance mixed from love and grief. I told her gently as we held on to each other 'We all know how much this hurts.'

She moved her head from my shoulder and with her eyes on the verge of exploding with tears she shook her head and then her head collapsed on to my chest.

Slowly we began to move to the lounge, where my parents, my great aunt and sisters Dee and Gurdev were. She tried so hard to compose herself before entering the room but when she saw them it was to no avail, as she just broke like a dam and hurled herself at my mother. She was unable to utter a single word throughout these few minutes of holding on to her. When she was able to look up, she began to wipe the tears from my mother's face and said 'Don't cry, please don't cry, Gurjit's here, I know he couldn't have gone.' Her words expressed the depth of shock and her desperate desire to believe that Gurjit could return.

My mother held Patty and cried out loudly 'God took him and he's not coming back to us.' Patty replied 'No Mom!' and then burst into a further deluge of tears as my father spoke to her as well, saying 'We can't do anything now, your brother's gone.'

They continued to seek desperately to comfort and console each other from the intense and immeasurable pain. Patty then turned to me and said 'Where are Dilly and the girls? I want to see them.' She was taken upstairs to where Dilly and the girls were, and the moment she saw Dilly she clung to her tightly, saying 'I'm so sorry'. They were merging into one as the harrowing sound of despair began to surface, because their grief could not be contained.

Then again, I wondered how anything could be structured when death takes place. It was a devastating language that they were communicating to each other and I could not intercede on their behalf to remove the pain.

Chapter Seven

Dilly began to try to comfort Patty, who was again unable to catch her breath. Jai was with the girls, who saw the pain their aunt was in and how their own pain was a constant reminder of their father's death. Patty repeated what she said, shaking her head as the tears were falling.

She then turned her attention to Baljinder and Suki. She put her outstretched arms towards them and they came to her. As she placed her arms around them it was like a mother bird protecting her young and not wanting any harm to come to them. Gently wiping their tears from their faces she said 'I'm so, so sorry' and then began to break down under the downpour of tears. 'I'm so sorry that your dad has died. I wish I could take all this pain from you,' and she burst into more tears.

This was her acknowledgement that death had taken place - death which she desperately wanted not to acknowledge, so understandable because none of us wanted to. Dilly then went to them and they all embraced together.

Watching them, it became more and more burdensome to know that literally every minute for Dilly and the girls was a constant search for wanting Gurjit to re-occupy his position in their life. This was set against the awareness of pain being ever-present because death had taken place.

We were all lost. There was no apparent route which would take us back to the way life had been before Gurjit's death. This was the frightening reality which we would have to face.

They all sat together on the bed and began talking about how they were all missing him. Patty began to talk about the last time she had seen Gurjit, which was the year before when she and her daughter, Kirin visited. She began to cry, as she felt Gurjit had treated Kirin as his own. She told them 'I know how much you all loved him and I could see how much he loved us all, because he was such a good man. I know how much we all meant to him and how kind he was with everyone. I'm so sorry.' Her tears were slowly trickling down her cheeks. Dilly responded 'thank you.'

Chapter Seven

Baljinder said to her 'Massi, it's good to know how much my dad meant to us. I'll always remember him because everything about him was so good.' She then sobbed in her mother's arms. Patty sat so close to them that her eyes lit with the fear of losing them. Bal remained with them as I went downstairs to see how my parents were.

Time appeared to speed up again, and before we knew it there was less than a hour before Gurjit's father arrived. We began to prepare for this by going to Gurjit's house. As we waited, Ami phoned to tell us that they were only a few minutes away, which I relayed to everyone.

When Gurjit's father arrived at his son's house everyone was waiting in the lounge, and as his little frame walked in he looked too numb to think, let alone speak. My father embraced him and his face looked as though it had been wiped of all his thoughts as he stood there, his eyes just fixed - his son was not there to greet him. My father and mother began to cry and say 'What has happened to our son? Who has done this to our son?'

Gurjit's father, still in deep shock, was unable to respond. He could only nod his head. Dilly and the girls approached him and he opened his arms to them, like a vacuum wanting to pull their pain away from them. Dilly and the girls cried as he stood trying to console them, understandably still not being able to utter a word. His eyes revealed his broken heart.

Dee, Bal and I went to him and embraced in turn and expressed our sorrow about Gurjit's death. All he could do was look at us, his eyes still revealing the depths of his brokenness. Slowly he began to speak.

'When you phoned me to tell me how ill Gurjit was I knew that he was going to die' he said. 'I just knew because my heart became so filled with fear.'

My father responded 'If only we had known, I would have given my life for him. I know he was your son, but he was also our son.' Gurjit's father replied 'I know he was your son as well.'

Chapter Seven

My father and mother sat crying while Gurjit's father tried to console them, not yet shedding a tear as I imagined that the shock was still surrounding him. He then spoke about the joy of knowing that he had at least spent one month with Gurjit, Dilly and the girls when they had been to India in November 2002.

His pain was so deep-rooted that it gave him no meaning at this time and his face showed dejection and desolation. He understandably did not know where he was in relation to what had taken place.

This showed how powerful a parent's love is. As he faced the loss of his youngest son and the disappearance of his eldest, he was an unbearable sight. It was as though fear was seeking to challenge his value as a father. Such distress called for our deepest and most sincere respect.

As he continued to reflect upon Gurjit's visit to India his eyes welled up, yet tears did not fall. He pressed his fingers against his eyes as a way of preventing the overwhelming distress flowing out of him. He sat motionless and silent and I felt so sorry for him having to face the death of his son. It was a sombre sight.

After a few minutes he turned towards my parents and placed his hand on my father's leg and said 'I know he was your son and I know that he always saw you as his father and mother.'

My parents burst into tears when these words registered in their fragile minds, because they knew deep down how much Gurjit loved and respected them. They began telling Gurjit's father about the last time they had seen him alive and how unsettled they had been, because they had felt that something was not right, but could not have possibly realised that he was going to die. My father said 'I wished I had called him back when he was leaving the house, so that I could look into his eyes to see if anything was worrying him, but I didn't – I let him go.'

He dropped his head into his hands and began to berate himself. Gurjit's father held my father's hands and said 'Only God knew.' Jai in turn said to Gurjit's father 'The last time I saw Gurjit was the Sunday before he died. It hurts us all so much to know that one day Gurjit was here and then the next day he had gone.'

Jai's tears were falling and his lips were quivering, for what he said reflected how we all had begun to recall the last words we had had with Gurjit before he died. It was locked inside of us and no one was going to take those precious memories away, they were our treasure.

The girls decided to leave the room and were supported in doing so by Dilly, Bal and Ami. Gurjit's father remained in silence with his head bowed. It was tough to contemplate his anguish, because to lose one child and not have any knowledge of the whereabouts of his eldest son would without a doubt be a horrendous and persistent nightmare with no obvious resolution. Then my father asked him if he wanted to go upstairs and sit where the religious ceremony was being performed, to which he nodded.

When he tried to stand up his legs were not moving, as though his feet had been glued to the floor. The look in his eyes revealed the severity of the pain which had totally caged him. Jai and I went to his aid and gently supported him to stand. My father began to get up and was supported by me as we all slowly made our way upstairs.

With every step, Gurjit's father paused as he fixed his eyes on another photo of his son. I knew at one level what he would have been feeling, because only days before Bal, Ami and I had gone through the same process. It was a very troubling walk and I began to wonder upon how he would be when he stepped into the bedroom. The moment he did so he placed his arms either side of the door frame and tried to turn back, his face covered with pain.

None of us said anything because reality was becoming more daunting for him, as it had for us all, for he knew that the ceremony symbolised an acknowledgement of the ending of life.

Jai gently placed his hand on his shoulder to signify his support and care. Gurjit's father turned around and shook his head sideways and then bowed his head and began to move inch by inch into the room. My father said to him 'Gurjit will always be in this home because he is in our hearts forever.' Gurjit's father nodded his head to acknowledge this truth. He engaged in the religious ceremony and then spent time sitting with my father and Jai listening to the religious scriptures. I went downstairs to see Dilly and the girls.

I found them crying and Dilly said 'I know how much Gurjit loved his parents and ours and it hurts because Gurjit would never have wanted to see any of them, or us, feeling so much hurt and pain.'

Her words were so true of the man I knew, because he was very sensitive to other people's needs and circumstances and would display a remarkable level of respect and consideration for others. Inwardly I was screaming, for I also knew that Gurjit would never have wanted to see any of us in such pain, yet I knew he would have known that being separated from him would result in despair.

After I had gathered my thoughts, I said to Dilly 'I know Gurjit loved us all so much and it hurts to know that we will never experience anything with him again.' Such expression of pain and vulnerability, as hurtful as it was, needed to be released, for time was required. We all embraced as this was one way to remain connected.

Then the doorbell rang. We were not expecting anyone, as night was beginning to fall. My sister Dee came to me and said 'There's someone at the door asking for you and I don't know who it is.' My mind became hyper-alert, thinking the worst, thinking that something else had happened. I nervously went to the door and to my total surprise found a friend named Sodhi with whom I had studied at college some fifteen years before. It was a complete shock to see him standing there. His smile upon seeing me began to slowly disappear as he saw what was written on my face.

'Sat, is everything OK?' he said. I took a deep breath and replied 'No, mate. My brother died a few days ago.'

His face almost swallowed him up as a agony came over him. He looked baffled, which was understandable. 'Oh no, Sat, I'm so sorry, I'll leave' he said. 'This is the wrong time, I'll come back another day, I'm really sorry to hear this.'

Sodhi was distraught, even though he had never met Gurjit, but I knew he had experienced many personal tragedies in his own family. I said to him 'Come in' to which he said 'I can't, I can't. I have to leave you with your family. Please let me go.' I appreciated that it was uncomfortable for him. He went on 'I went to your house, and when no one answered I asked your neighbour, who told me you were here. I came to share some good news with you but if I had known I wouldn't have disturbed you at this time. Please Sat, let me go, I'm so sorry to hear this.'

I had to respect his request, and he left.

As night fell we began to make our way to my parents' home, while Dilly and the girls stayed as they wanted to sleep in their house. Dee, Bal and Ami stayed with them. The final few hours of the day were spent attending to Gurjit's father by ensuring he had eaten and got some rest after such a harrowing day. He and my parents carried on talking about Gurjit. It was their way of expressing their love for him. I left them alone, as I also wanted to be alone, trying to prepare my mind the best way I could for the forthcoming days of preparing for Gurjit's funeral. I thought about the day, which had been very emotionally difficult for us all. Its effects were beginning to take place and tiredness was taking hold.

The next thing I remember was waking to the sound of my parents and Gurjit's father making their way upstairs. Once they were settled, I went downstairs to try to get some proper sleep. However my sleep was interrupted throughout the early hours by many thoughts and questions running around my mind. Could something have been done to stop Gurjit from dying? How come I never saw this coming? How can we truly respond to this pain?

Chapter Seven

I now felt my mind battling with the 'what if' question - what could have been done differently which might have made a difference to Gurjit surviving? I felt that this was already affecting us as a family and that it was threatening to bring deeper pain.

Even though I had thought this had been discussed, I realised that it was by no means fully explored, and the realisation that it would have to be discussed in a lot more detail was pain in itself. Yet it would have to be done, because within me there was a deep sense of knowing that the 'what if scenario' would be plagued by feelings of guilt and even hatred towards ourselves in thinking we had failed Gurjit, more so as I knew Dilly would be battling with this.

I knew we would all need to express our grief about this, for we had to face the pain of Gurjit's death and of not having known how ill he was in the days before his death.

With this in mind I got up and saw my parents and Gurjit's father. I was listening to them talking about Gurjit as well as about their life in India. They shared so much personal history, which revealed their very deep emotional connection to the past. Their eyes showed how hard it was for them to see Gurjit as part of the past. There was not much I could say. It was their time to express their grief, and listening to it was evident how much they treasured and loved Gurjit.

As the morning passed, Dilly, the girls, Bal, Ami and Jai came over to my parents and spent some time with Gurjit's father. After this we spoke about supporting the girls with regard to visiting the funeral directors' and the crematorium.

However Dilly began to cry, and was speaking so low that it was difficult to hear what she was saying. It again showed how distressing this was, because it was not something we could just put into a box and look at when we felt ready.

Jai, Bal and Ami and I remained silent, while comforting Dilly in turn by hugging her and shedding tears with her, knowing her plight was bleak. She then spoke clearly, which on the one hand was a surprise, because I had awoken with a similar thought, and on the other it showed how guilt had set in for us all as she said "I keep thinking that if I had taken Gurjit to the doctor's or the hospital earlier he might have survived. She kept breaking down in tears and wiping them away. 'I feel so bad for not seeing how ill he was and not understanding what was happening when he was at home with me' she went on, her body shaking and her words being spoken brokenly 'I feel that... I let him down... I wasn't there for him. He needed me.'

The echo of her pain was worse than being hit by a bullet, because usually a bullet's effectiveness is instant and allows no room for thought, whereas her words meant that we had no choice but to embrace her continual pain.

Simply saying to her that she should not be thinking this way would not have been the wisest action to take, so we adopted a sensitive approach by acknowledging her pain. We said we also had the same thoughts and that our minds would certainly be thinking this for a while. I said to her 'Dilly, hard as it sounds, you need to realise that you did not cause Gurjit's death. We know how much this is hurting you to think whether you could have done something different. You did all that you could. None of us could have known that Gurjit was going to die.'

She replied 'I know, but the thoughts still come into my mind,' to which Jai interjected 'You did everything you could. You could not have known how ill he was because you are not a doctor. There was no way you could have known how the illness was working, not even the doctors knew. I only wished they had. You did everything you could and you did it well and Gurjit knew how much you loved him.'

Dilly's tears continued, though a soft smile arose when she was reminded by Jai that the time she had spent with Gurjit was intense and extremely supportive and that she had responded to him with so much care. We continued to comfort her as Bal said to her 'Massi, we've all had these thoughts and will carry on having them because the pain hurts so badly. It is frightening because it looks like this will never go away, but I know there is hope even though it is difficult to see.' His words reflected his insight and his maturity.

I reflected at this point that the sudden change caused by death made it look as though there could be no opportunity ever again for any development in our relationships. Everything appeared bleak because it felt that death had made such an assault on our entire beings revealing a level of vulnerability which when looking into a mirror reflected a different image staring back. There was no doubt that uncertainty would continue to challenge our thoughts of grief as a wind had hit our foundations, shaking them to the core.

After a few moments of silence Baljinder said 'if we had stayed home on that day we could have at least spent the day with Dad and we could have told him how much we loved him.'

We told them that their father knew how much they loved him and that wanting to have stayed at home was an indication of their love. Baljinder said 'I'll never forget seeing my dad at the doctor's surgery, he looked as though he knew something terrible was about to happen, and I feel so bad,' and her tears erupted. 'I feel so bad for not telling him that I loved him when I saw him like that!' Jai held her as she began to curl up and scream out loudly the intense pain locked inside. 'I can't get that picture out of my head. I knew he was ill but I didn't know how ill he was' she cried.

As she was being comforted, Suki, already in a stream of tears, gushed out her words intermittently. 'When Dad left for the doctors I feared the worst, and I don't know why I said goodbye to him. I wanted to say, don't worry you will be fine, but I said goodbye instead.'

Their pain and love so intertwined and its depth was so great, as they bravely expressed their fears and despair at such tender ages. It was a sight that burned sharply into my memory. We spoke about the times that their dad had spent with them and the fun they used to have in travelling to various venues. We talked about how the lasting memory of their father would remain forever and that it would be a valuable treasure, as they would often be able to look back at this as they grew older. They gently smiled, as they had a lot of good memories of being with their father, and I believed it would provide them with positive meanings about their relationships.

In light of their words about not knowing how ill their father was, I said to them 'remember there was nothing you did or said that resulted in your father dying. You loved him so much, as he loved you. It is important that we share what is so frightening us all. I know how much you want him back and I wish we could bring him back. Remember, what you said to him was because you loved him.'

Bal and Ami embraced them. Baljinder then revealed more of her pain as she said 'I know I really wanted him to hear me on that day. I really wish I had told him I loved him, but I didn't know he was going to die.'

There was no doubt that this was their time to continue to express their pain, and we had to listen and support them through it. I knew that a lot of repetition would be required. They were supported in sharing their feelings and thoughts no matter what, because no-one was going to ignore them or tell them not to say what they had said or to have the feelings and thoughts they had felt. Yet we would support them in talking about this because we knew how much they loved their father.

The reflection of the message that they loved their father was so important to reinforce, because I thought it was one of the immediate hopes that they could rely upon when grappling with what their thoughts and emotions meant.

After this Jai and I spoke privately, as throughout our conversation with Dilly and the girls his face had shown so much distress and pain. All I had to say was 'Jai, I know what you're feeling,' and he immediately broke down in tears, expressing his thoughts about not fully knowing how ill Gurjit had been before his admission to hospital, and about how he felt that some of Gurjit's symptoms should have been given more attention by the general practitioners who had seen Gurjit.

Our struggle as to whether to show our emotions or shut them down was identical. For me the closeness that such emotions brought was the desire to ignore what I was feeling and only focus on others. For me this was understandable, to the extent of allowing us to undertake various tasks, yet we knew this would have to be faced, because in order for us to bear each other's pain we needed to face our own as well. In the midst of all of this as a family we could provide comfort to hold on to each other, offer encouragement through our interactions and show our compassion to reach each other's needs.

I felt so bad, because I thought Jai had been robbed of not being there at the hospital and I blamed myself for that as I said to him 'I'm really sorry that you weren't there when Gurjit died.' We embraced, as the reality of death would always be with us in such an immovable way, knowing that in an hour or so we would be supporting the girls in preparing to visit the funeral directors' and the crematorium.

CHAPTER 8

FUNERAL ARRANGEMENTS

TUESDAY 4TH FEBRUARY 2003

The time that had been spent talking to Baljinder and Suki about the funeral was to support them with regard to their wishes and feelings as to how much they wanted to be involved. We ascertained their views so that they would not be put under additional distress.

As we began to make our way to the funeral directors, Baljinder and Suki spoke about the flower arrangements they had chosen. Suki said she felt slightly happier knowing that she and Baljinder had chosen the flowers for their Dad. Her beautiful words reflected her love.

This was a terrible tribulation they were experiencing at such a tender age. Baljinder started to cry, saying 'at least after the funeral I will be able to fully grieve for Dad and I look forward to the time when it is just us together. I need the time to grieve because the number of people who have come to the house has meant I've not been able to do this in the way I wanted.'

Her honest remark was a reminder to me that it was going to get even more intense once the funeral had taken place. I knew that as a family we were mourning and our grief had not even began to become fully expressed, for the fullness of the effects of death were still unknown. I said 'We know what you mean, and we will be together when we continue to grieve.'

Allowing a few moments to consider what this meant, it was a bit of a surprise to then hear Suki begin to talk about the disappearance of her

Uncle Parmjit. 'I know Granddad and Grandma are hurt by this and this makes me upset as well' she said. 'I'm angry about this, and I feel sorry for him not seeing Dad at the funeral' she said, beginning to cry.

She was revealing honesty about how her uncle Parmjit's absence was hurting her, and made me realise even more how much they were contending with. As I looked in the rear view mirror of the car, Baljinder was comforting her. I said 'Suki, your Titha (her paternal uncle) is going to be really hurt when he finds out, but there's nothing we can do, just as there was nothing we could have done to stop your dad from dying.'

Such discussions revealed that our minds' capacity to grasp the entirety of the event was clearly searching for knowledge to act as a bridge that we could all cross to lead us to partial recovery. The hope of being sustained to provide the best relief we could for each other was the tie that would keep us firmly knotted together.

I said to them 'What you have both have said is true. It is hard to know that there is nothing we can do at the moment to try and find Parmjit, but we can continue to support you. Your love for your uncle is good and we all need to remember that as well.'

Their tears began to trigger each other as my own eyes welled up. They remained huddled in the back. It was as if they were seeking refuge for each other. In continuation I said 'after your father's funeral, we all will spend a lot of time together.'

When we arrived at the funeral directors' we were greeted by Rajinder. Her compassionate and caring nature was again evident as she firstly expressed her condolences to them and told them that they looked like their father, which made them both smile. We went into the main room, where she went on to explain to them the funeral arrangements. The girls told her that they were aware of them through the family but were thankful that she was explaining it again.

Rajinder spoke to them that if they wanted to, they could provide any memorabilia of their father after the funeral, which could then be kept as a photo, a book etc which they would design. It was delightful to see the girls smile when Rajinder asked them what their father's likes and dislikes were. They were immediately able to tell her the main ones. They told her 'Dad loved watching football, even though he supported Manchester United. He did not like doing the hoovering but had to because Mom would constantly nag him. They laughed. 'He did not like having to take Mom and us shopping for clothes as he would just suffer in silence wandering the shops having no idea what we were buying or doing. But he was a good cook and liked spending time with us.'

Rajinder then told them that the flowers that they had chosen were really beautiful and expressed great love and attention. Their eyes were filled with tears. She then gently placed her arms around them as she looked at me and her eyes acknowledged the experience the girls were enduring. The girls responded by saying 'thank you.'

After showing the girls where their father's body would be viewed she went on to say 'Death is hurtful, and living with the memory of your father will be more hurtful, but because of the love you shared you will begin to heal the hurt that you are experiencing.'

Her words were very sensitive, considerate and gracious as she was acknowledging their pain as well as trying to offer hope for the future. Just watching how Rajinder was interacting with the girls was so refreshing and positive as she clearly understood what their experience of loss signified. Her willingness to show what the longing meant, through talking about her own experiences of bereavement, offered stepping stones towards the bridge that we as a family would need to continue to build.

The girls told her that they would be visiting the crematorium after this, so they could see the building and know what would happen. She again expressed her condolences and her warm smile lit up their faces as we left.

Chapter Eight

When we got into the car the girls talked about how understanding and kind Rajinder was and how they felt that she knew what they were experiencing and that she was very helpful in explaining again to them the funeral arrangements without rushing anything. Though it was so overwhelming for the girls to undertake this visit, Rajinder had made it less so by her ability to sit with them in the midst of their pain. I said to them 'Yes, she really is a nice person who knows what is happening for you and it was nice to know that she wanted to know more about your father.'

They gently giggled, and Baljinder said 'Can you imagine if we told her about Dad's driving?'. She was implying that he was not the best driver, to which I responded, 'You're telling me!'

As the funeral directors and crematorium were only a few miles apart, we arrived there in no time. As I pulled into the car park there was no other vehicle in sight, which was strange. As we stepped out of the car there was total silence, which was even stranger. Not a single person could be seen. Slowly we moved to the foyer area and once we entered in, we found people making various changes inside the hall.

I introduced myself to one of the men, who went to fetch Craig, the gentleman with whom I had arranged the visit. He was a young man, and he stretched out his hand to me to shake which I did. He then turned towards the girls and said 'Hello, my name is Craig and I'll be showing you around the crematorium. I'd like to say how sorry I am to hear about your father's death.'

He proceeded to show us around the hall and began to explain what would take place when their father's casket came into the hall, in terms of where it would be placed. To this, Baljinder asked 'Can we put a framed picture of Dad on top of the coffin when the service is happening?' to which he responded 'Of course, that's a very nice thought.'

We then left, thanking him for his time in showing us around the crematorium. Again as we walked out of the foyer area, the same strange silence was present. It felt as if everything around us stood still.

Chapter Eight

Glancing at the girls I asked 'how are you feeling?' to which Baljinder replied 'all right, but it's weird because I didn't think coming here would be so calm.' Suki said 'I feel better now I've seen where Dad will be.'

In the car the girls were initially silent, as it was clear that the enormity of their father's death was beginning to take another step in their minds and hearts. When I looked into their eyes all I saw was the deepest longing to have him back.

Baljinder then spoke. 'Mama, I found the visits very useful and helpful because at least I'll know what is going to happen' she said. I reassured them that on the day of the funeral that the immediate family would be with them every step of the way.

When we arrived home they spoke to their mother and family members about their visit and about how they felt it had been more helpful to them than they had expected.

The rest of the day began to repeat itself, with more relatives visiting to pay their respects to Gurjit. Time whizzed by, and before I knew it evening had fallen and my mind began to ponder upon the next day, which would be about preparing Gurjit's body for the funeral. I felt some ease knowing that the girls were prepared as best as we could in order to begin to contend with the most tragic experience of their young lives.

By this stage tiredness was slowly creeping up on me, and the heaviness on my eyelids finally submitted. My mind went blank.

* * * * * * * * * *

Snow had fallen during the early hours of the Wednesday morning and the day began with the awareness that preparing Gurjit's body for the funeral was going to be extremely emotional and sorrowful. It was part of the Asian culture, so it was viewed as an important role to be undertaken, as it would be signifying the utmost respect and honour for Gurjit's life.

Chapter Eight

Discussions had taken place with relatives who had undertaken this demanding task through their own experience. Jai and I spoke to our cousin, Chima, who told us that even though his father had died fifteen years ago he could not forget the image of his father when he washed his body the day before the funeral.

He told us that it was important that those involved understood that this would stay in their minds for a very long time and suggested that everyone was spoken to clearly about how distressing this would be. Such words of wisdom and experience had to be heeded.

Hence it was identified that those who wanted to be involved in this were: Jai, our cousin-brothers, Laker and Harjinder, and our nephews Bal, Ami, Bobby, and me. Gurjit's father and my father would also be involved, though it was initially thought that this would be too traumatic for them both; however it was realised that they had more experience of death than all of us put together.

Jai and I spoke again to Bal, Ami and Bobby and told them that the task of preparing Gurjit's body for the funeral would be difficult and that we needed to ensure it did not cause them undue distress, as we knew that the day would forever remain with us all.

Bal and Ami had been present when Gurjit had died, and said 'we want to honour him and we know this is going to hurt, but we are in this together and we will all support each other. Our dad's not here and we are saddened knowing that he does not even know his brother has died, but we want to focus on Chacha who was like a father to us.'

Bobby wanted to be involved for the same reason, and more so for him as on the day Gurjit died Bobby was in Preston as his mother, father and little sister, Kiran came to us. He told me 'I stayed at home because Mom thought Chacha would be fine, so I went to work thinking he'd be fine and I felt so bad not coming to the hospital. I never got the chance to see him.'

Jai and I looked at each other and knew that the lads were as prepared as could be, even though I felt that none of us wanted to really prepare for the funeral, because it was not something we thought we would ever do. Death had seemed a million miles away from my family, but its impact was now within us.

A couple of hours had elapsed and my prevailing thoughts shifted from preparing Gurjit's body to trying to take on board how everyone would be feeling when they viewed him. I felt that only through being unified would we be able to prepare ourselves for this.

The time had come for us to go and prepare Gurjit's body and as we travelled, there was silence throughout. When we arrived at the funeral directors' we were sensitively greeted by an Asian gentleman named Jaswinder. He spent a few moments with us all in the foyer explaining that he would be here to offer support and assistance at any stage.

Jai and Bal stood holding Gurjit's clothes and personal items. Jai's fists were clenched on the bag, knowing that these clothes belonged to Gurjit. He looked as if he did not want to let them go.

Jaswinder then took us into the room where Gurjit's body awaited us. Gurjit's father and my father initially waited outside while we began the preparations. They were visibly distressed. As we walked in and saw Gurjit's body lying on the table none of us could even muster a sound, let alone any words. We spent a few moments gently holding his hand and the tears began to surface as it was so daunting. There was no language that could have been spoken to offer any immediate comfort.

Though we knew that Gurjit was not with us, Jai still spoke out of love and what he said clearly represented what we were all feeling, 'Gurjit, please get up,' he said as he embraced him, weeping. I just stood shaking my head and wondering how this could be, and the bulge in my throat tightened as tears began to fall.

For Bobby the shock of seeing his uncle was so hard-hitting that he stood in a gaze, his eyes totally distraught and his body like an icicle. The only movement was his lips quivering, desperately battling the tears that were about to be released. He lifted his arm to move forward but his legs were rooted as though in concrete.

We approached Bobby and spoke gently to him to say it was OK to feel what he was feeling, and we all understood if he needed to leave the room for a few moments. At this point it was as though he awoke as he looked at us and then moved his hands to his face to meet the tears racing down. He stood still crying as Bal and Ami comforted him and then he moved to the table and held Gurjit's hand as his tears fell on to his uncle. Bal and Ami began to stroke Gurjit's head and hair and their tears were falling all over the floor as they shook their heads simultaneously and said 'Chacha, we all love you. Can you please come back to us, we miss you, please come back.' Their heart-felt, heart-wrenching plea was shredding me into pieces, for when I looked at them I saw a reflection of my own despondency.

Laker, though he was putting on a brave face, was unable to hide the emotional pain as the years of his relationship as Gurjit's cousin-brother were flooding through his eyes and he was shaking his head in disbelief. Jai approached him and they embraced and Laker said 'we need to begin to prepare Gurjit's body, otherwise it is going to get harder to do.'

We began to check to see how everyone was feeling and whether anyone wanted to take a few moments out, which none of us did. At this point we decided to bring in Gurjit's father and my father. The moment Gurjit's father saw his son's body it was clear that reality had begun to sink in for him as he stood shattered and broken-hearted. His eyes were bloodshot and red and the tears were swirling around. His hands trembled, the tragedy of seeing his son was so profound. My father placed his arms on his shoulders to gently move him closer to his son's body. It was as though he did not want to move any further in the hope that it was not his son lying there.

When he made the steps forward he grabbed Gurjit's hand. He was ready to collapse and had to be held by Laker. He fought hard to stop the tears like a dam ready to burst, but they began to trickle down and he placed his hand over his face as if somehow to take them away.

My father held Gurjit's other hand and began to talk to Gurjit, saying 'son, it should not have been you who God has taken, it should have been me.' Laker went to my father and comforted him and said that Gurjit would not have wanted that to happen.

We quietly proceeded to prepare Gurjit's body and everyone periodically spoke words of comfort to each other. Yet in the main there was silence. When it had been done, Jai placed the new shoes he had selected on Gurjit's feet as he knew they were the style that Gurjit liked. We all smiled knowing how much Gurjit liked his shoes.

Then a red turban, representing honour, was prepared by our cousin Laker. This was to be placed on Bal's head first, (as Bal was representing his own father, Parmjit) and then on Gurjit's head. When Bal walked in with the turban on, we were all amazed as he resembled his own father and uncle so much. We expressed our acknowledgement that it was a courageous act through a warm smile, yet his eyes were redder than the turban.

As Bal took the turban off his head, he held it with the uttermost respect, his grip displaying the determination that his uncle should look peaceful and dignified. Once this was placed on Gurjit, he looked splendid.

The final, and by far the most difficult task was, to place Gurjit into the casket. As I looked at Bal it was amazing to think of Gurjit's humour at this time. I had a flashback of the times Gurjit used to play-wrestle with Bal and how Bal (even though he was a lot younger) was able to pick Gurjit up like a little baby. Gurjit would always pretend that he was letting him, yet he was never able to explain how he allowed Bal to pick him up. Gurjit's humour was certainly something else.

These thoughts began to disappear as my father and I stood back and everyone picked Gurjit up and gracefully placed him into the casket. This was it, this was how Gurjit would be seen by the immediate family and extended relatives. We briefly commented that even though this image would remain with us for a long time, there were many living memories and images that we had of Gurjit which would also stay with us for a long time to provide comfort.

As we stood around Gurjit the crying then began, for pain was becoming manifested and it was incredibly awful.

We knew that we would have to go back and begin bringing every immediate family member back. As we drove back, the lads all said pretty much the same thing: 'This has meant a lot to us, to be able to prepare Chacha's body, because we loved him so dearly and we want to tell everyone at home how good he looked.' Their words carried so much compassion.

We would not be staying long back home, as there was a total of twenty of us (a big family) to go back to the funeral directors': Gurjit's father, my father and mother, my sisters Dilly, Dee, Patty, Mangender and Gurdev, my brother Jai, my cousin-brothers Harjinder, Laker and Chima, my nephews Bal, Bobby and Ami, my nieces Sunny, Baljinder, Suki and Kiran, and myself.

We were again greeted with sensitivity by the staff. The mourning was already beginning and tears ran freely as we waited in the foyer area. Everyone was so admirable as we all sought to give each other warmth to begin to deal with our shattered hearts. Then the moment of our love and pain arrived as we were about to enter the viewing room.

Dilly and the girls were totally broken as they walked in and the realisation crept in that the person they loved so dearly would never be with them again. Such a daunting, dreadful and formidable reality was like being in a desert searching for a glimmer of life to reach out to, in order to be sustained.

Yet they wanted something more powerful than being sustained at that time, they wanted him back. Gurjit's father and my parents followed, seeing their daughter's and grandchildren's absolute devastation, for they had been assaulted by the bleakness this had brought upon them.

When we were all in the room, the realisation of how painful this was became ever more clear as the shock, affliction, battery, dread, insecurity, disbelief, separation, brokenness, despair, outrage, and tragedy just smacked like a hurricane rising. If there was any doubt about what the pain meant, it was certainly removed by such a sight, because there could not be any containment to the emotions being expressed.

Throughout the time we spent there everyone cried. Our distress was in unison, and so was our comfort. Every tear shed, every shaking in our bones, every plea for Gurjit to be with us, every desire to take away each other's pain, was etched all over our faces. The vulnerability was inescapable and undeniably irreversible, for there would be no relief for a long time.

Every time I looked at everyone it was like a mirror image, each face expressing a longing for the separation from Gurjit to be undone. The pain was that no words were going to make a difference to the reality we were facing. I knew words could only remind us of our relationship with him.

I noticed that the longer we stayed the more degree of peace began to rise like a mist. It was captivating, because it was like being sprinkled by a hose on a very hot day. I began to feel that the distress was no longer taking central place - Gurjit was, when we talked about his personality, his character and his loving determination to see other's supported. This was the peace. We all talked about how much he meant to us and how much we knew we meant to him and that it was such a privilege to have known him.

Time had passed quickly and now we knew we would have to leave. As everyone began to vacate the room it was time for Dilly to spend her last private moment with her husband. This was her treasure, and extremely valuable as I hoped it would give her the strength to face her grief.

Everyone waited outside, and I approached Baljinder and Suki. Baljinder, in tears, said 'there's so much love for Dad in there and it hurts to know we can't have him back.' When we all heard what she said, the embracing of the truth was so tragic yet so uplifting, for I knew that difficult as it was, there was still hope to respond to each other. Jai came across to Baljinder and Suki and hugged them as they cried alongside Bal, Ami and Patty, while I went back into the viewing room as Dilly had asked me to return.

As I went into the room she was clinging to the casket and when I approached her her eyes were so full of tears that it looked as though a tidal wave had arisen within her. She grabbed me and cried her heart out as my tears fell on to her head. Then she turned towards Gurjit and in a final intimate act she leaned over the casket to kiss him and wipe her tears on to his face. This I knew would be a lasting memory of their relationship.

I moved slowly to her as she held on to Gurjit and felt how hard it was for her to leave. As I gently touched her on the shoulder she looked at me through the wall of tears that had submerged her eyes and turned her head towards my body as I held her. I told her 'Gurjit knew and experienced your love and that of the girls and the entire family, and we certainly know his love was experienced by us all.'

Her crying rose to a squeal and her body began to slip through my arms, almost collapsing to the floor. No words, only tears, could be spoken.

We walked very slowly towards the door and Dilly thanked the funeral directors for the time they had given and their support. They were very sensitive and told her that they were very moved by what they had seen today and it demonstrated to them how special Gurjit had been to her and the family. Their words gave us comfort as we prepared for another journey back home.

Chapter Eight

When we got home we all spoke about how the time spent at the funeral directors had helped us and Dilly said 'I'm so grateful to have known him and to have had him in my life and to see him dressed so beautifully will always remain in my heart. He was so good.' Then her tears began to overflow.

I spoke to the girls, and Baljinder said 'Seeing Dad has made me feel a lot better. I would have found it difficult if I had only seen him on the funeral for a few minutes.' Her tears began to fall. 'He looked really nice. Seeing Dad today was different from when I saw him at the hospital. In the hospital I felt that he was in discomfort, but today I know he was at peace.'

Listening to how much they thought of seeing their father was so tender and their views about what it meant to have spent that time with him was so valuable. Baljinder said 'We are so glad to have spent the time with Dad, it is very special and no one can ever take that away from us.'

Another evening had fallen among us and we spent this trying to get some rest before the ultimate acknowledgement of Gurjit's death - his funeral.

CHAPTER 9

THE BREAKDOWN & ACKNOWLEDGEMENT OF LIFE

THURSDAY 6TH FEBRUARY 2003

The snow of the day before had already begun to melt, but we made sure that the drive was clear as well as the entire entrance to the house. Relatives and friends began to arrive and as customary all the men, besides Gurjit's father, my father and Jai, waited outside the house, while all the women were in the house.

As we stood outside the tears from inside echoed deep sounds of wailing, which sent a shiver throughout my entire body, mind and soul. The cries roared louder and overshadowed the silence outside as all the men stood, many with heads bowed and many with quiet tears. Waiting and listening to such pain needed to be endured as it felt as though we were all casualties of the war of separation. This terror was not fading but increasing as we knew the hearse would be arriving soon.

Then came the reality of the arrival of the hearse. My heart sank further, and as I looked around I saw a mirror image in Jai, Laker, Bal, Ami and Bobby. Not even a bottomless pit could compare to the inner turmoil of the severance of attachment that had been experienced. I couldn't even begin to translate what this meant for my sister and nieces.

As the hearse reversed on to the drive, Bal, Ami, Bobby, Jai and Laker waited, as they would be carrying Gurjit into his house. My mind, battling to understand, was seeking refuge, but none was forthcoming. Rather there were just thoughts of enquiring what has happened, but there was no response.

When the coffin was placed in the lounge with the uttermost sensitivity and care the crying was loud, yet magnified with deep pangs as the coffin lid was removed by the funeral directors. The entire room erupted like a volcano at the realisation that there would be no more interaction with Gurjit.

Dilly, supported by our sisters, was beyond despair. Total devastation surfaced within her as she curled her body towards Gurjit as a symbol of wanting so desperately to be next to him. Nothing could bring any relief to her. Baljinder and Suki, supported by their, aunts were also being upheld as their little bodies began to collapse, for the foundations of their life had been ripped from underneath them. Such a sight was intensely penetrating to the mind, leaving scars which were compounded by watching my immediate family's burden and bleakness.

Gurjit's father was at the top of the coffin, and he could not have been more broken. He stood physically quaking, tears bouncing off his face like a heavy downpour of rain hitting a road. He was being held by Laker, who was trying ever so hard not to cry. Jai approached them and said 'Gurjit was your son and our brother and we are all hurt.' Laker's tears exploded, landing on Jai as they held on to each other firmly.

My mother's distraught face painted a picture of her love which none could remove. Her hands trembled at the sight of her son as she frantically held on to him and Dilly in the hope that all her pain would transform into life. Screaming at the top of her voice 'Gurjit get up, my son you can't go, look at your daughters! Gurjit please come back to us, don't leave!'

Such overwhelming pleading was so afflicting, for there was no liberation that could be brought, no matter how much it was longed for. Love's protectiveness could not undo what had happened, yet it would hopefully sustain us. The entire room was packed and everyone was in tears. I stood by my father gently supporting him as he remained firmly clutching Gurjit's arm and shaking his head sideways, his tears dropping like lead weights. He whispered through his tears 'Gurjit, what has happened? Gurjit, stay here... you are young and we are old. Come back!' He could not utter another word as the enormous power of death had taken its stronghold. All I heard was my father's teeth rattling.

In the midst of all of this the religious ceremony commenced, while relatives and friends all came through the house to pay their final respects in viewing Gurjit's body. The crying did not stop at any stage during the ceremony, and my mother embraced Gurjit again and would not let go as she kept on saying 'take me instead,' her words again echoing the sincere love for her son.

My mother was gently supported as she let Gurjit go. As she stood by him she placed a flower by his side and leaned over to kiss him on the forehead, her last physical contact with her son. As she turned away she clung on to relatives, saying 'God please give him back to us, please, please take me!'

Dilly and the girls had embraced Gurjit and placed a flower with him. Their tears fell on to his face, and they gently rubbed them on to him. Dilly shook her head in disbelief, saying 'I love you too much! Please do not go without me, please stay with us.'

Baljinder and Suki were unable to utter many words, yet the ones they did were like thorns firmly pushed into the flesh: 'Dad, we love you. Don't go, please don't go.'

The development of their relationship reflected the significance of their respect and love. My prayer was that this would sustain them for the days, weeks, months and years to come, and that the belief in hope would remain even though we had all been pierced by the sting of death.

My father held Gurjit's hand and placed a flower with him. Then he put his hand on Gurjit's forehead and said 'My son, you are going home now.' The words ran deep, because as they say 'Home is where the heart is', and I knew our hearts had been broken. With such words from my father, I leaned forward and embraced Gurjit, and as my last physical act of respect and honour for him I kissed him on the forehead. I said 'Gurjit, I'm so sorry that you have gone, we love you so much and I know how much you loved us all.'

I then placed a flower by his side. No more could be done, and my tears ran down my face and on to my lips. They could be tasted, for they engulfed a sorrow which swirled inside me like a ship in the sea being tossed between rocks by high winds.

I turned around and saw Jai's eyes looking like a hurricane raging over the sea, but he stood lifeless, his arms by his side, unable to move. He looked lost, as I knew we all were. All of a sudden he moved quickly, leaned over the casket and grabbed on to Gurjit to the point Gurjit's body was no longer visible.

It was so hard to visualise the acute brokenness of his heart, so many pieces that could not be put back together. Even with the tribulation caging him, the empathy manifested in every fibre of his being as he screamed out his loyal love for his brother. 'Please get up Gurjit, please I beg you, please get up, Gurjit don't go, please don't go!' he shouted

I felt a tap on my shoulder and when I turned around my cousin Chima whispered in my ear 'I need you to come outside. The funeral director needs to see you.' As I stepped outside, Jaswinder, the funeral director, looked as though something terrible had taken place, and I was wondering what could be worse than the death we had experienced. He said 'I don't know how to say this' and took a deep breath. He was not able to say another word. I just told him that whatever it was, he should just tell me. He then composed himself and said 'One of the funeral limousines has broken down en route and the breakdown company is trying to repair it. The other one will be here within minutes. I am really sorry about this.'

My cousin Chima, a competent mechanic, volunteered to go, and I turned around to Jaswinder and told him 'this is not an issue, today is about Gurjit and nothing else. It doesn't matter about the vehicle, don't worry about it.' I told him that I did not want the hearse leaving for the crematorium until all family members who were to be in the funeral car were in alternative vehicles. He looked at me and said 'I'm very sorry about this,' to which I replied 'There's no need to worry.'

When I went back into the house, Jai was still holding on to Gurjit and Laker gently held Jai saying 'Jai, it is OK to let Gurjit go.' Jai did so, wiping his tears. Jai turned around as I was behind him and his eyes filled with of burning love, with a quest for answers.

We stood together embraced, crying in the knowledge that our brother was not returning. I softly whispered in Jai's ear 'It's OK to show our love this way.' We looked up and saw Gurjit's father place a flower by his son's head and touch him, and then he exploded into tears, trying to cover his face as though trying to remove the memory of his son's death. I could only wish that none of us had to have such an afflicting memory.

As the religious ceremony was coming to an end in the house after about half an hour, Jaswinder came into the room and stood by the casket, preparing to place the coffin lid. He tried to keep a composed stature, but when he heard the high-pitched cries, so intolerable and indescribable, he looked as though he had frozen.

I glanced at Dilly and the girls and saw tragedy written all over their faces as Dilly and my mother were trying to cling on to the casket. Jaswinder slowly began to move to place the lid on the casket, and as he did so my mother, who was opposite him, placed her hand against the lid, stopping him from doing so. He looked at her, as Jai moved across to support her. Jaswinder said to her 'Aunt, he is going to God's home now.' My mom, if not already broken, was now disintegrated by these words of truth.

Jaswinder then managed to complete what was required and the high-pitched sounds of cries continued as Gurjit's casket was being transported to the hearse by Bal, Ami, Bobby, Jai and Laker. The lads then placed the flower arrangements that they had chosen which had an inscription in the corner 'GBH', which represented a personal memory for them.

While everyone else was coming out of the house I informed Jai what had happened with the other funeral car, so we hurried around making the alternative arrangements. When Dilly, the girls, my mother and Dee came out of the house they were supported in getting into the funeral car. Their crying was so desperate and incredibly compassionate for each other.

We then began to make our way to the crematorium. I chose to drive and had my cousin Harjinder and my nephew Bal with me. As I was following the hearse and the funeral car my thoughts centred upon how everyone was coping with this as I knew that there was a lot of effort to be implemented in order for us all to come to terms with Gurjit's death. Nothing else entered my mind. It was a strange feeling to have after what I had seen.

The journey was very quiet. I felt none of us were able to say anything because I think our minds were battling with the raging emotions inside. On arrival at the crematorium the majority of the relatives and friends were already there as the funeral directors took a longer route to get there. At the appropriate time Gurjit's coffin was carried in by Jai, Bal, Ami, and Bobby. I remained with my father, walking slowly with him due to his own ill health.

The religious song that had been chosen by Dilly was being played. It was extremely peaceful and I believe it enabled everyone to focus for a few moments. Even amid so much distress, hope somehow felt closer than before; I did not know how or why.

My father and I began to follow, and as I held him, he looked lifeless. As we got close to the main entrance doors he stood still and began shaking his head and tried to turn around, crying. He said 'I can't do this.' Pausing for a while, I replied to his despair 'Dad, this is our final farewell to Gurjit,' to which he bowed his head, tears dripping like water from a tap and we began to walk. My cousin Chima saw this and came across to help.

When Gurjit's coffin had been put down, Baljinder went up to it and placed a framed photo of her father on top. The picture was such a lovely representation of his life as it displayed his warm and caring smile.

The crying continued throughout the service and my mind again tried to focus on ensuring support was there for everyone, while another part of my mind was trying to focus on the magnitude of the loss experienced for us as a family.

Every part of the funeral process was going to be difficult, and it did not get any easier when the time came for Gurjit's body to be cremated. Gurjit's father, Bal and my eldest cousin brother stood by the side as they would be the ones pressing the button to lower the coffin. Bal looking totally crushed as he held on to his grandfather's hand and they pressed the button together. As the curtains began to encircle the coffin the same high-pitched sound of crying returned, again intolerable, for it was a plea for Gurjit not to be taken. Yet once the curtains closed the physical realisation could no longer be ignored. Gurjit had gone.

All manner of emotions and thoughts arose within me as I was trying to fathom the event of death. I felt totally useless, unable to bring about any change, and feeling unable to offer anything tangible.

Everyone began to walk outside and the crematorium staff approached me and asked who from the family wanted to view Gurjit's coffin being placed for cremation. I had forgotten about this as I was holding my father from collapsing, and just directed them to Jai, who arranged for Bal, Gurjit's father, Laker and my eldest cousin-brother and himself to be there.

Chapter Nine

The thought running through my mind at that time was that we had seen enough distress, and to now have to consider this was an immense struggle because I knew those who had gone to undertake such a task had already poured out their professed love. I felt it was like the final straw was being placed on to their back. What an alarming position to be in.

All I could do at that point was to remain with my father up until I saw Dilly, who was completely and profoundly wounded. Dee was comforting her in every way possible. I just had to go to them, so I left my father with Ami who was standing with me with tears pouring down his face.

I quickly approached Dilly and Dee as had a number of family members and friends who were seeking to console them. I embraced them, but their fragile bodies began to crumble in my arms and we had to hold them up.

There appeared no structure left to her life at that point. All I could say to her in repetition was 'Gurjit knew your love, you knew his love and we all know that. Our love for him will keep us all together.' Slowly moving out of the crematorium and seeing everyone's faces was the familiar visualisation of dejection, pain and a quest for change.

Time then felt it had speeded up as we began to make our way to the Gurdwara (Sikh Temple) for the final part of the religious ceremony. This time I had Baljinder, Suki, Sunny, Kiran and Bal in my car. They were all in tears. Bal said to his cousin-sisters 'I can't believe we are never going to see your dad again, it's so hard to believe this.' Baljinder said 'I know, it's unreal,' and curled up. 'I want him back, I miss him so much!'

Sunny was just holding on to Baljinder and Suki, saying 'I'm here for you,' as her tears fell over them. I then said 'we are all going to miss him so much and this hurts so much to know. But I want you to know that all our love for him and his love for us is still in us and we can hold on to that.'

Suki, still crying, then spoke. 'Mama, can you play that song that Dad liked?' she said. It was amazing to hear what she said, because the song she was referring to was an Asian song which her father certainly did like and would often sing to make her laugh when he tried to also dance to it. It was incredible that she was hanging on to this memory of her father. I replied 'of course' and played the song all the way to the Gurdwara while tears were still being shed.

When we arrived at the Gurdwara, many family members and friends were already in the hall. Only immediate family members remained in the foyer area. We waited for Dilly, who had gone home from the crematorium as part of the cultural tradition prior coming to the temple. Jai, Dee, Patty and Mangender went with her, as Jai would be driving them to the Gurdwara. Knowing it would be a while before they arrived, we used the time again to give and receive the emotional strength that was needed.

This was the deepest and most desolate experience faced within the family, it felt like being captured in a cage ready to be devoured by my emotions. There was no escape and no expertise that could handle such an impact. As this thought continued to spin around in my mind, Jai pulled into the car park, and my thoughts stood still because everything around me seemed to slow down to the point where I began to wonder for a split second whether this was all still a dream.

However, as Dilly stepped out of the car she was frozen with the overwhelming realisation that she was separated for ever from her husband; the devastation had its last say. It became apparent that in spite of whatever resolve was imparted to us all, the trauma was too deep. We all approached Dilly and spoke to her the few words of comfort and support we could, which was that we were all there as she walked in these difficult and lonely times.

As we entered the hall the ceremony commenced. It was spoken in Punjabi and focused upon how God is central to life and death, a message which I know many people believe and many people disbelieve in the midst of their pain. For Gurjit's death was painful indeed.

When the ceremony finished and everyone stood up, many family members and friends approached my father and Gurjit's father to offer their final words of sympathy and respect. About three hundred people then began to move upstairs to a hall where there would be a Langar (a communal gathering of the family and friends eating a meal, equivalent to a wake).

As is traditional, the food was being served by volunteers within the temple to the family and friends. I knew there were a lot of people there who did not want to eat, including myself, as all my energy was being focused on what to do next, and how.

The only reason I ate, which applied to all those who like me did not want to eat, was tradition. This signified that this was the last meal being provided by Gurjit to us all and we had to embrace this.

When the meal was done, it was time for the immediate family to go home. When we arrived back at Gurjit's house, the atmosphere was cold. Dilly walked past me and went into the back lounge with my parents and sisters and the girls, and the crying continued, for the acknowledgement of Gurjit's death was becoming even more evident.

I stayed only a few moments before leaving to take a great aunt to the coach station, as she needed to go back to London. She showed tremendous strength in being at the funeral and was a source of encouragement throughout. Ami went with me and we all talked about the funeral and about how we knew that there were many of Gurjit's friends who were extremely hurt but were trying so hard not to show it as they wanted to remain firm to give some hope to the family.

After we arrived at the coach station, I assisted my great aunt to get on to the coach before leaving. At this time Ami remained in the car. When I got back to the car he was crying and his blood shot eyes rippled with an immense intensity of grief.

Chapter Nine

'I can't believe that today Chacha has just been cremated and is no more' he said, bowing his head and holding his hands together in prayer as the tears came streaming down. 'This thought has been going through my mind over and over again. I keep wondering how I could have stopped this from happening.'

He continued in his distress, spurting out his words. 'I know there is nothing that we can do for Chacha now, but I know there is something that we can do for everyone who is left, but it's too hard to think about it.'

His words reflected how torn up he was with the battle between acceptance of death and acceptance of the pain caused by death. We spoke about how strength at this time could only come through knowing that the painful truth was the need to touch each other's pain. Our relationships were now being tested by the whirlwind of turmoil.

Our conversation continued about the reality of what we believed about Gurjit, about us as a family, and about God, and the reality of the pain being experienced. Then silence fell. We travelled back as though the volume had just been muted and this I believe allowed a few moments of private space. When we arrived back at Gurjit's house there was a different atmosphere, a peace which I did not consider could be there. It was like being given a strong dose of medication, relaxing the body and bringing the mind under control for a short time, which was welcomed.

Such a sensation meant the consuming and piercing day began to slow down. Everyone sat and just spoke, checking out how each one of us was.

As the day drew to a close I took my parents and Gurjit's father home and began to support them in the best way I could. After a couple of hours I returned back to Gurjit's house. Dilly, Baljinder, Suki, Dee, Bal, Ami, Patty, Sunny, Bobby and Kiran were all sitting down and reflecting upon not only the funeral but the day of Gurjit's death. I sat intently listening to where we all were in relation to such loss. Then suddenly something was heard that most would feel offended by as it is not perceived as part of grief or respect, whereas the reality is that it is part of love and truth: laughter.

Baljinder and Suki were laughing about the limousine breaking down and it made them think how only a few weeks ago their father's car had experienced the same problem – a failed alternator - and Jai, Bal and Chima had stood in the freezing cold weather sorting the problem out. They laughed about how crazy their father was at driving, not literally but in the things he used to get so badly wrong, such as the time he broke the key in his car door, not once but twice, and to make it more interesting he then broke it trying to open the boot. The fact that they could look at the memories at this time was evidence of their love.

As night began to close they ordered a Kentucky Fried Chicken meal, one of Gurjit's favourite fast foods, for he could eat the chicken pretty fast to say the least!

We all then began to speak about how we felt that everyone's support was so gratefully appreciated and that it was going to be very important that within the coming weeks we would be able to sit down and talk openly about Gurjit's death and the effect it had had upon us all.

Baljinder said 'It's hard to imagine what my life is going to be like without Dad being here. I love him so much and it frightens me to know that he's not here.'

Suki said 'I keep dreaming that this will all go away and that Dad will come through the door and tell me that he is back.'

As we sat and cried, providing support in the midst of their heart-felt messages, together we all reinforced Dilly's and the girls love for Gurjit and his love for us all.

Dilly's message I thought was befitting as the final statement of the day about Gurjit's life. She said 'I want to thank you all for all your love and support. I know how much every one of us loved Gurjit and how much we would love to have him back'. She paused as her tears fell. 'It's hard to know that he is not coming back and it's hard to think about this, but I know he gave me the best years of my life and I'll never forget that.'

The day was over, and I pondered upon what the reality was. It was shaped with doubts and hopes, as we had been living it. It was within us, because the memory of Gurjit was still alive in us. It was the realisation that the wounds were deep, yet it was also the belief that our relationships were deeply secured by love.

CHAPTER 10

FAREWELL TO GURJIT

SUNDAY MARCH 9TH 2003

Sunday 9th March 2003 was to be another extremely significant day, as it would have been Gurjit's birthday (he would have been 44 years old), and his ashes were returning to India with his father. Dilly, Baljinder, Suki, Dee, Bal, Ami, Jai, my cousin Chima and I left Gurjit's house with his father alongside us. My cousin Laker was unable to go to the airport, but his presence provided comfort to Gurjit's father as he ushered him to my car. Jai and Bal were also with me.

Gurjit's father was shedding tears, as he would have known that whenever he visited again his son would never greet him. The tears I felt were also an acknowledgement of knowing that Dilly would be without a husband and the girls would be without a father.

There was total silence as we travelled to the airport, not because we did not want to talk; rather it was part of a tradition to pay respect to support Gurjit's father to gather his thoughts in preparing himself for the release of his sons' ashes. To enable him to do so, the religious song chosen by Dilly for Gurjit's funeral was being played throughout the journey.

Upon arrival at the airport and once all the usual procedures had been followed, time began to whistle by and we sat and waited. Though weeks had passed since Gurjit's death, the pain was ever present. In looking around at everyone I saw how difficult this was and how much we needed each other. I felt inside that there was no way we were going to be able to respond on our own to the effects that death had upon us and within us.

Chapter Ten

Then came the moment for Gurjit's father to board the plane. Jai, holding on to him, said 'Don't worry about Dilly and the girls' as his tears began to roll. 'Tell everyone back at home how much Gurjit meant to us all and that we will miss him dearly.'

Gurjit's father responded, with his tears also rolling down into his beard: 'I know Gurjit was also yours and I'm glad that he had known all of you.' I echoed the same sentiments that Jai had to Gurjit's father, because such words could not have been added to.

After we all embraced, Gurjit's father cried and held on to the bag tightly as he walked slowly towards the departure lounge. When he was about to pass the point of not being able to see us he turned around and acknowledged everyone through a gentle nod.

All that could be done was to stand and wave to him with all our love. We then made our way very slowly to the side of the departure lounge, where the runway could be seen, even though at that stage it began to rain heavy. In looking at the downpour of the rain, I felt it resembled the downpour of our hearts.

Dilly, Baljinder and Suki wanted to go home as they did not want to see the plane leave, and the girls said something that was very special to them about their father which was 'Our dad's home is in our hearts.' This was part of the hope that we all needed to take refuge in. We all embraced, even though we would all be going back home, yet Bal, Ami and I remained to see the plane take off.

We stood silently in the viewing area, but the rain and mist made it difficult to see outside. When the time came Bal saw the plane slowly moving towards the runway and we knew this was it, that Gurjit had died and would never return, but it was important to say goodbye. When the plane took off we said it with all our love. Bal and Ami said 'Goodbye GBH,' and I said 'We'll see you in heaven.'

Let me tell you why we called Gurjit 'GBH'. In the late evening of my brother's wedding in July 2000, Gurjit had had a bit too much to drink.

Chapter Ten

As a result Bal, Ami and Bobby walked him home, after the wedding celebrations had ended. The day after the wedding Bal, Ami, Bobby, Dilly and the girls all played a trick on Gurjit. Dilly told him he had been so drunk that he had actually hit Bal and given him a black eye.

Gurjit was panicking, as he was wondering what my parents would be thinking about him and what we must all be thinking about what he had done. He rang me and asked 'is Baljit OK?' to which I queried why he was asking.

He hesitantly then asked 'how's his eye?' At this point I thought he had not recovered from his hangover and asked him what he meant, to which he blurted out 'I didn't mean to hit him.' Coincidentally Bal then came into the house and I could see that he did not have a black eye. When I asked him what Gurjit was on about, Bal placed his finger on his lips and gently laughed, whispering 'tell Chacha that my eye is badly hurt.'

It became clear they were trying to play a prank on Gurjit. I didn't have the heart to prolong his anxiety, so I told him they were only joking.

Since then the lads had nicknamed their uncle GBH, which was the personal inscription they had placed on the flower arrangements they had chosen for his funeral.

How strange that the nickname they gave him means grievous bodily harm, for death certainly does cause this.

When we arrived home we all spoke briefly about Gurjit's ashes returning to India and about how as a family we would need to continue to support each other in looking at 'moving forward' with such tragedy in our hearts. In considering this, in May 2003 Gurjit's and Parmjit's mother died in India. Her death compounded the grief that Dilly, the girls, Dee and the lads were experiencing.

As I attempted to explore the 'moving forward' I began to wonder what had moved within us. This moving on came to be tested by another significant and traumatic event.

PART 2

PARMJIT

In the previous chapter I mentioned that Parmjit, Gurjit's eldest brother and my eldest brother-in-law, had left the family home in January 2001 due to alcohol-related difficulties and was reported missing to the police. Unfortunately their efforts to locate him had been unfruitful; at least that is what we thought.

In January 2003 and over the months after Gurjit's death every effort was made to locate Parmjit, but he unfortunately proved elusive. Then, just as we were learning to contend with the tragedy of Gurjit's death and the impact it had upon the family, we were hit by a tidal wave. Our search for Parmjit bore fruit in a tragic way, revealing another personal and deep tragedy for my family. Nothing could have prepared us for what else was to unfold.

The names of the police officers and non-family members in this account have been changed to ensure anonymity.

CHAPTER 1

DEVASTATING NEWS

THURSDAY 11TH DECEMBER 2003

I was sitting in a dental surgery waiting room to see the dentist, because I had a toothache which had persisted for a few days, when my mobile phone rang. It was my nephew Bal. 'Mama, the police have come out to see Mom and they told her something about Dad' he said.

When I asked him what exactly the police had said, he paused and I detected in his voice a deep brokenness.

'The police told mum that they believe they have located Dad, but that they think that he has already died' he said.

Realising the significance of what he had been told, it was no surprise that he sounded dejected. My immediate thought was 'what?' My mind tried to grab hold of the thought, but it was difficult to grasp. I pondered on what Dee, Bal and Ami must be feeling, knowing what the police had said. I asked him 'What do they mean?'

'I don't really know' he said. 'They spoke to Mom first and it doesn't make sense.' He sounded even more dejected, and my emotions were travelling too fast for me even to recognise what I was feeling. My heart sank even further than I thought possible, considering that I thought there was no more room left for pain. Yet my pain was of insignificance in comparison to the intense and despairing pain that my sister and nephews would be experiencing.

Hence my thoughts began to focus upon what pain they were experiencing and how would they be able to deal with this. It felt as though we were going to have to go back to square one to look at what we had learned about Gurjit's death.

As I gathered my thoughts I told Bal that I would be on my way back home. Forgetting my toothache, I left the dentist. It felt as though not only did my mind begin to feel numb, my entire body did, for the toothache began to disappear.

The thought that began to reign in me was 'How can we ever take refuge and receive relief from the distress that is appearing to descend upon us?' As I searched all I heard was the heart's silence. Again there was no safety. Rather there would be more sorrow, as I knew our voices would echo more agony from which we would need healing. The experience of being worn out from weeping was about to return, and it felt like a flaming arrow piercing the heart's shield.

On the way home I began to think in further detail about how my sister and nephews must be feeling and thinking. This I knew would have been more shocking, knowing that they, along with the majority of my family, would be going to India the next day to undertake a memorial service for Gurjit as part of cultural traditions. How on earth were they going to be able to go and engage in such an important custom while having knowing that Parmjit too has died?

Beyond comprehension would not even begin to explain the heavy burden that had arisen. The feeling of having no peace was terrible. I felt like a piece of wood in the sea being tossed back and forth by the wind.

In thinking about Parmjit as my brother, the tears came to the surface and my throat became dry. The thoughts at first were somehow blocked as though a hedge had grown to obscure my view of what was going to take place. Then tears began to slowly drop as I was driving. 'What's happened to him?' I thought. 'Why haven't I thought about him more? Has he really died? Where is he now?'

Yet the prevailing thought centred on what we needed to do now to support Dee and the lads to deal with this news, which in itself didn't appear too clear. How were they going to be able to respond to this? What could we use to face a reality that appeared to promise only more pain? Had we responded to the pain of Gurjit's death, and could we learn from this, even though death doesn't appear to be something that one would really like to learn from? Could death teach anything, and if so what? Such thoughts ran riot in my mind.

They came to a standstill when I arrived at my sister's house. It became evident that the sheer shock had already started to devour her. Dee looked bewildered as she opened the door. Her entire world had been shaken and her body slumped with the burden of death. She could hardly stand. I felt that if a feather had been placed on her shoulders she would have crumbled. Her face was contorting, every muscle seeking to contain the emotional impact that had been delivered to her by the police.

I gave her a gentle hug, but neither of us was able to utter a word. The feeling of powerlessness was certainly present. With the information she was about to share with me, it was ever more apparent why she looked so distressed.

As I tried to maintain eye contact, I wondered how I could possibly even begin to ask how she was. Her eyes were distant; fear had captivated her. I wished she did not have to face this and I felt we needed another fortress to protect her and ourselves from further hurt.

Turning my attention to Bal and Ami, their appearances were gloomy as they stood in the lounge. They, like me, were putting on a brave face to hide the pain. Their eyes were in a state of alarm and their body posture was like that when one is preparing to engage in a battle - a battle between the thoughts and the emotions.

I knew they experienced ambivalence in their relationship with their father and I felt that this was going to create apprehension in what they were feeling; this was going to be another troubling experience for them. When I continued to look at them I saw what appeared to be anger rising in them as their bodies were tensing up, fists clenched, as though they were waiting to erupt with an intense rush of outrage - outrage that I was going to hear.

The feeling of hopelessness stared me in the face again and laid down a gauntlet which I knew we would all have to confront and challenge. There would be no hiding place, rather a lot of wrestling with thoughts, because once again the ground we were standing on felt slippery.

We sat down and I asked Dee to tell me what the police had told her. This I knew was a difficult task for her to undertake, knowing that the information pointed towards the loss of her soulmate.

Dee gathered her breath, and with her voice echoing both her love and her innermost agony, she bravely said: 'I rang the police to ask them if they had any information about Parmjit because we would be going to India tomorrow. As I asked this, Detective Constable Price sounded as though I had caught him off guard as he went totally silent. I thought the phone line had been cut off as it seemed a while before he spoke. When he did speak, he told me that they had some information that may suggest that Parmjit is deceased, but they needed to clarify this with me and wanted to take a further statement from me. He wanted to come out to see me today, which he did.'

Seeing her inner longing being hampered by overwhelming dread was inconsolable. An anger arose in me about how such sensitive information had been shared with her - how dare this police officer say that over the phone? I was annoyed because she deserved to be told that in person, but I had to put such anger to one side for that moment. For as I looked at her I saw every part of her slowly breaking, her body trembling with fright and uncertainty as to how to respond - she was not alone in that. The life that was in her began to fade like a burning candle and her tears flicked off her cheeks on to her laps.

She needed a remedy to the onslaught of information given to her by the police. I felt that she had already begun to enter a place of soul-searching and that the intense pain was causing much unrest. I wondered how it could be stopped, but inwardly I knew it could not be - it was going to be felt by us all again.

The next piece of information she shared with me completely shook me. I could only imagine this would have shaken her entire world, for the profound impact that this had upon her and the lads was devastating.

'When Detective Constable Price came out to see me he told me that they had made further enquiries into Parmjit's disappearance' she said. 'It appears that he died in December 2001. He was found drowned in a local canal.'

Her lips were quivering and tears were streaming towards her mouth like an unstoppable river. It brought flashbacks of Dilly when Gurjit had died, and now Dee was caged in with nowhere to flee.

Her words sent a spine-chilling, icy feeling into my mind. I felt she was being left to hold on to very little, because nothing seemed rational. I began to realise why they all looked so desolate with the knowledge that Parmjit might have already died before Gurjit, and none of us had known about it. It was a hammer blow to them, threatening to crush their spirits. I could understand why the lads looked so angry.

The few seconds that had elapsed seemed like an eternity. I just looked at her and the lads and felt such emotion for them having to contend with such dread. Coupled with this came a surge of anger. I would need one heck of an explanation from the police for what they had told her.

It felt as if someone had pushed me into a deep pit. Everything seemed clouded and the realisation that the longing for clarity was going to intensify did not make it easier, because hope was being snatched from me. Yet the pain of considering what their thoughts were made the inner cry louder.

I thought what else could possibly be needed to attend to such trauma when part of me felt that all strength was being dried up. Silently I questioned how we could even consider thinking about getting over this experience when we were already trying to re-build from the separation we had already endured.

My mind was trying to make sense of the information. Again the anger re-surfaced and inwardly I was questioning what on earth the police had been doing. How dare they, I thought, say what they had to my sister and nephews without providing a reasonable explanation of what took place?

'What do they mean? What are they talking about?' I asked. 'How do they know it's Parmjit?'

'He told me the body had a tattoo on the right hand, similar to Parmjit's.'

'Is that all?' was the thought that flashed by me. Surely they'd had more than that.

'He couldn't tell me anything else, besides the fact that they believe it's Parmjit.'

I was horrified to think that the police thought by sharing such limited information that we'd accept that Parmjit had died. I felt annoyed as I thought about how Dee and the lads were in such anxiety and that it had been caused without clear information. There was no certainty, and I felt for them having to hear what they had been told without having the proper information to begin to prepare their hearts and minds for the possibility that Parmjit had in fact died. It felt as though we were just trapped.

'What did the detective say about how they were planning to give more information to confirm whether it is Parmjit or not?' I asked.

'He told me that he'd come back out when we've returned from India in the New Year and that he should have more information then. He also wanted me to give a statement about when Parmjit left the home in 2001' she replied.

Chapter One

Her eyes looked so burdened with the thought of whether Parmjit had actually died. She went on 'He also told me that they were waiting for some photo evidence from an expert and they they'll refer this to the Coroner's Office to open an Inquest. They can't say it's Parmjit until the coroner confirms it's him at the inquest.'

Again I wondered how the police could make such a statement without being definite in their conclusion. I felt it was unacceptable because of the uncertainty. The tremendous intensity of apprehension they would have to endure was enough to break anyone's resolve.

We were all struggling to process the information. On the one hand the police were indicating they had evidence only to 'suggest' that Parmjit may have died in December 2001, and on the other hand they were stating that they could not confirm this as only the Coroner's inquest could do so once they had all their evidence. This evidence had not even been fully disclosed to my sister and nephews.

For Dee, Bal and Ami to be left in total limbo like this was a horrible position to be in. At a crossroads you have a choice of which direction to go, but for them it was another desolate experience with the burden of inconclusiveness.

The thought of them having to contend with such uncertainty was unfair and seemed very cruel. It was very hard to see them in such distress, though the lads were trying ever so hard not to show it. This was another torment for their minds to deal with.

As we sat perplexed by the information the police had given us, and battling with the family's trip to India the next day, we were considering what, if any, information could possibly be shared with Parmjit's family when we could not be sure Parmjit had really died.

We felt a mixture of emotions, mainly uncertainty and anger, along with feeling shut down by the numbness of having to wait for confirmation of death. It was a terrible place to be in. We spoke together about how we felt knowing that Parmjit might have already died two years ago and as a family we were not aware of this. Dee, tears streaming on to her hands, said 'This is my worst fear coming true as I thought he had already gone. I felt this more when we could not find him after Gurjit had died.'

Sitting in disarray and knowing the high probability that her husband's death had taken place two years ago was an immense ordeal. Her body seemed to shrink even more as she disappeared under the cloud of tears and anguish that had engulfed her. There was no canopy to cover her and I imagined the loneliness she was feeling would have been excruciating.

Life appeared barren and we felt as though we were living in a land of oblivion as this dark despair was attempting to dwell in our hearts again. Yet I felt that a little hope was still holding us from underneath to withstand another profound and terrifying reality. The hope was that we had already begun a painful yet supportive journey towards facing Gurjit's death, but it was certainly going to be a challenge.

Dee's body was shivering with the horror of the knowledge of death. Bal, his face contorted with longing for peace, said: 'I don't know really what to think besides the fact that it hurts knowing that all the information given by the police suggests that my dad died two years ago. It hurts even more because Chacha is also no longer here.'

His eyes ready to open the floodgates, he breathed hard to control the torrent of emotions that were waiting to sweep him off his feet. It was agonising to know that there was very little control that could be brought to this situation.

Their words reflected the need for healing, because the void was threatening to become even bigger. Yet I knew that our love would not relent, rather we would be willing to reach out to touch each other, through the hardship being endured; hardship which was evident in Ami's eyes as he sat shaking his head.

His eyes were red, and I imagined they had been dried out by pain.

Softly he said 'I feel sorry that Chacha never knew that most likely his own brother had already died, this is too difficult to understand.'

As he sat, I felt the numbness that surrounded him. He looked like a submarine going under water, not wanting to be seen. After pausing he said 'I'm going out tonight with my friends, I've got to go, I've got to get my mind off this, I can't really think about this now, it makes no sense, I need to go out.'

Bal replied 'Ami, it's OK to go, but we're going to have to think about this at some time. I know it's very hard for us all to even understand Chacha's death, and to think about Dad when we don't know what has really happened is just as hard.'

Listening to such hurt and disbelief was so devouring. I understood how difficult it was to even try to make sense of the significance of the information that had been shared with us. I also understood how difficult it was to know that we could not respond until the Coroner's inquest had taken place.

The devastation was insurmountable and there was no way we were going to be able to avoid contending with the emergence of new emotions. This was going to cause unrest as the reality of another family member's death was beginning to burn into our minds.

The only way, and not the ideal way to even begin to try to look at this, was to do the opposite for a while, which was to put it to the back of our minds until my family returned from India. For there were too many questions to be asked, and so little we could do at the moment. My mind was grappling with the impending tragedy that would touch us all. We were entering the unknown of more pain.

When I looked at them there was so much shame, not that they had done anything wrong. I believed their compassion would provide the anchor as they would begin to look deep within themselves and see the remedy that was present in the midst of the suffering they were facing. It was going to be head on, and no more so than when speaking to Dee and Bal about how they felt about going to India along with the whole family, knowing the probability that Parmjit had already died. Bal immediately said 'It's still important to go because it's about a memorial for Chacha and to see the family.' He paused, expressing for the first time some anger about the information given by the police. 'The police need to confirm that the body that they recovered two years ago is Dad's rather than telling us that it might be, it's not good enough.'

Dee remained quiet, as I imagined she was still registering the impact of what was unfolding. How could she seek to defend against a barrage of fear? Bal's face expressed the desire to run away from any current knowledge pointing to his father's death. This was not a surprise, because it was such an ordeal.

In apprehension, Dee understandably was emotional and began to express her despair. 'I'm struggling to understand this and accept that he might already have died.' Her tears interrupted her speech as she was trying to gather strength. 'I believe it's still right to go to India as I want to support Dilly and the girls. But there is also a part of me that does not want to go because I'm afraid that I won't know what to say if anyone asks me about Parmjit.'

When looking into her eyes I saw her inner battle. It was as though she was trying to run with her feet tied. I knew her mind would have been tormenting her, even though she had done all she could to help Parmjit - she had cared for him. Yet with the way guilt surfaced I knew she was being plagued with memories of her relationship with him.

At that point we spoke in detail about Parmjit, the positive features as well as the limiting factors of his life and how we all felt about this. It was acknowledged that this would require a lot more exploration. We had already begun to explore the impact of Gurjit's relationship and death upon us all, and we recognised that looking at Parmjit's life in the same way was necessary to enable us to gain some understanding of what had taken place. The realisation that tears were to be shed for the fullness of our words would need to be withheld until confirmation of death was so demanding and difficult to tolerate, yet we needed to withstand the inner conflict this created.

With all this information, Bal said 'In spite of the difficult circumstances we are in, we have to get on with life, but we know we can't ignore what has happened in our life and in our family. We can't let the circumstances dictate to us. We're slowly coming to terms with Chacha's death, and to think that Dad has died is not something we want to have to also cope with at the moment, until we know.'

Thinking about their words revealed to me the torment of their uncertainty of having to wait for answers. Yet I knew that their innermost love could not be taken away or removed.

At this stage I reflected upon the few minutes of information that the police had shared with Dee and the lads, which surely had given rise to an anxious state. This hurt would take time to rehabilitate, yet awareness of each other's presence was the most important involvement that we could have.

With all this in mind, we began to talk about what if anything we could tell Parmjit's extended family in India. The main question was, what exactly could we tell them when we ourselves didn't know or have the full information?

As we explored this, Dee and Bal decided that it was not appropriate to disclose any information to Parmjit's family in India until the police and coroner's office were able to confirm the identity of the body. Bal summed up their thoughts saying, 'What if the police have got it wrong and the coroner does not agree with them? We can't tell the family until this has been sorted out.'

As they began to offer each other comfort, I phoned Jai and told him what the police had told Dee. The shock of the information was tangible over the phone as Jai said 'You what? When did the police now this? How did he die?'

'At the moment we are not sure because the police did not tell Dee,' I replied.

Jai's silence then made me think how he was feeling, knowing the high probability that another brother had died. Jai then said 'I'm coming up. Tell them I'm coming to see them.'

Pausing after the call ended I prepared my mind for calling Dilly. The ringing tone was only brief, and then I repeated what was becoming a familiar but unwelcome story. Her response was 'How's this happened?' What I had said was certainly going to take some time to register, so I told her what I knew. Dilly interrupted. 'How is Dee going to be able to go to India tomorrow?' she said. She began to cry, and asked how Dee and the lads were.

I could still hear the tone of Jai's and Dilly's voice in my ears when the calls ended. It was as though they had been cut with a razor. Their few words summed up what we were feeling, shattered all over again. From this I wondered how we could possibly protect each other from what was unfolding before us. With this battle raging, the struggle was also to mend the pain that was beginning to tear at us again.

Walking slowly back to Dee and the lads, Bal and Ami were talking about how even though they loved and respected their father as a person, they did not accept his behaviour due to alcohol. 'We know he cared for us and loved us but he struggled to tell us' said Bal.

For Ami, though he believed his father did care for him and love him, he was angry that his father had left the family home. 'This will not stop me from getting on with life because I know as time goes by I will have to look at the love I had for him and the anger of him leaving, but I don't feel it is the right time' he said. 'I'm just learning to adapt to Chacha's death.'

Their words were a truthful reflection of their relationship with their father and echoed their love for him and annoyance about his behaviour. Their eyes contained a combination of dread and empathy as well as anger. They knew how complex this pain was, for they were trying their best to focus on a year's journey of exploring the impact of death and now they were going to face another tragedy.

Dee looked drained of all energy. Every fibre of her being was being attacked with an incomprehensible despair, which had quickly surfaced to challenge any refuge she was seeking. It was so awful seeing her like that, and it was multiplied as we weren't able to offer her any real comfort. The intensity of her pain was making me squeal inside, knowing that death was again seeking to conquer our minds.

Glancing at his mother, Bal said 'Mom, I know this is hard, and it is very hard to wait until we come back from India to find out, but we have to be strong for each other, even though it is hurting us.'

Dee's tears poured as she broke down, even though she was already broken. Shaking her head she said 'I know he's gone, I can feel it in my heart,' and she held her chest. 'I knew when he left that I wouldn't really see him again. I shouldn't have thought that, but I did.'

Ami interjected 'Mom, you've not done anything wrong and you're not responsible for Dad. He left because he made the decision to leave. He could have stayed but he didn't.'

Dee held her head up high when he said that, and replied 'I know, but I can't help thinking about the times I prayed that God would help your dad and I thought the best thing that God could have done was to take him away. Now I can't believe that this happened without any of us knowing. It's hard to understand anything.'

They responded simultaneously 'We know it is hard to cope with this but we have to wait. If the police have got it wrong, where would it leave us?'

I didn't feel the lads were trying to dismiss the possibility of their father's death; rather they appeared to have adopted a strategy to allow their minds to prepare for the eventuality. In contrast I felt that Dee was already at a stage of knowing deep down that there would be no relief from the news that Parmjit had died.

I said 'This is very difficult to even begin to think about and I feel so sorry for you being left with this uncertainty. We have to remember we will all have different thoughts about this, because I know your hurt took place a long time ago, before this news.'

Bal said to his Mom 'I'm sorry. I don't want you to think we don't care, because we do. I'm sorry if you feel we don't understand what you are feeling. As Mama said, we are all going to have to face this one way or the other. We do care for Dad, but I can't really think too much about him because I'm trying to stay strong for the visit to India. But I'll never forget Dad.'

These feelings and thoughts were a tidal wave pounding against the shore, unstoppable and seeking to erode our foundations. It was impacting upon everything we had learned in relation to death and the piercing consequences it imposed upon our lives. Dee's words made it even clearer how painful it was as she said 'I just don't know how I will cope with all of this.'

Her words captured a truth of the ruin that death creates. Thus I admired her honesty and the significance of this for us all. It felt as though we were all being pulled in every conceivable direction, knowing it was an impossible task to fully comprehend and respond to all that was taking place.

Silence fell upon us, soon interrupted as the door bell rang. I knew it was Dilly and as I opened the door she moved past me, grabbed hold of Dee and began to sob, saying 'I'm so sorry, I'm so sorry.'

Dilly was still bearing the marks of grief over Gurjit's death, and her face remained contorted with pangs of pain, knowing they had felt this for her when Gurjit died. Her tears when she embraced Dee appeared to gush over her, trying to wash away her suffering and provide a healing touch - a touch we all needed. She looked at Bal and Ami and with her tears streaming down her face like rain said 'I'm so sorry, I'm so sorry.'

Chapter One

She then flung her arms wide open and they came to her. Her muffled cries were creeping through as they embraced. The lads upheld her as her legs began to buckle under the weight of what this meant - another death in the family - the death of her husband's brother. 'I can't believe he's also gone - what would have Gurjit had thought?' she said. Shaking her head, she went back to Dee and embraced her, saying 'I'm here for you in the way you were there for me.' Dee tearfully replied 'I know, but it's so hard to understand why this is happening, it's just so hard to believe.'

Dilly was supported by the lads to sit down, but before she did we embraced and the level of despair she expressed when Gurjit died had resurfaced. She held me tightly, crying aloud 'This can't be happening to us all over again!'

After managing to sit down, the doorbell rang again and I guessed it would be Jai. As I went to the door I heard the lads say to their aunt 'we just don't believe it yet, it's not sinking in, and it won't until they can fully prove that it is Dad.' Those words revealed again the depths of the wound that had begun to rise within them.

Jai shook his head when he saw Dee and the lads, and looked bewildered as he slowly began to walk into the room. Physically shaking he asked 'what did the police say?' There was no doubt that he was trying, just as we all were, to digest the enormity of the information we had received. He needed to hear it again to contemplate the profound significance.

Bal responded to him with more detail of what had taken place when Detective Constable Price had visited. Dee at this stage was so overwhelmed by the severity of pain she was unable to speak. Yet her tears could be heard as they fell. She looked as though she was in deep reflection about Parmjit as she leaned on to Dilly's shoulders, finding comfort from someone who knew what it meant to have her heart so deeply wounded by death.

Once Bal had finished, Jai sought to mobilise hope, saying 'So they don't know then whether it is Parmjit'

'Everything so far suggests it's him' said Dee. 'They just can't confirm anything until we come back from India and the coroner agrees with them' said Bal.

Jai sat down, placed his hand on his chin and bowed his head. Every time he looked up at Dee and the lads I saw the tears build up in his eyes. It reminded me of how I had felt when battling with the thought of knowing Gurjit was dying and refusing to acknowledge that it was taking place.

'Jai,' I said 'Everything so far points towards it being Parmjit, the difficulty is that we don't have any clarity about what actions the police took because it is very confusing as to what caused the delays in identifying him. At the moment the police haven't told Dee this, but we'll find out soon. This is very difficult because as Bal said we can't do anything until the coroner confirms it is Parmjit.'

Looking at Jai, I saw that this was causing immense frustration because strength appeared to disappear like a rug being pulled from under his feet. It was another shock to the system, for death had dealt a body blow and we could only block this for a short time.

This was a tug-of-war between the questions that would need to be asked and the response that could be provided. Either way we were vulnerable, carrying emotions from which we could not flee as the sorrow began to tie itself around our hearts. The weight of holding on to this was what we had to contend with.

Again silence fell upon us as somehow I believed we had all begun to briefly reflect upon the entire year we had endured and how our current reality was indicating that more pain was unfolding in our midst. It was going to be another ordeal. It was 'déja vu'.

Having to contend with the partial information given by the police was I felt a major hurdle to cross, for fear was trying to paralyse my mind, coupled with anger as to how after two years death was the conclusion that was being drawn.

Such emotions were like a tornado. Within me thoughts of deep regret arose, questioning what could have been done differently to have located Parmjit earlier. Feelings for him became central, but it was unbearable to hold on to this. The frozen silence was lifted when Jai asked Dee and Bal 'How do you feel about going to India tomorrow?'

Dee softly replied 'We're still going because it's about Gurjit's memorial and we can't do anything here besides wait. I'd rather go and support Dilly and the girls, but I know it's going to be hard to keep this out of my mind.'

Upon hearing this Dilly's tears overflowed. I imagined she was broken by Dee's empathy in such turbulent times.

'Are you sure?' Dilly asked her. Dee replied 'yes.'

'Massi, we have to go for Chacha and as much as this is going to hurt we're not going to let you and the girls be on your own. I want to go,' said Bal. Dilly cried as Bal embraced her.

We all agreed not to inform our parents, as we felt that such uncertain news would place them under undue strain. All that could be said was said and Ami reminded us that he was going to go out with his friends as he had pre-arranged this. His interjection enabled us to bring the evening's profound discussion to an end, and we all embraced, expressing our love. Dilly stayed with Dee and the lads, while Jai and I left and went to our parents' home. In doing so, Jai said to me 'first Gurjit, then his mom and now Parmjit. How's their dad going to cope with all of this? How are Dad and Mom going to cope with this?'

'It hurts' I said. 'And it's going to get a lot deeper for all of us.'

As my mother had already gone to India a few weeks earlier, it was half the weight of having to see just our father. It was awful to withhold such pending tragic information from him, but we had no choice. He was still in grief for the loss of his son Gurjit and we didn't want to compound this. Jai and I spoke to him about the memorial service for

Gurjit. He knew more about its cultural significance than us and he began telling us about how he had done this for his father, our grandfather.

After such discussions, the evening fell fast as Jai left. The initial physical discomfort I felt from the toothache reappeared. It was insignificant when thinking about what Dee and the lads were wrestling with.

A part of me was still very annoyed with the way the police had shared the information with Dee. I felt it was not sensitively managed because of the lack of information that had been given to Dee, and I certainly wanted to discuss such conduct with the police. With such thoughts, I felt my eyelids becoming heavier and I nodded off. I was woken in the early hours by a sudden shuddering that went through my body.

Everything was dark and I realised I had fallen asleep on the sofa downstairs. My mind was still in overdrive, and thoughts about Dee and the lads were the first to spring up. 'How cruel this is! How are they going to face this? What can we do? How are they going to manage this?'

The tiredness crept up very quickly because my heart was so despondent with the heaviness of the emerging reality. Emotionally exhausted, I fell asleep again.

CHAPTER 2

A VISIT TO INDIA

FRIDAY 12TH DECEMBER 2003

When morning broke, it was raining and cold with dark clouds. It looked a bleak day. It was certainly going to be uncomfortable knowing only Ami and I would be staying behind as my father, Dee, Bal, Dilly, Baljinder, Suki, Jai, Mangender and Sonia would be flying out to India within a few hours.

My mind appeared hyper-alert, for I was trying to challenge the emotions that were threatening to cause fear and anxiety to reign in my heart. I began to wonder what I would do if something else happened while they were in India. This, along with additional 'what ifs', were circling my mind, producing additional pain as I remembered Gurjit's death. The tormenting reality of losing two close family members was threatening to take hold of me. Yet I knew deep, deep down that we would all slowly respond to the enormity of what remained ahead of us.

The journey to India was discussed with Dee and Bal again, to which Dee said tearfully 'I've got to try not to think about this. I know in my heart he's gone but I wish it wasn't true. It hurts me because I can't really think about it at this time.'

Embracing her I replied, 'Dee, we know how difficult this is. There isn't a good time to be told anything like this. Are you sure that you want to go? Dilly would definitely understand if you don't want to.'

Shaking her head with tears falling and her hands raised to catch them, she said 'I want to go and be with Dilly and the girls. They need all the support from us. I can't let them down. I have to be with them.'

She rested her head on my chest and Bal said 'Mom, we'll support each other and we'll think about this when we get back, because we still don't know whether it is Dad or not. I have to think about Massi and the girls now and face this later. We're going because of Chacha.'

His words portrayed the reality of what we would all be facing, because we were all touched by death and none of us were immune from its grip - a grip that was now seeking to trap us in a cage of desolation.

'That's all we can do at the moment,' I interjected as Jai walked in with Sonia. Bal went to Sonia and took her into another room, not wanting her to see his mother's distress. Seeing Dee in that state Jai said 'Dee are you really sure you want to go? Because if you don't that's fine.'

'I know it's going to be hard, but I have to be there. It's going to be hard because I can't tell his family,' replied Dee.

Jai said 'OK, we'll pull through this together,' and hugged her.

Leaving them, Ami and I began to load up the cars with the luggage, aided by my dear friend Dal, whom I welcomed as though he was my brother, while heavy rain poured down. Slowly everyone began to get into the cars, yet my father's face was swollen with pain as his eyes continued to reveal the inner longing for relief from sadness. Gently Ami and Dal assisted him to get into Dal's car, yet his tears had started to fall as he joined his hands in prayer.

Silently we then set off for the airport. Knowing it would take a while to get there Dee and I briefly spoke as Sonia was also in my car, along with Jai and Mangender.

'Dee,' I said 'we know this is very hard, you need to remember that you did everything in your power to help Parmjit. I know you're going to think you could have done something else to help him, but you did more than enough. We all miss him just as we miss Gurjit, and we know your heart has been wounded. Going to India is a brave thing to do under these circumstances and I need you to know that we're all going to be here for you and the lads.'

She somehow kept composed as she gently replied 'I know there's a lot to think about, thank you for your support.'

'It's true that there's a lot to think about and we'll be with you all the way,' Jai said to her as her tears slowly trickled down her face.

It was now a time for silence, as I imagined she needed to reflect privately on the emotional battle she was coming to terms with. A continual battle it was going to be for Bal and Ami, and for all of us in varying degrees. Yet the ability to even begin to somehow negotiate with the reality that was emerging was going to be immense and overwhelming.

However hope still existed, knowing we were already exploring the vulnerability we had experienced and that again we would need to support each other in such a traumatic time, for hope would still connect us in our relationships. This thought kept going round in my head, until I realised we were only minutes away from the airport. The dark clouds continued to pour down a heavy and miserable rain.

Trying to avoid getting totally soaked upon arriving, we hurriedly got the luggage together. Fortunately the queues and waiting times for my family were short and we quickly made our way to the departure lounge.

Time began to fly by and I spent the precious moments with my gorgeous little niece Sonia. I was struggling with the notion of not being able to see my family for three weeks. I sought to continue to embrace the comfort of knowing they would all return then.

That was all that I could consider, it was like trying to hold on to a thread dangling from a garment. But I was not going to let go of it because it gave me strength at a time when distress was seeking to rule my heart. This I felt was the way fear continually attempted to grip me and make me become anxious.

I held Sonia's little hand, we walked around the lobby area. Those few moments were amazing as her little presence was so calming and reassuring, and this provided me with the peace I needed at that time to respond to everyone going to India. Her little eyes were observing everything, as she soon would be travelling on an airplane for the first time at the tender age of two.

When I walked back to everyone I knew it was only a matter of minutes before they would be entering the departure lounge. Looking at each of them I had a mixture of thoughts, ranging from being proud that they were there for each other and had shown how they were enduring the tragedy together, to being concerned about the emotional impact caused by death, which was so vast and nowhere near fully explored.

Though these concerns would linger for a while, I focused on my relationship with my family, in particular the love and support we had all shown to each other. This I knew would continue.

As departure time drew near we all began to embrace. I approached Dilly and the girls and hugged them, as they were crying. The thought that this was the first time Gurjit would not be going with them was earth-shattering.

I said to them 'remember you know deep down how much he loved you and he knew the same about your love.' Dilly replied 'I know, but it still hurts so much to know that he's not here.' Our embracing continued in silence and looking up I saw Ami comforting his mom as her head was resting on his chest.

I felt so sorry for Dee having to go with such a heavy burden of knowing that nothing could be done about Parmjit. Her body looked exhausted as her energy drained out of her. As I hugged her she said 'Why has this happened? Why?' I responded 'I don't think we'll ever know. What I do believe is that we're going to get through this together.'

Time began to run out and I briefly spoke with Jai, for he knew the enormity of what the trip meant and I didn't need to discuss that with him. Instead all I could say was 'keep safe and we'll see you all in three weeks,' as we embraced and I gave Sonia a little kiss.

They all began to walk into the departure area, turning around at every opportunity. All Ami and I could do was smile and wave at them. Yet strangely even though they were getting further away I felt their eyes were still piercing my heart.

Ami and I waited for the plane to leave before we left the airport; I suppose it was an instinct that we did not really want to leave them. We talked about how we felt, a mixture of being tense as there was a void within us due to this difficult time, while we were also feeling an element of peace, knowing that they were all together and that the support they would provide each other would be great.

The journey home was quiet, not because we wanted it to be. Rather I had forgotten my driving glasses and didn't realise this until leaving the airport, so I felt I needed to concentrate due to the heavy downpour. When we arrived home it brought back memories of returning after Gurjit's funeral, in that everything was quiet. Then Ami spoke in depth about everything relating to his uncle Gurjit and father Parmjit and how this would never go away. He said 'my heart is hurting and it is difficult to feel this and hold it at the same time, because it's a struggle and I feel that I'm closing down and that hurts even more because I really want to help everyone else.'

'You've been a great help to everyone,' I responded. 'The pain you feel is what we all feel as a family.'

He began to cry, uttering words when he could. 'It's so hard to understand....it's so hard to understand what's happened. I keep trying to think, could this have been different?' His tears rolled down his face. 'But it's not going to be and that's what really hurts.'

I said 'You're right, that is the real pain that we are living with and it will never really go away. All we can do is to support each other and talk openly about the effects it has had upon us.'

Ami replied 'I want to make sure my mom, Bal, Massi, Dilly and the girls are supported, I want to be there for them.' His tears continued to fall rapidly on to his lap, his head bowed.

'Ami we are not alone in this and as we give support we are also going to need support' I said.

We spoke about how we were all feeling the effects of death and would do so in different ways. I told him his thoughts were an expression of such pain. In detail we spoke about what we had learned after Gurjit's death and how this could support us all in looking at his father's death, even though we had to wait for final confirmation of this.

'Ami, this shouldn't stop us from talking about your dad and your relationship with him and us all' I said. 'It's going to hurt when we think about it because deep down I know he loved us, and yet the difficulties he had with alcohol were too much for him and this stopped him from being a bigger part of your life. It's such a shame that it's ended this way when you think about the times when your dad was able to make changes to his life and how that was positive. I understand that this is going to be a struggle and we'll continue to support each other.'

His face was withering away, his eyes dwindling, his lips trembling as he tried to keep his hands still. His heartbeat could be heard pounding, somehow seeking a deeper refuge from the profound sadness that had befallen upon us.

Slowly he replied 'I know, but it really still hurts thinking about Chacha and to think about this as well is too much. I don't want to think about it until I have to.' He paused and bowed his head. 'I just hope Mom and Bal are OK, I can't wait for them to all come back.'

'What you've said about how difficult this is so true. We know it will take some time to sink in,' I replied. We remained quiet, imagining what we'd ultimately have to face. At such a reflective moment, the tragedy caused by death was uncomfortable and I continued to wrestle with the despair it had wrought.

As I focused briefly on this I began to dwell upon what resolutions we had sought and how this had supported us in making any recovery. Then it dawned on me that the key was not in recovery (because how could we recover from death when we couldn't control death?), nor was it about resolution (because how could we seek to rationalise the experience that has forever changed our relationships?). Rather the issue for me was knowing that we would be living with the pain and this would need to be questioned and explored in order to begin to release the deluge of emotions that had been captured, so that hope could surface. This I believed would take place through love, compassion and empathy, which would be the fortress that comfort would bring. The comfort was the knowledge that as a family we could continue to explore our experiences together, even though we were at different stages in looking at the impact death had had upon our relationships.

As I was thinking this, Ami said 'I can't wait for them to phone and I really can't wait for them to get back. I already miss them so much.'

I expressed the same sentiments, and we then continued with the day, hoping that time would speed up, even though this was going to be the first Christmas and New Year that we would spend a part as a family.

For me, I focused on getting some sleep, only to wake up within a few hours to the silent house. I was alone. It felt very weird when I gently got up. Evening had fallen and I knew nothing could be done as I waited in anticipation for Jai's call to say they had arrived in India.

Then Ami decided to come back over, as he didn't want to stay at his own house. So we spent the remainder of the evening just talking and watching TV until tiredness took its toil upon us and we called it a night.

My eyes remained heavy because my heart was heavy. However throughout the night my sleep was disrupted. It was as though my mind was not permitting my body to rest. I felt another experience of loss revealed more vulnerability which would have to be gradually unmasked over time.

I knew I was once again in a battle between my thoughts and

emotions. The pain was death, having to live with the impact of death and then realising there was more pain in knowing someone else's pain and not being able to respond. This was pain at its height.

Then I was startled by a phone call at about 6 am. Rushing to the phone I picked it up and paused. 'It's me' said Jai. 'We've arrived safely and under the circumstances are doing OK.' I asked 'How's everyone?' to which he replied 'we're as OK as we can be.'

Ami came to the phone moments after and spoke with Jai, saying 'Mama, we're already missing you all, can't wait for you all to get back. Tell everyone I love them and am thinking about them. Tell them I love them all.'

A little more peace arose in my heart as I thought that at least it was one day less to wait than it had been yesterday. Ami also looked more peaceful and less fearful, and he was smiling throughout the conversation.

Just hearing Jai's voice at that time, was a joy as it provided uplift for my heart, mind and soul. In ending the phone call, I said to Jai 'As always we are thinking about you all, you are all close in our hearts and we will see you all very soon,' to which he replied 'likewise,' and we said goodbye.

After the call I felt able to get some sleep, for the heaviness which was present slowly melted away like an icicle.

The next ten days or so picked up quickly in many ways, as Ami and I just got on with daily work. We kept ringing to see how everyone was in India, but at times we experienced technical difficulties in getting through. It was frustrating because on occasions the phone calls cut off during conversation.

Strangely, one call that did not present any technical difficulties was the call we made on the day of the memorial service, even though the call in itself was going to be emotional. Jai answered the phone and I quickly said 'Jai, how are you and everyone else?' How did the service go?' After a pause he replied 'it was very hard because it's still really sinking in that Gurjit is not here.' He went on to tell me how everyone was doing. 'Dilly and the girls' pain was very difficult to see, but we all offered support to them. But other things have happened which I'll tell you about later.'

In his voice was a deep sadness and a further grief as my mind pondered upon his words, trying to understand what he meant and questioning whether something else had happened to a family member. Unable to leave such thoughts in my mind I replied 'Jai, what's happened?' 'I can't go into detail, everyone's safe', he said. My mind was racing, trying to control the apprehension that was slowly creeping in of the unknown.

This time I remained quiet and after a lengthy pause, he explained 'it's just that Gurjit's extended family have been very insensitive towards Dilly.' The moment that registered with me, I inwardly shouted 'how dare they?'

'What do you mean?' I asked.

'They've tried to make Dilly think that someone caused Gurjit to die and that she has to find out who that was, and they've tried to frighten her with religious talk. I've told Dilly that it's just their way of trying to cope, and what they've said must be ignored, because we know that no one caused this. I've reminded her that she did everything she could have done because she then started to think again that it was her fault. But we've spent so much time with her to stop this from affecting her and I've also spoken to Gurjit's extended family members about how, even though they are in pain, they have no right to make Dilly feel guilty or frightened.'

Part of me was at peace, after listening to Jai knowing he and everyone else was supporting Dilly and the girls. But another part of me now contained a mixture of feeling sorry for Gurjit's extended family, whom I felt were struggling to face the reality of his death, and feeling very annoyed that they had caused Dilly so much distress.

I said 'You're absolutely right, Dilly needs to ignore their nonsense and we'll discuss this when you all return.'

There were a few seconds of silence and I thought the phone had been cut off until I heard Jai say 'in truth, Dilly has been very hurt by many things they've said because they've tried to create arguments.'

Now I was thinking 'what on earth are they playing at? Even though I had no doubts that they were in emotional turmoil, they had no right to cause anyone to feel distress by their behaviour. This was unacceptable.

Jai went on 'So what we've done is make sure that none of them even attempt to start any conversation like that. Don't worry, we're going to get through this. Dad and I have spoken to Gurjit's father and family and told them that this is not what Gurjit would have wanted and they had to remember that. Since then they've not spoken about this, so don't worry about it.'

His words provided hope that Dilly and the girls would not be adversely affected, and I also hoped Gurjit's family would be able to look beyond their own pain. I asked Jai 'Is Dilly nearby? If she is I would like to speak to her.' He replied 'I'll go and get her,' but before he did I said to him 'Jai, I'm so glad to know you are there with them.' He replied 'I'm glad as well.'

I could hear Dilly crying as she approached the phone. When she picked it up I said 'Dilly, Jai has told me what has been happening,' to which she cried even louder. 'Dilly, as Jai has said to you, you provided Gurjit with all your love and support and no-one is going to take that away from you' I said. 'Hold that truth and when you all return we will talk about this.'

She replied 'they've really hurt me because I loved Gurjit so much and would have done anything to keep him alive, and they've tried to put doubts in my mind. They should have supported me and the girls, but they hurt me instead.'

Chapter Two

The annoyance again arose from within me when I heard her distress and in response I hoped my words comforted her. I said 'Dilly you know what is true no matter what other people say, and when you doubt it is not because of you, it is because they have tried to shift their pain on to you. You have never done that and you have not done anything wrong. Please remember that.'

She began to sob. 'I know' she said.

'Then you hold on to what Gurjit left within you, because that is going to support you in dealing with this' I replied. Through her tears she said 'I know Gurjit is always going to be in my heart and that's the strength I know he's left inside of me.'

I believed that she would be able to respond to this and that it was not going to undo the foundations of support that were in her life. Nor was it going to create a stronghold of fear in her mind.

Knowing that Jai was by her side I asked her to pass the phone to Jai, and said 'We all love you. We'll see you soon. You know what you are doing. Tell Dee and Bal thanks for all their support at this difficult time for them as well.' He replied 'Don't worry, we'll be home soon.' We then said our goodbyes.

After this I spoke to Ami and told him what had been taking place, to which he reacted with some passion. 'How dare they even think of talking about my Chacha and Massi like that, have they got no respect? If I was there I'd sort them out.'

His frustration was evident in his face as his eyes welled up at the thought of his aunt and cousin-sisters being subject to such an insensitive approach. I said to him 'Ami, I know you are upset by this and so am I, but they're going to be fine because they are all supporting each other and it's only going to be about a week before they all come back.'

'I can't wait for them to be here' he replied.

We then spoke about how people react differently to circumstances, in particular death. Yet it was important to know that we all need time to adapt to our experiences of the pain caused, including how people can at times be insensitive to another person's experience. I felt that this only reinforced the importance of ensuring we continued to support each other.

The rest of the day was spent completing what needed to be done, and Ami went out with his friends, as he certainly needed them.

* * * * * * * * * *

Before Christmas Day, Jai's best friends Carlo and Julie, who were also close friends of my entire family, rang and asked if Ami and I would like to spend Christmas Day with them and their family. Their kind gesture was much welcomed because they had known Gurjit well.

We spent Christmas with them and it was incredibly peaceful, and, difficult as it was, enjoyable. Ami and I managed to relax, something we had not had the time to do over the past year. Just being with them was a joy, as it reminded me that normal life could continue.

As evening fell we spoke around the warm fireplace and reflected upon our families. We actually laughed about the happy, funny and beautiful memories we had all experienced with Gurjit. Ami told us a story of the time when Gurjit was so tired after working a double shift that Bal, Baljinder, Suki and he decided to put women's make-up on him while he slept and then took a picture of him.

Ami said 'The funny part was that when Chacha got up late in the evening to get ready to go out to the pub and washed himself, he didn't remove all the make-up or nail varnish because he didn't see it.'

Carlo, Julie and I were roaring in laughter and I thought it was typical of Gurjit, who would rush to get somewhere, more so on his one night out with his friends.

Ami laughed at how when Gurjit entered the lounge everyone was giggling and he had no idea why. They didn't even stop him from leaving the house with nail varnish and lipstick still on.

Ami went on: 'Massi couldn't bear the thought of Chacha leaving the house like that because she knew his friends would have teased him for a long time, so she tried to tell him by saying to him 'have you seen your face?' and Chacha said to her 'What's wrong with it? You married me didn't you?'

Ami was laughing so hard it was like tears of joy being released. 'Massi then said to him, 'You'd better look properly in the mirror before you go out and also look at your hands'. I tell you when Chacha saw the nail varnish on his fingers he ran to the mirror and saw the lipstick. He quickly rubbed it off, but we couldn't stop laughing. It was one of the funniest times with him, because he didn't get annoyed with us, he was just moaning that he was going to be late getting to the pub. He told Massi that because of this he would come home late. Trust me, Massi stopped laughing then. It looked like Chacha got the last laugh!'

Listening to him telling that story revealed that even though the pain of death was ever present, so was the memory of Gurjit, and I felt the story was timely. After such a strange yet lovely Christmas day, Ami and I headed back home and my mind for once did not feel as though it was racing all over the place. The day reminded me that hope was still present and that we would be able to rise up and respond, because we had love and belief in our midst.

* * * * * * * * * *

The significance for Ami and me of New Year's Day was the knowledge that our family were coming home the next day. The three weeks had at times felt as though it had been a thousand years and now it was only moments until they would return.

As the day of their arrival dawned, we received a phone call in the early hours of the morning. It was Jai to say that the flight had been delayed for up to twelve hours because of dense fog and that he would contact us if anything changed.

Chapter Two

Having to wait at least another twelve hours was a mission in itself and as the waiting passed by, I periodically thought about Dilly and the girls, considering they had engaged in a very difficult and painful memorial service for Gurjit. Yet I believed it was going to be a memory that would reveal even further their great love for him, because his nature and character I believed would assist them in always remembering the significance he had in their life. Likewise I thought about Dee and Bal in the light of the emotional burden they had been carrying for three weeks about the probability that Parmjit was dead.

All we could do was to wait. When the afternoon came the phone rang and it was Jai to say that they were about to board the plane within half an hour. I was engulfed with joy, knowing we would see them within a few hours. The time couldn't come too soon, and when it did Ami and I left to go to the airport on a cold and dark evening. We spoke about how good it felt knowing that they were on their way back home.

After waiting at the airport, which was packed with so many people, Ami, being taller than I, saw everyone as they came out of the corridor. When we could get to them, we all embraced in turn. Dilly was already crying and I embraced her as her head rested on me, the girls also approaching me. We huddled together as I said 'it's so great to have you all back.'

I never really got the chance to speak to Jai, Dee and Bal, as after the delay in the flight they had felt unwell and just wanted to get home.

All we spoke about in the car was about how great it was to have them back home and how every day was difficult being apart. Then my mom said 'In my heart I know Gurjit was there with us and that's what mattered the most.'

It was an interesting statement, and I dwelled upon how she was coping. It really struck me that coping couldn't actually deal with the pain, for it was an expression of the vulnerability experienced.

She went on 'I went to the river where Gurjit's ashes had been released and pictured him as he was, standing there smiling at me. I wished I could have reached out and grabbed him so that he wouldn't go.'

'Mom' Dilly said, 'Gurjit's always going to be with us and I know this will give us the strength to face this,' and she slowly began to cry.

Sensing that they were tired I tried not to engage much in conversation, but listened to what they were saying. It made me think about the ongoing support we all needed. I didn't feel uncomfortable with this. Rather I felt a peace that we were going to be able to continue to respond to each other's pain through facing the painful truth.

Then Dilly said after composing herself 'I'm glad I went because I know I went for Gurjit and just like you said Mom, I also saw him every time I closed my eyes. I wanted to grab him as well but he'd disappear. But he'll never leave my heart.'

Her tears fell on to the girls who were resting on her, not crying, and Baljinder said 'I'm glad we all went and that we were together because that really helped me. But I still wish this was all a dream and Dad would come back to us.'

At this point I responded, 'What you all did was so amazing. I believe it will always stay within you, because our love for Gurjit will never change.'

Silence then descended as I imagine we were trying to think about everything that had happened, but my heart was heavy as I knew that my mom and the girls were not aware that Parmjit was probably dead. We couldn't tell them yet - it would have been too much for them to have to contend with this knowledge before the police could confirm that it was Parmjit.

Many of them were feeling unwell with symptoms of headaches, high temperature, sore throats, colds, and coughs, so once we had sorted out the luggage I rang the emergency doctors' on-call and was advised that they should see a doctor. I took Jai, Mangender, Sonia, Dilly, Bal, Baljinder and Suki, and they were all diagnosed as having a viral infection and told to rest. As it was late evening, none of them wanted to eat, rather wanted to just sleep as they were all very tired. Then again so was I but at least this time I had more peace of mind knowing they were at least home.

In the early hours of the morning my dad, mom and sister Dee began to develop the same symptoms. Even Ami did, and he hadn't even been to India. So it was another journey to the emergency doctors' on-call, and they too were diagnosed with a viral infection.

During the week each of them slowly began to make a recovery. However it had been tense watching them exhibiting similar symptoms to those Gurjit had displayed when he had become seriously ill. This came to the forefront when Jai was the only one who was not getting better. In fact he was admitted to hospital. While in hospital his symptoms began to become even more like Gurjit's. Naturally our anxiety began to increase. There appeared to be no rest from the continual emotional battles being endured.

Having to go to the same hospital were Gurjit had died and the same Emergency Assessment Unit brought back flashbacks of the night Gurjit had been admitted. The waiting in the emergency assessment unit became ever tenser. Jai looked as though he was deteriorating and I thought 'This can't be happening again!' I began to pray to God for intervention because this was too much to contend with - Gurjit's death, the high probability of Parmjit's death and now Jai being seriously ill.

As Mangender and I were by Jai's bedside she looked fearful, though she tried her best not to show it. Rather she was trying to keep optimistic as she said 'he's going to be fine, it's just a cold and he'll get over this in a few days.'

Her words were a genuine hope for restoration for her husband, my brother, but her eyes did not reflect the confidence of such words. She reminded me of Dilly. It was difficult to somehow remain calm when everything about Gurjit's death kept flashing through my mind. The pain of knowing that Mangender was now facing this was difficult to hold on to.

This time I didn't want to miss the signs of what was taking place in the way I had before Gurjit's death. But strangely, while I knew this was trying to create anxiety in me, there was a deep conviction within me that Jai was going to get better. Even though it provided me with comfort it also caused me distress, because I had thought Gurjit was going to get better as well. I said to Mangender 'Jai needs to rest and we've got nothing to fear.' She just nodded, holding Jai's hand tight as he drifted in and out of sleep.

After half an hour or so, which to me was long enough, I approached the doctors who were at their desk and politely questioned the reasons for the delay in them seeing Jai. To their credit they did respond when I made it clear that Jai had just returned from abroad and had appeared to have picked up a viral infection.

A female doctor got up and walked back with me to Jai. She introduced herself as Dr Reid. Jai was continuing to drift in and out of sleep. She then asked 'where did he return from and when?'

'India, and we came back on Friday 2nd,' Mangender replied.

'Was he sick while in India?' she asked. 'No,' replied Mangender.

She asked 'So how long as he been like this?'

'He was unwell when we came back and was taken to the doctor's on the same day and the doctor said he had a viral infection. I thought he was getting better, but he's been really ill since yesterday and he's got worse today,' Mangender nervously responded.

Further questions were then asked regarding Jai's medical history and whether he had shown other symptoms such as fainting, losing consciousness, nausea, difficulty keeping his eyes open, whether the lights hurt his eyes and whether he had any rashes on his body. Mangender told the doctor that Jai had vomited and that bright lights did hurt his eyes.

'I'm going to arrange some blood tests and hopefully we'll find out what's going on,' she said, and walked away. Returning within a few minutes, she prodded Jai with needles, which momentarily woke him up. She took some samples and sought to reassure us that she'd get the results as soon as she possibly could.

Mangender and I thanked her and stayed by Jai's bedside, as all we could do was watch and wait in silence. We breathed a sigh of relief when within an hour Jai woke up and the first thing he said was 'how's Sonia?'. Tears fell from his eyes and slowly moved down the side of his face. Mangender held his hand and said 'She's OK, and so will you be.'

Dr Reid came back to us and said 'It's a good job he was brought in because he has pneumonia. It's a good thing we've detected it early on.'

She gently then said to Jai, as he was still not fully awake, 'We're going to give you a course of antibiotics which will clear the infection within a week, but we're going to be keeping you in hospital for a few days to make sure that you are all right.'

She then left, and I smiled at Jai and Mangender and tried to reassure them in the way the doctor had just done. I went to phone home and spoke to Dee, telling her what was taking place. The tension I at first felt from her over the phone began to disappear. I sensed that she, like us all, was conscious of the last time we had been at the hospital and how it had ended. We certainly didn't want to contemplate the discomfort that had caused.

A nurse gave Jai some medication and then he fell asleep again. Mangender decided to remain the night at the hospital, and I went home reassured that he would get well soon. Pneumonia is a serious illness if not treated early, so I didn't want to be complacent. But I was confident that he would be OK, and that was the message I conveyed when I got home, to which everyone appeared to slowly relax.

Two days later Jai was discharged, as he had begun to make a full recovery. The tension we felt as a family over those few days was split wide open when he came home. But the intensity was going to continue, as that day the police were planning to visit Dee to obtain a statement in respect of Parmjit.

CHAPTER 3

POLICE STATEMENT

FRIDAY 9TH JANUARY 2004

Before Detective Constable Price's arrival Dee, Bal and Ami and I briefly spoke again about what it meant to know that the police considered that the evidence strongly suggested that Parmjit had already died. Dee's tears had already sprung forth as she said 'There can't be a worse nightmare than this, knowing he has died and we didn't know about it. It's so hard to believe that he's already gone and none of us saw him.'

Very little could be done to soothe her pain. It was very difficult, yet my full empathy was for her and the lads because their hearts revealed even more brokenness. The tragedy and despair was once more reinforced as Bal and Ami remained silent and the look on their faces was enough to convey their anguish at their father's death. They began to melt with the realisation of what was taking place, as Bal asked the vital question - 'How could the police not have not known earlier?' His question could not be answered at that time. Ami shrugged his shoulders in anger and said, 'Well, let's see what they've got to say.'

They sat trying to remain focused on the pending visit from the police, their eyes visibly overwhelmed by their mothers' plight as they looked at her crying. Unable to bear this for long, they got up and sat next to her and tried to comfort her. Bal said 'Mom, we're going to face this together,' and Ami added 'We've been facing Chacha's death, and we'll face this as well.'

Chapter Three

Their words certainly tested what support could be provided when their world was once again beginning to shake and fall apart. So was mine, by the very nature of my love for them. This I knew would be a painful sight, for it was incomprehensible to focus on, let alone understand and accept. With my heart sinking into the gloom with what we were experiencing it was difficult to scratch the surface of their emotions. It seemed so unjust that this was unfolding.

As I was feeling this, the doorbell rang and Bal answered it. Detective Constable Price entered. He was a tall man, big in build. He walked into the lounge clutching a folder under his arm and I noticed that his hands were shaking. I wasn't sure whether this was due to it being cold or because he was nervous about the information that he was going to share with Dee and the lads.

He smiled at Dee, and as he had already met her and the lads, she introduced him to me. He sat down and apologised for being late. He was definitely nervous as his hands continued to shake when he tried to open the folder and pull some papers out.

His next words set the scene for the confirmation of Parmjit's death. He said 'I am ever so sorry to have to break such tragic news, but the evidence of facial imagery has confirmed that the body recovered from the canal in December 2001 is that of Parmjit.'

Dee immediately began sobbing, and this stopped Detective Constable Price in his tracks. The look on his face was of deep empathy and his eyes slightly welled up. He was seeing the intolerable tribulation my sister was facing. Bal and Ami held on to her and gently whispered 'Mom, we can't do anything for Dad now, but we are going to get through this.'

Dee had been mortally wounded, and her body knotted up as she placed her arms around her abdomen, clinging I imagine, to her memory of Parmjit. Detective Constable Price sensitively waited for her. Only when she was able to sit up and look at him did he continue.

He then said 'I am so sorry for the mistakes that were made by us in identifying Parmjit's body. The expert who did the facial imagery has confirmed that the body we recovered from the canal in December 2001 was that of Parmjit. But the actual confirmation of Parmjit's identity cannot be given until a Coroner's inquest has been held.'

When he said that, he was unable to maintain eye contact with Dee. He quickly moved on and explained that the purpose of her providing a statement was for the inquest. He told her that they felt it would assist in the overall identification process.

Not even silence could have explained the void that was present in the few seconds that elapsed after his words. The thought running through my mind, influenced by an utter anger and bewilderment, was 'how do you expect us to respond when we are not fully aware what the mistakes were?' Yet whatever they were it would not reverse the sting left by death through the agonising separation.

With this in mind I allowed the thought to get the better of me and asked him what mistakes he was referring to. He looked at me startled, as though he had not been anticipating such a question. He paused, took a deep breath, and said 'We missed opportunities in identifying Parmjit's body but I don't have the full details. My Supervising Officer, Detective Constable Warrington, will be able to explain what happened.'

There was something about his body language that suggested that he knew more than he was telling us, but I also wondered if I was 'over-analysing' his responses. Either way it didn't rest well with me, because it was an unfair position for Dee to be in. I thought, knowing her relationship with her husband, the positives and drawbacks, that the circumstances of his leaving home were going to have to be summed up and presented as part of the overall evidence to confirm his death.

I felt for her, yet also believed it would allow grieving to begin. What tremendous strength she was displaying at such a distressing time, strength to express her love and uncertainty. I believed her vulnerability was not going to master her.

Dee began to provide a detailed statement describing the circumstances of Parmjit leaving the family home in January 2001 due to his alcohol difficulties. She informed Detective Constable Price that as a family we were aware Parmjit sought support from an Asian voluntary agency in Birmingham. He was hoping to have dealt with his personal difficulties related to alcohol misuse and then return home.

As she spoke her brokenness came forth. It was incredibly touching as she fought the tears while describing what took place. This revealed her consuming yearning for her husband. It was dreadful, yet she managed to hold the fragmented pieces together as she told him that in October 2001 the voluntary agency had contacted her and told her that Parmjit had gone missing from his rented property in Birmingham and that she had had to report him missing to the police.

The tears rolled fast as she went on 'I didn't report him because I was annoyed with him. But in December 2001 the voluntary agency contacted me again and told me that since October Parmjit had not turned up for any support sessions and no one had seen him. So I decided to report him as a missing person to Belgrave Police Station. That was the station the agency told me to contact.'

Her eyes continued to release the unlocked tears. Bal and Ami, seeing their mother's distress, held her hand, fighting back their own tears. As she held firmly on to their hands she said 'I wish I had reported him missing earlier, I should have. I feel guilty that I didn't.' Bal replied 'Mom, it's not your fault.'

Detective Constable Price paused from writing, his hand still shaking. He gently said to her 'Do you want to take a break? I can imagine how difficult this is for you.' She shook her head and said 'I keep thinking that if I had done this differently, if I had done something, he'd be here today.'

'Mom, you did everything you could for Dad, we all tried' said Bal. 'You're not responsible for this.' He looked at Detective Constable Price with a hint of anger in his voice.

Dee continued to give further details about Parmjit. Seeing her so immobilised by the havoc resulting from such a tragedy was so cruel. She required the deepest sympathy and the highest empathy to support her in facing her void. We were all going to have to endure it, more so the lads, who sat by her like pillars of support. Their eyes would wander every time she spoke and their jawlines would tighten every time she expressed her pain - pain they were also feeling knowing their father had died.

I felt as though our foundations were being shaken again - the foundations of love. Yet I believed that the experience of our love would strengthen us to face another painful and traumatic experience. It was strange, I felt, to have such a thought at that time, but I couldn't deny that I believed it was sustaining me and my hope was that we would all be sustained. But I couldn't ignore the reality of seeing her in such a state.

I gently asked her 'Dee, do you want to carry on, or re-arrange another time to continue talking?'

'I want to carry on' she replied. She turned to Detective Constable Price. 'I contacted Belgrave Police Station at the end of January 2002 to find out if they had found Parmjit' she said. Her tears poured down her face as she held Ami's hand tight, 'It hurt me when they told me that they didn't even have a missing persons report on their computer system. I had to report him missing again, even though I had done so in December 2001.'

When Dee said that, Detective Constable Price's face was a picture. His eyes widened and he looked fearful. I had the same feeling as before; he knew something, but wasn't sharing it. My stomach churned, but I didn't want to interrupt Dee because it was difficult enough for her to share the information. But my mind didn't want to rest, for that feeling was getting stronger, and I wanted to ask him why he looked so shocked with the piece of information Dee had shared with him. This time the temptation didn't get the better off me. I restrained my tongue, because I didn't want to prolong the meeting for Dee. She finalised her statement by telling him 'Some police officers came out after that to get a photo of Parmjit which I gave them.'

Again Detective Constable Price's face was giving off alarm signals, ranging from shock to fear. This was the first time I had noticed that he was maintaining eye contact with Dee. It was as though he was trying to convey a message to her. Yet the thought lingered that for whatever reason, he was withholding information.

Dee looked drained after she had completed her statement.

'Once again I'm ever so sorry about this and would like to express my condolences to you and your family at this difficult time' said Detective Constable Price. 'I'd also like to thank you for sharing this information with me.'

He was ready to say something else, but Bal interrupted him by asking 'what happened to my dad's body?'

Detective Constable Price appeared to have frozen. His eyes stared back at Bal and with a bulge in his throat he slowly said 'I am really sorry to have to tell you that Parmjit was cremated in October 2002. It didn't allow you the rightful opportunity to have said your farewell to him. I am so sorry, because we made a number of mistakes in the identification process.'

His words came across as sincere. They also expressed a degree of remorse. Whatever the mistakes had been, he was unable to specify them and the implications this had.

He went on 'I am also very sorry that I can't give you answers to many questions which I imagine you've got. I am really sorry about that.'

Dee and the lads had every right to ask him whatever question they needed to about Parmjit, to which they did.

'Where was he cremated?' Bal asked. 'I think it was in Rowley Regis, but the funeral directors can confirm this,' he replied.

'Have you got their number?' asked Bal.

'Not on me, but I can get it for you' he replied.

Dee was crying as she listened to this and her tears were running freely. 'Why has this happened?' she said. It was a question which didn't have an answer. The lads held her tight and Detective Constable Price's face said it all. He knew he could say nothing that would make any difference to Dee.

'I'm so sorry, I wish we could have identified Parmjit earlier' he said.

A few long seconds of silence fell and I knew that there was no real point in asking him any more questions, because we needed time to think about what else we needed to know.

'When will the coroner's inquest be held?' I asked.

'Detective Constable Warrington will take this evidence to the coroner in the next few days and the coroner will then arrange the date' he said. 'I'm not sure when that will be, but they will let you know as soon as they can. You can talk to my boss and he'll be able to tell you a lot more about the investigation and the Coroner's inquest, as well as answer any other questions you may have as a family.'

He then reiterated to Dee that her statement would be incorporated as part of the evidence that would be submitted to the Coroner's Inquest. He got up and moved slowly to Dee and gave her Detective Constable Warrington's contact details, his hand still shaking. Then he then said 'I have to leave now. Once again I would like to express by sincere condolences for your loss.'

Dee replied 'Thank you.' The lads didn't say anything at that point and then Bal got up and silently showed the officer out. All we could do was again sit in silence, contemplating the magnitude of the awful, confusing and despairing event of another death.

I was dejected when I looked at Dee and the lads, because I felt that mourning and grief were still in limbo, until the Coroner's inquest had been concluded. The pain of death was tormenting, the pain of having to wait was challenging. On top of that we still didn't have any clear information as to how Parmjit died. Then to add to the emotional pain being experienced was the knowledge that the police had made mistakes, even though we were not aware of the exact details.

At first my breath felt it had left my body as I tried to speak, and then from somewhere the strength arose as I said to Dee and the lads 'This is very hard because it is very painful. To think that Parmjit has already died is such a shock, just as Gurjit's death was. We're going to have to face death again. This is tough to accept as it feels so hopeless, but I believe with all my heart that we can face this together.'

Dee's lips were quivering, her tears were sliding down her cheeks and her hands were trembling. 'I'm already finding it difficult to cope knowing they've cremated him without us knowing. I really want someone to tell me that it's not true!' The dam broke as her tears ran riot.

Bal, Ami and I rallied around her and did our best to offer words of comfort in a situation that was anything but comfortable. They simultaneously said to her 'Mom, we know you loved him and you're hurt. There's nothing we can do for Dad, but we can for each other.'

Her sobbing got louder, in what appeared to be recognition of her son's love for her and awareness of their love for their father. Then silence fell again and it was the space for releasing some of the emotional pain that had built up, because words alone could not suffice against the intolerable and immeasurable hurt.

For me the fact that we had known about the high probability of Parmjit's death for about four weeks did not make this any easier. The memory of my relationship with Parmjit had begun to come to the forefront of my mind and this gave at least some meaning to inwardly acknowledge the loss that this separation had caused. I knew deep inside that they had also began to experience a similar process of reviewing their relationship with Parmjit. However the full emotional release was still contained, because we still had to wait for official confirmation of Parmjit's death.

Chapter Three

The silence began to break as we talked more about how our current experiences in exploring Gurjit's death could give us strength and hope to face the grief that had arisen again.

Having to leave them to go home and tell Dilly, Jai and my parents the outcome of Detective Constable Price's visit felt like a hindrance, because I didn't want to leave them alone. We were left dumbfounded by what looked like an endless hardship. I then said to Dee 'I'll come back later once I've told everyone and then we can talk about making contact with Detective Constable Warrington, if that's OK with you?' 'OK, and thanks for being here with us,' she replied.

We embraced and I kept thinking about what she and the lads would have been feeling and thinking. All I knew was that there was so many unreleased feelings which needed to be heard. The reality was it was so complex at times to grasp the roots of such deep pain, because grief just confirmed that there was a big hole that remained within us. This hole I imagined was bottomless, for they had another intimate void to battle with.

As I arrived at my parents' home I thought 'how can I share with them more tragedy?' I knew I couldn't really give any hope, because all the evidence was pointing towards Parmjit being dead. With Gurjit, at least I had felt that there was a possibility of survival, even though I realised it was more of a desperate plea.

As I got home my parents, Dilly and Jai were waiting in anticipation. My mother was already crying, her eyes red and her face swollen with affliction. Dilly was also crying. Her glasses were steaming and her lips quivering as she held my mother's hand.

Jai's look communicated pain as his jawline contorted and his hands clenched, somehow seeking to release the tension within him. In contrast, my father had his head bowed down and was silent. I began to relay all the information Detective Constable Price had given to Dee and the lads. My mother and Dilly cried loudly as they embraced. It became difficult when they realised that as a family we would have to wait for the inquest.

My mother, now engulfed with tears, shook her head as though she was trying to get the thought of Parmjit's death out of her mind. She cried 'Why, why is this happening to my family, God why don't you tell me?' I certainly had no answer, besides knowing that death was not evidence that God did not exist, rather a reminder that God is God. My father continued to sit in total silence with his head bowed, as though he wanted to avoid all forms of contact with us. Yet I knew he was in deep anguish, knowing that his eldest daughter was also now a widow and that his two grandsons had lost their father.

Jai, drained of all energy, asked 'When will the inquest be held?' to which I informed him that the police would be arranging another meeting with us first to give exact details of their investigation, and they would then speak to the coroner, who would set the inquest date.

I saw my father muttering under his breath and slowly shaking his head, his hands lifted to his eyes. 'How are Dee, Bal and Ami?' asked Dilly. 'What have they said?' I told her briefly about their views and feelings. Dilly knew how traumatic it was for them, as she was still responding to the effects of Gurjit's death.

Every time I spoke or thought about Parmjit, a numbness arose. It was as though I was standing outside myself looking in, only to observe that words were depleted. Seeing everyone's distress once again began to occupy my mind, and I wanted to reach out and wrestle with the pain and force it into submission. Yet I knew it was not going to suddenly go away for any of us. This became clearer for me when I looked into Jai's eyes and saw the adversity we were all experiencing being reflected by the glare in them.

They needed a few moments to gather their thoughts, and so did I, though I had heard Detective Constable Price. The silence continued to fall upon us like a blanket which might provide warmth and shelter from the harrowing knowledge of death.

Chapter Three

It was interrupted when my mother turned to my father and said 'Why aren't you saying something?' to which my father responded 'What can I say?' His face was perplexed. He shrank back into his chair, clasping his fingers tightly together as though he was trying to hold the feelings of hurt.

'Dad' said Jai. My father looked up in uncontrollable tears. He moved his hands to cover his face and curled forward, sobbing. His response revealed how the dreaded hurt was entangled within our hearts and reminded us that it could not be undone. We were heart-broken again, once again touching the centre of despair.

Jai looked at me, not yet shedding a tear. 'I'm going over to see Dee and the lads' he said. Dilly followed suit. Before she left she hugged my dad tightly and kissed him on his forehead, then did the same to my mom, saying 'You've both been strong for me and the girls, now you have to be stronger for Dee and the lads.'

After they had left I sat with my parents, who continued to cry, every tear shed causing my body to ache as I felt their love being tested again. My mind couldn't bring any words to the forefront. But some closure was required. I said 'Dad, Mom, Dee and the lads know how much this is hurting all of us and they know we'll be there for them.'

My mother replied, 'My heart has been completely ripped out of me, and my eyes have seen so much pain. To see my daughters hurt so much has destroyed me inside.' Her words were a combination of her love, compassion, sympathy and empathy for her daughters and grandchildren. I couldn't add much to what she said. It was another shock to the system that would require a response. The only words of comfort that came to mind were 'Mom, Dad at this time there is very little that we can say, besides knowing we all love each other.'

She asked me to pass the telephone to her as she wanted to phone Dee. When she got through, their crying became simultaneous. Mom was saying 'Why is this happening to us? Why? I can't understand this.'

She kept on repeating the question, then asked Dee to come over and see us, the tears falling on to the phone.

I bowed my head, thinking how to support her in making contact with Detective Constable Warrington. I knew Dee and the lads would visit in a while because Jai and Dilly were with them. So when the phone call ended I repeated what I had said earlier to my parents, then left the room to try and focus.

This resulted in my actually falling asleep for a while, to be woken by my mother's loud cries. Dee and the lads had arrived. When I went downstairs and opened the lounge door Dee was consoling them, while Bal and Ami sat side-by-side, their grandfather remaining bewildered.

I gently smiled at Dee and the lads. She turned to my parents and said 'I know you loved him as a son, and even though he did what he did, I loved him and thank you for helping me.'

My mom's hands began to tremble and her cheeks wobbled as I imagined Dee's words had reminded them of true love. Dee and my mom sat next to each other, holding hands. Bal interjected, saying 'Nan, none of us can do anything about Dad dying.' She stared at him and shaking her head replied 'That's what hurts me the most, I can't help him and we've lost him.'

She kept crying as Dee continued to console her, while my dad was shaking his head and his bewildered eyes shed tears. My mom's anguish was so deep that her breathing became heavier and her eyes showed intense sorrow as she tried to speak. 'Where is he? I pray, I pray every day... I asked God to help him.'

Then she turned to my dad and said 'What are you going to say to our daughter?'

He looked up and initially tried to avoid eye contact, shaking his head, and then the lads put their arms around him and he said 'When he went I knew I wouldn't see him alive again, I never wanted this.'

'Baba don't worry, we all tried to help him. It didn't mean we didn't care and love him because we did,' Bal said to him as my dad covered his face with his hands.

We sat still and the evening began to draw in as Dee and the lads prepared to go home grappling with the knowledge of death. I knew they were exhausted. I was certainly shattered and felt so moved by everyone's tremendous efforts to remain hopeful of the support we could provide. We all embraced as they left to go home.

The tiredness again crept up slowly and my mind felt as though it was going blank. The heaviness, of such tragedy began to take a tighter hold on me. Woken again by the physical shaking of my body, I sprung off the sofa I had fallen asleep on and stood in the lounge, thinking again about how Dee and the lads were. It was dreadful to hold on to such thoughts.

I had just managed to get myself off to sleep when morning came. It was the start of another weekend. However I began to think about how within two weeks it would be a year since Gurjit's death. It was so hard to fathom how fast the year had gone and to grapple with the knowledge of Parmjit's death just compounded the distress.

After completing the usual routines I went to see Dee and the lads. When Dee opened the door, her face reflected anguish and it was clear that she had had very little sleep. Her eyes were like a furnace, yet they also appeared distant as though I imagined she yearned so deeply to push the pain far away, as far as the east is from the west.

I gently smiled at her as I entered and hugged her, saying 'I know this is difficult, but we are all going to get through this together.'

'Yes, I know' she said. 'I can't stop thinking about Parmjit and keep thinking he's going to turn up and that the police have got this all wrong. But deep down I know he's gone and I can't do anything about that,' she replied. Her tears were rolling like a train down her cheeks and she wiped them away as I hugged her again.

The lads came downstairs and embraced her as she cried, and Bal said to her 'Mom, it's OK to cry.' Ami repeated what Bal had said and added 'Mom, this is going to hurt for a long time, but we are in this together.'

We did not enter into a lengthy discussion, as we were all still very tired, in particular Dee, who said 'I haven't really slept because I keep thinking about how to believe this when I can't even see his body.' Her inconsolable and immense despair was so much part of her, alongside her love for Parmjit.

My words stuck in my throat, unable to project any relief to her as she remained so broken, tears falling rapidly. The truth of knowing we would not see Parmjit's body was going to be a major obstacle in our minds, for the tragedy continued to unfold like a peeled onion, as each layer of despair would always point towards more pain which could not be undone.

As we sat, we knew that further dialogue was required with the police, which also meant having to wrestle with more distress. Hence I asked Dee, 'How do you feel about having to speak to Detective Constable Warrington about the police investigation?' She initially responded by shaking her head and then said 'I want you to do it,' as her tears poured down again. I replied 'fine.'

It was very strange to think that with all these difficulties we would have to continue to get on with all the responsibilities we had. Thinking about this, knowing all we could do was wait, only added to the suffering. And on top of that I thought about my family's visit to India when Gurjit's memorial had been undertaken. The reaction of his family made me wonder how they would cope with the pending reality of Parmjit's death.

As if reading my mind, Dee then said 'What's his family in India going to think? I know they'll try to blame me for this.' Bal replied 'Mom, you don't have to worry about them, forget what they're going to think. We all know what has happened and they didn't live with Dad, we did, so they can say what they like, it's not going to affect us. We know that we loved him even though it was difficult at times, but that didn't mean we didn't care for him because we did. You did everything you could, so don't worry about them.'

Ami turned to them and said 'I wasn't with you when you were in India, but I know they had no right to say what they said to Massi Dilly and they certainly have no right to say anything to us about Dad. If what they say is not helpful then I don't care what they say. Mom, we've got plenty to think about without having to wonder how they'll react to the news of Dad's death.'

The dread on Dee's face began to reduce as her son's words reached out and upheld her. They were united in their response and I felt this was cushioning the blow that had been delivered to them.

I felt strength when I listened to what the lads said, because they had already started to show a very clear view with regards to their love for their father. This love was being given to their mother as well. It also showed me that they were going to face the reality of their experience and would do so truthfully.

With such thoughts in my mind I said 'Dee, the lads are absolutely right. Even though Parmjit's family are most likely going to struggle with his death, we have to understand that this may be part of their way of coping. But it's not right for them to shift this on to you, because as you know you haven't done anything to cause Parmjit's death, just as Dilly couldn't have stopped Gurjit from dying.'

'I know it's going to take a lot of time to accept this' said Dee. 'I've got many fears and doubts about what to do. I believe I'll survive this, but I can't ignore how much it hurts.'

I was amazed by her resolve to believe that she would stand up against the challenge death had brought to her.

'You're right,' I said. 'It's going to hurt and this hurt will probably be more so after we find out all the details of what happened. Our love for each other will give us the added strength to face this.'

We then began to talk briefly about Dee's and Bal's experiences while they had been in India. In recognition of our not having had the opportunity to explore this in detail since their return from India due to many of them recovering from illness, we decided that we would talk with everyone later on.

This discussion took place with Dee, Dilly, Jai, Bal, Baljinder, Suki and Ami (even though he had not been to India). We spoke about this sensitively, because it was important for the girls to hear appropriate expressions of care and not blame.

Even though Jai had intervened by removing the girls from the situation, the hurt had been caused through them overhearing their father's extended family's insensitivity. After that it was positive to know that Jai and Bal ensured they remained with the girls and that no adult was able to commence any conversation which was inappropriate.

Upon reflection I thought that even though such insensitivity had been shown by Gurjit's family, due I imagined to their own emotional hurt, there was a positive side the importance of sharing the emotional pain with people that can be trusted and not for the purpose of trying to seek blame. I believed it was an important message to convey to the girls and that it was the reason for their inclusion in family discussions.

I said to them 'I know it's been a while since you all returned from India and that undertaking the memorial service for Gurjit would have been emotional yet special, and that this will always remain with you. It's important to hold on to that because it will give us all some strength. I also know that it was difficult to find how Gurjit's family reacted, but no one has the right to cause us to feel fear and seek to blame us, because no one could have known Gurjit was going to die. This is the hard truth that we've faced all year, that there was nothing we could have done. Whatever they said was out of hurt. We all know our love for Gurjit and his love for us and nothing is ever going to change that.

No words will ever be able to challenge that truth which is in us all – that's what I believe we need to focus upon.'

Dilly began to shed tears which could have filled a bucket within minutes, and she was comforted by Dee, who said to her 'Your love for Gurjit will never fade, just as mine for Parmjit will not.'

Their tears became synchronized as Baljinder edged forward to speak. She said 'I know Dad would never have wanted us to feel we let him down, I know we didn't because we loved him so much. I don't care what anyone else says when it tries to hurt me. I won't listen to them, because I know we all loved Dad and I don't have to explain myself to them.'

Such powerful conviction was expressed with a maturity which revealed that she had begun slowly to develop some positive strategies in facing the reality of her father's death.

Suki followed on, saying 'I know they also loved my dad, but they were wrong when they tried to say that someone was to blame. That frightened me, but I know it's not true, because I know we all loved Dad.'

It was incredible to see how they were able to think in a way which was calm even though they had experienced insensitivity.

'I'm not even paying attention to what people say if what they say is not helpful' Bal said as he turned to the girls and held their hands. 'If anyone wants to try and hurt someone by saying hurtful things then I'll just ignore them, because I'm only focusing on how to support each other.'

In response to Bal, Dilly said 'You're right. But when they started to question what I did it hurt because they were blaming me and I started to feel maybe it was my fault that Gurjit died. Deep down I knew I had done all I could, but I still felt it when they said I should have helped Gurjit because they were really trying to say that I didn't care and that hurt me. I've only realised how much they didn't know me, but I find strength in the truth that Gurjit knew me and I can reject what they said.'

Her new confidence was like seeing a caterpillar transform into a butterfly. It was so positive to know that she was not prepared to allow doubts to remain in her mind about her love for Gurjit, for the actions she undertook had been based upon such love.

Ami then quietly spoke. 'I'm so glad that you all were together supporting each other, because it doesn't matter what people say when we know what's in our hearts. I don't have to explain this to anyone outside the family because it's personal to me. Listening to what you've all said has helped me know even more how much we loved Chacha and my dad and how much we love each other. That's what really matters.'

'Everything that's been said is so true,' Jai said as he turned towards Dilly and the girls. 'It's important to remember that Gurjit belonged to us and no one can take that from us. We will always remember all the good things about him. So forget people's views when they don't really help you.'

I felt that what Ami and Jai had said reinforced the belief that our love was deeper than the wounds we had suffered.

CHAPTER 4

MOMENT OF TRUTH

THURSDAY 22ND JANUARY 2004

As the days went by I tried to focus my mind on the coming meeting that had been arranged with Detective Constable Warrington to ascertain the precise details of the police investigation into Parmjit when he had been reported as a Missing Person.

Jai was supposed to attend the meeting with me but was unfortunately unable to do so; he was still recovering from pneumonia. We had spoken earlier about whether to seek a re-arrangement until he was well. He said to me 'It's better for the meeting to go ahead, though I would have wanted to have been there. I don't think it is fair for Dee and the lads to wait, because we don't want to delay this any further.'

It was awful to know he wasn't going to be with me. Awful because the thought that flashed through my mind was that he hadn't been present when Gurjit had died because I had asked him while he was returning to the hospital to bring our cousin-sister. Those few moments when he had returned to my parents' house to bring our cousin-sister to the hospital had haunted me, because I felt I had deprived him of the honourable right to have been with Gurjit at the time of his death.

All I could say was 'OK'. I was left rehearsing in my mind the issues which as a family we required clarification on. As I arrived at the police station, I felt the tension rise in my body through the level of concentration running through my mind.

I breathed slowly as I entered the reception area, knowing deep inside that a major part of me didn't really want to be there. I was hoping that the meeting would be quick, but knew that it would not be.

As I sat down in reception, I began to think about the number of times I had entered a police station in my role as a social worker. This was very different, because I was nervous.

After I had waited a few minutes a very tall gentleman walked in and introduced himself as Detective Constable Warrington. He stretched out his hand to shake mine. His face was probably reflecting mine as I sensed his nervousness. He said 'Thank you for attending. Please follow me this way' and led me to a room adjacent to the reception area.

Once we entered the room he said 'I need to go and fetch Parmjit's files. I'll be back shortly, please take a seat.'

The room was small but not cramped. It had one table and a couple of chairs and the window had bars on the inside. It seemed a clear reminder that there was no escape from death, as it created a feeling of being trapped.

Detective Constable Warrington then came back into the room with two large folders, which he gently placed on to the table. As he sat down and looked at me, it seemed as though we both wanted to speak at the same time. Knowing this, I think we tried to give each other the opportunity to say something. As he clearly showed respect for the reason I was there, I felt he provided the time for me to speak, which I took.

'Thank you for coming to this meeting' I said. 'As a family we have a number of questions relating to four specific areas. Firstly, the precise issues surrounding Parmjit's death eg when was his body found? Where exactly was it found? Who found it? What was the cause of death? Secondly we would like to find out more about what investigations were undertaken by Sparkhill Police Station and Wednesbury Police Station, as we know they covered different areas. Thirdly, we would like an explanation as to what went wrong during the investigations resulting in the delays in identifying Parmjit's body. Fourthly, we need more information with regard to the Coroner's inquest.'

Before Detective Constable Warrington provided any details he looked at me and his eyes displayed genuine consideration as he said 'Before I answer you I want to sincerely apologise to you and your family, in particular Parmjit's wife and sons, for the manner in which the investigations were handled.'

I thanked him for his comments. Yet there was not much I could say at that time, and I believe my silence enabled him to begin talking.

How Parmjit's body was found

Detective Constable Warrington began to tell me that Parmjit's body had been found on the 28th December 2001 in a canal in Smethwick. He said 'Parmjit's body was found face down in the canal by a member of the public who was taking his dog for a walk. We believe from the decomposition that had set in that Parmjit's body had been in the water for some time.'

The atmosphere in the room changed as I struggled with the information that Parmjit's body had been in a canal for a number of weeks before being recovered.

It was so horrendous that the pain had to catch up with me to contend with what my mind was seeking to register. A feeling of tremendous sadness coupled with anger rattled through me. How could this be? What had he been feeling and thinking? How could I even begin to truly think about what he was feeling and thinking at that time? It was horrifying.

He went on to talk about the cause of Parmjit's death, saying that the Coroner had recorded an open verdict, as the cause of death could not be determined.

He took a long pause and a deep breath before going on to say: 'At that stage the investigation was being managed by Wednesbury Police Station, and I'll explain what went wrong in a moment. What I know is that a toxicology report was undertaken but it did not reveal any evidence of drugs or alcohol in Parmjit's body, and there were no findings to suggest trauma or fractures, or disease. Furthermore, even though Parmjit's lungs were not filled with water, the Coroner could not exclude death by drowning. Neither could he say that he definitely had drowned. Rather the Coroner believed that the moment Parmjit landed in the canal, due to the freezing temperatures at that time, his body had gone into immediate shock and shut down, a condition known as vascular inhibition.'

This was quite a lot to take in. Maybe I felt this was because Parmjit's cause of death was unknown and from what I heard, would continue to remain unknown. It was terrible to think about his death and to know that as a family we would not know how he died.

I said 'Parmjit always used to like walking by canals, it was something he had done when he was growing up in India. It's even more strange to think that he was found approximately four miles from where he lived and the canal route would have brought him within yards of his house.' I had to pause at the next thought I had. 'I wonder whether Parmjit was planning to return home? I just wonder.'

Thinking about what Parmjit might have been going through was too intense to want to hold on to. My stomach churned and I felt sick inside. Detective Constable Warrington must have seen my distress, for he asked 'Are you OK to continue?'

'Yes' I replied.

The rest of the interview would not alleviate such despair; rather it would compound it, as he moved on to telling me about the police investigations that had taken place.

Chapter Four

Police investigations and what went wrong

With regard to the police investigation, he said that Wednesbury Police Station had investigated the finding of a body in Smethwick between December 2001 and July 2002. However at around the same time a second body was found in a canal close by, which was the subject of a murder enquiry. This was where the confusion had set in. Wednesbury Police Station were unable to identify Parmjit's body and because of that they passed the file over to the Coroner in July 2002, as they did not have a missing persons report.

Hearing what he was saying, in particular about the missing report, I replied that my sister had reported Parmjit missing in December 2001 and again in January 2002 to Belgrave Police Station in Birmingham. Furthermore we had told Detective Constable Price about two weeks before that Belgrave Police Station had told my sister that they did not have a missing person report.

Detective Constable Warrington looked totally stunned, as it was clear he was not aware of that. He said 'I need to check that out, because it concerns me that we might have known earlier. I thought Parmjit had been reported missing in July 2002.'

I sensed that he might have felt slightly embarrassed, as he might not have read Dee's statement to Detective Constable Price. The shock on his face showed that he was aware of the implications for the police, because they clearly could have responded to that information. He looked totally helpless, yet this was just what we a family were experiencing. The thought that went through my mind was to demand an immediate response, because it was unacceptable to think that Dee had reported her husband as a missing person and the police had paid no regard to such reports.

I did not hold back. I said to him 'It's becoming clear to me that the missing person reports which my sister filed in December 2001 and

Chapter Four

January 2002 to Belgrave Police Station appear not to have been recorded, nor even circulated to any other police station. Furthermore it also appears that neither police station liaised with the other, so they missed an opportunity to identify Parmjit's body.'

I felt my jaw tighten as I tried to manage my anger. I went on 'As a family we are very concerned about how this has been handled by the police.'

Detective Constable Warrington sat shaking his head as he realised what this meant, a total shambles. My information had thrown him off track and I could see that he was trying to gather his thoughts. While he was doing so, I was gathering mine. I was wondering why the respective police stations had not spoken to each other. Surely this should not have presented a communication difficulty, though it obviously had. He looked at me, slightly shaken, and said 'I'll certainly have to check this out.'

The seriousness of the situation was evident to me and I imagined to him, for his right hand began to shake as he held on to one of the folders. I knew that there was no purpose in trying to debate the issue at that time, because he acknowledged that the implications were quite serious and needed time to clarify this. However the thought that went through my mind was that it might not be known what had gone wrong with the police investigation and this was something that we would have to struggle to accept. This level of uncertainty was cruel, and I was left questioning how we would embrace this. Silence elapsed as we processed the information and it felt as if the room had been frozen.

Detective Constable Warrington tried to explain the police investigation. He said that although the missing person report had been filed at Belgrave Police Station, it was Sparkhill Police Station which had undertaken the investigation. Sparkhill Police Station had begun its investigation in July 2002 when they were contacted by Parmjit's wife.

I told him, 'I'm more concerned because the only reason my sister rang Sparkhill Police Station was because she was told by Belgrave Police Station that they were dealing with the case.' He acknowledged that if Dee had rung in July 2002 for an update, it indicated that a missing person's report must have been filed before that.

He said 'I'm going to need some time to check this out, and I'll be honest with you I'm also very annoyed by what has been a total breakdown of communication and lack of co-ordination by the police. I'm really sorry for Parmjit's wife and sons and for your entire family.'

The implications of what was unfolding could not be underestimated. I felt it was crucial for him to ensure that for Dee's and the lads' sake every effort was made to clarify what had gone so drastically wrong.

He went on 'Sparkhill Police Station undertook an investigation into Parmjit as a missing person, and the detectives involved contacted Wednesbury Police Station in July 2002. However when they enquired about the body in the canal, Wednesbury Police Station thought the enquiry related to the murder inquiry that they conducted. This was the main error made by the police, because Sparkhill Police Station and Wednesbury Police Station had failed to consider the second body that had been found, which was in fact Parmjit's.'

Again I was shocked as I wondered how the police officers could not have thought about this. What on earth were they thinking? Couldn't they have explored the enquiry further?

The annoyance inside me was building up like a volcano ready to erupt. I looked directly at him, and he would have seen this all over my face. He said 'It is unacceptable that we did not follow up all the details. If we had done so Parmjit would have been identified earlier. More so, I'm very concerned as we might have had the information for a while. I will fully understand if as a family you decide to place a formal complaint about the way this has been managed and our failure to combine enquiries and follow up on the investigation.'

Chapter Four

I felt his words were genuine, as he made no attempt to seek to minimise the errors made by the police. His acknowledgement of them reinforced my belief that he was trying his best to explain what went wrong. I said 'That's something my sister will decide, please continue.'

'From July 2002 to October 2003 Sparkhill Police Station had no information about Parmjit's whereabouts' he went on. 'As a result my Supervisor asked me in October 2003 to review the case, which I did. My field of work is fraud investigations, but I was approached as I had several years of experience working on missing person cases.'

He gently smiled as he continued to talk about the investigation. 'Because of my experience it was not hard for me to identify the shortcomings in the way Sparkhill Police Station undertook the investigation. As a result my supervisor gave me the case in November 2003 and asked me to progress to a conclusion, as it was clear that a number of errors had been made in identifying Parmjit's body.'

I saw the annoyance on his face; he was clearly not impressed by the previous police investigations. 'When the case was given to me I contacted Wednesbury Police Station' he went on. 'I did this because I was not happy with their response or with the enquiries made by detectives from Sparkhill. They told me the same thing about the body recovered being part of a murder enquiry. When I asked about the second body, they realised that they had failed to realise that this was what Sparkhill had initially been enquiring about.'

He sighed deeply and continued. 'After it was established that they had failed to consider this, I requested the photos from the Coroner's Office which had been taken by Wednesbury Police Station, as I wanted them to be sent for Facial Mapping and for this to be compared with the picture that we had of Parmjit which had been given to us by his wife.

'I have to apologise again, because I know that the photograph she had given us had not even been circulated between the police stations. If it had been, Parmjit would have been identified earlier and as a family you would have been able to attend to all the cultural requirements for his funeral. I am deeply sorry that this was taken away from his wife and sons.'

Sitting there knowing that the entire police investigation had been a failure increased my determination to seriously challenge their actions as my mind sought to register each serious failure. First they had not registered the missing person reports in December 2001 and January 2002. Second, they had failed to competently liaise between themselves when making enquiries after Parmjit's body had been recovered from the canal. Third, they had failed to circulate the photograph of Parmjit.

I was very annoyed about what had clearly been a total mess-up. I was infuriated that there had been so many chances to identify Parmjit, and all were missed through their failure to investigate properly.

The only reassurance I felt was that Detective Constable Warrington was conscientiously seeking to help us as a family to find closure, and was doing so without playing down their failings.

He must have seen the annoyance that was written all over my face. He apologised again, saying 'I know this will be difficult for Parmjit's wife and sons to cope with. It should never have happened. We failed them and there is no excuse for the shockingly poor standard of police investigation we provided.'

This man's apologies came non-stop. I felt that he was actually seeking to put himself in Dee's and the lad's shoes, trying to think about what they would be feeling and thinking and how this would impact upon them.

Detective Constable Warrington now went on to talk about the inquest and viewing Parmjit's photographs.

He said he would take Sparkhill Police Station's investigation file to the Coroner's office, where the coroner would look at the evidence and contact him to open an inquest to formalise Parmjit's identification.

'I've already spoken to the coroner's assistant, who has told me that the coroner is absolutely livid about the errors that were made in the initial police investigation' he said. 'The coroner's assistant wanted you to know that the coroner will be liaising with the police about their failings.'

Hearing those words gave me some strength, knowing that someone else had seen the effects this was going to have upon my family.

We moved on to what was going to be a very sensitive and heartbreaking issue; viewing the photographs of Parmjit. Detective Constable Warrington told me: 'These photographs are very distressing. I can't stop the family from seeing them, but in my opinion and experience the photographs should not be seen by Parmjit's wife or sons as I believe the photographs will haunt them.'

I noticed that his eyes had welled up and I thought for a moment that he was going to shed tears. He managed to compose himself. I was touched by the tremendous compassion and empathy he was showing for Dee, Bal and Ami, considering he had not even met them. His words were very caring and considerate.

'Thank you for your concern for them' I said. 'As a family we have already spoken about viewing the photographs. My elder brother Jai was unable to attend this meeting because he is not well. At the moment we have decided as a family that my brother and I should see the photographs. That way we would at least have some peace knowing that the body you've identified really is Parmjit.'

'OK' he replied. 'I think it will be better than his wife and sons seeing the pictures. I can imagine how much they would want to see the photographs, but please tell them it will only cause them more pain and they've already suffered enough by our failings. To tell you the truth I'd feel distressed if I knew they were to see the photographs.'

I was taken aback by these words about how he would feel. It made me think about what could be done to reduce the impact this was having on Dee and the lads. I also wondered what would have happened if this detective had investigated Parmjit as a missing person when Dee had originally reported Parmjit as missing.

I nodded to acknowledge what he had said, and he then slowly moved to the folder and took out a small blue album. I sat there thinking, oh my life, a photo album! I was thinking that such albums are usually a reminder of all the brilliant, fun and loving times you have with your family and friends, yet here I was inwardly shaking at the thought of what I was about to see.

Detective Constable Warrington placed the album on the table and gently opened it. As soon as he showed me the first photograph I knew immediately that it was Parmjit. Even though decomposition had set in, it did not prevent me from recognising my brother. I turned and looked at him and said 'That's Parmjit. I don't need facial mapping to confirm it.'

My immediate thought was of empathy for poor Parmjit. What had happened before his death? What had he been thinking and feeling?

I sat in silence and I touched the photograph, knowing now that we would never see Parmjit alive again. The photograph was the closest we could ever come.

It was horrible to know that this man whom we loved had died under such tragic circumstances, and I felt an immense sadness that he had been alone. Irrespective of his shortcomings, he was still my brother and I wanted him back so badly for my family.

As I continued to turn page by page it was distressing. It felt as though I was on quicksand, sinking down with very little to hold on to. The thought of Dee and the lads seeing the photographs was terrifying, as each photograph was burning into my consciousness.

Then I came to a photograph that really got to me. My eyes welled up on the brink of tears. It showed Parmjit holding his hands crossed as a sign of prayer, his fingers tightly interlocked.

I questioned whether he was seeking forgiveness from God and from us as his family. It felt as though he was longing for wholeness, because deep, deep down I knew he loved us and it was crushing to know that he had died.

My mind froze with the question - 'Parmjit what happened?' Then I thought 'Parmjit, I want you to know that we love you and miss you, and I'm sorry for not being there for you. Parmjit, this is hurting so badly and I know it is going to cut so deep into Dee, Bal and Ami.'

After I had finished looking at the photographs there were a few seconds of silence as I tried to gather the rest of my thoughts. The main one was - how on earth was I going to be able to tell Dee and the lads about this?

Detective Constable Warrington gently took the photo album from me and placed it back into the big folder. He then asked me 'Would you like a few moments alone?' to which I replied 'That's a good idea.' He left the room.

Sitting there alone could not even be compared to the loneliness that Parmjit would have experienced, and what Dee and the lads would have to contend with.

More questions arose in my mind, such as 'what happened to you, Parmjit?' 'God, were you there for him?'

My prevailing thought was about Parmjit being alone. I knew nothing could be done now. Not even trying to focus upon the failings of the police would assist. The only thing that was becoming evident was the knowledge that we would have to come to terms with his death.

The door opened and Detective Constable Warrington returned. 'How are you feeling?' he asked. I replied 'Under the circumstances I'm managing the best I can. I'm just trying to prepare myself for sharing this with my family.'

'Can I ask you, and I know it may be difficult, if you would be willing to provide a statement expressing your belief that the photographs you saw were of Parmjit?' he asked. 'Sure' I replied. I gave a statement stating my belief that with complete certainty the pictures I had seen were of Parmjit.

As I was giving the statement I thought it should have been Dee's right to do so. Yet I felt that she would have endured so much agony in seeing the photographs. I knew she could not be protected from the reality of her husband's death. However I also knew that if she had seen the photographs they would have tormented her.

After I had given the statement, it was time to leave. We got to our feet and stretched our hands towards each other. I said 'Thank you for sharing such information truthfully. On behalf of my family I would like to truly thank you for the efforts you have made in bringing us closure over what happened to Parmjit. Thank you for everything you have done and for today's meeting.'

He replied 'I wish that they had given me the case a lot earlier. I'm deeply sorry for the distress that I know it will cause Parmjit's wife and sons because we got this so wrong. I'm also going to be looking into the specific issues you raised about Parmjit's wife reporting him missing a lot earlier than what we have got recorded.'

'Once again, thank you' I said. No more words were uttered, as our eyes made final contact and I walked out of the room.

Knowing that I had been in the police station for about two and a half hours, and that it would take about an hour to get back home, I began to process the information to make sense of it again before I could communicate it to my family. The recurring thoughts going through my mind were: how are Dee, Bal and Ami going to cope with the knowledge that when she had reported Parmjit as a missing person it was not recorded by the police?

The images of Parmjit were stuck in my brain, immovable. I wondered how I was going to be able to describe them to my family. This thought made my stomach twist in knots and I felt trapped and sick. The spine-chilling pain shuddered through me as I held tightly to the steering wheel. Every fibre of my body was battling against the thoughts that were careering round my mind like a racing car.

As I drew close to home the thoughts were not diminishing but becoming more upsetting. I was trying desperately, but failing miserably, to 'block' out for a few seconds the battering my mind was taking. I felt weary, and as I turned into the avenue where I lived my legs seemed to have disappeared. However the awful feeling of having to go into detail about the police investigation was compounded by my annoyance with regard to the police handling of the case.

I parked and gently opened the front door, knowing that Dee, Bal and Ami, Dilly, Jai and my parents would be waiting in the lounge. As soon as I walked in and saw them my words were blocked by pain, and the tears were brewing inside of me. I was trying to find the strength to share this heartbreaking news.

Looking at their faces was enough to reinforce my sense of being trapped. Dee's expression was one of utter despair. She just glanced at me and then closed her eyes, waiting for the earth-shattering confirmation of her husband's death. The feeling of awfulness just got more awful.

Bal's and Ami's eyes pierced me with a knowledge that another separation was in their midst. My mother was already sobbing quietly, while my father sat with his head bowed and his hands intertwined.

Jai, still recovering from his illness, sat with his face contorted, the sides of his jaw straining, and Dilly, sitting by Dee, sought to provide support, her eyes already red.

I attempted to summarise what had taken place in the two-and-a-half-hour meeting with Detective Constable Warrington. I told them that it would take me a while to explain in detail all the areas that we needed clarification on. I began to tell them about the circumstances of Parmjit's death. The shock on their faces could not be concealed as they stared at me, trying to register the horrible fact that Parmjit's body had been in a canal for a long time before being recovered.

Furthermore, the belief that Parmjit might have been on the way home became unbearable for Dee to hold. 'Was he coming here?' she said. Jai interjected 'I think he was, he had to have been,' offering some hope at such a desperate moment.

I said 'Thinking about it, he may have been, because he himself said that after he got support that he would return home. We will never really know.'

Dee was trying hard not to shed her tears; her fingers were rubbing against each other. This frightful reality was difficult to accept. I felt so much for her and the lads having to battle with this.

Jai then asked 'how long do they think Parmjit's body had been in the canal?' I felt my vocal cords tighten as I uttered quietly, 'The police think he might have been in the canal for six to eight weeks.'

The horror of that was unbearable for Dee, and she began to cry. 'How could that have been?' she asked.

I had no answers. 'No one knows' I said. 'The police think that because it was so cold during that winter, when the ice set in it would have prevented any passer-by from seeing his body.'

This was very difficult, because the feelings that were arising could not be contained. Once I disclosed the information about the police investigation, I knew it would be even more uncomfortable. The reality was that I was still trying to process the information myself, along with the catalogue of errors made by the police.

I told them as clearly as I could everything Detective Constable Warrington had said about the police investigation. Bal immediately identified what this meant in terms of his dad's funeral. He said 'So we could have done the funeral then? If they had done their job, we would have been there, like we were there for Chacha.'

His anger was visible as he clenched his fists. His jaw line contorted and he stood up and breathed heavily, shaking his head. 'They took that from us, how dare they take that from us! What were they playing at, can't they just do their job?' he said.

Ami reacted just as angrily. 'How could they have messed up so badly? What were they doing?' There was no reasonable explanation for the questions they were asking.

Dee's tears were restricting her voice. She stuttered, 'Why, why didn't they listen to me? Why didn't they pay attention when I reported him missing? I feel they are saying it's my fault, but I did report him missing. Why?'

Of course she was not guilty of anything but loving her husband. I could only glimpse what she was feeling in having to accept such loss under such desolate circumstances. Her entire being was crushed by the thought of the lack of action by the police. I knew this because this thought was also tearing through me. Listening to her plea was even more heart wrenching.

Dilly turned to Dee. 'We know you did, and you are not at fault' she said. 'I know what you're feeling, because I went through that when Gurjit died. You haven't done anything wrong.' Dee's head rested on Dilly's shoulder as Dilly placed her arms around her. Dilly's words of comfort were powerful, for she had her own personal experience of how guilt causes havoc in her own life.

Jai asked 'How did that happen? How could they have made those mistakes? If they had done their job, Gurjit would have known what had happened. What are they going to do now?'

There was a righteous anger in Jai's eyes. He was correct in pointing out that Gurjit had also been deprived of the right to be involved in the procedures required for Parmjit's funeral.

My mind was tired. It felt as though I was caught up in a whirlwind as their statements reflected the pain reigning in their life. What could I possibly do to move from such a dark place? For the ground was not firm and focus was hard to grasp.

Feeling so let down was consuming, as I knew our hearts loved

Parmjit dearly and that we were struggling to think clearly because of the shock, anger and disbelief at what had happened to him.

I said 'This is extremely tough to have to accept that Parmjit has died, and on top of that knowing that the police investigation before Detective Constable Warrington's intervention was so woefully lacking. Yet the police have not tried to minimise such incompetence. Rather they have acknowledged how their mistakes let us down as a family. We have all been thinking that we could have been involved in the funeral process, and that this was taken from us. We have every right to be annoyed about this. We'll have to revisit this again, as well as other aspects of Parmjit's life and our relationship with him.'

Explaining what the Coroner's inquest would entail was far easier than explaining the police investigation. This was a procedure that we knew would bring about the finality of knowing that Parmjit had died. Yet it became very tough again because now it was a matter of going into detail about the photographs taken by the police. To this I said 'I've seen the photographs and there's no doubt in my mind that it was Parmjit. It was not an easy task to view them and Dee, you would be very distressed if you saw them.' She began to cry louder. I imagined that the thought of not even having the opportunity to see Parmjit was beginning to have its full effect on her.

'There was one photograph which was so heartbreaking' I said. 'I need you all to know this. It showed him with his hands intertwined as though he was praying.' My eyes began to well up, and it was difficult to maintain eye contact with them because I saw so much distress in their eyes.

Dee remained collapsed in Dilly's arms, sobbing. My mother's tears had not stopped, and her face was visibly shaken every time she looked at Dee. My father, who until now had remained quiet, suddenly stretched a hand towards Dee and placed it on her head. He then stretched his other arm towards Bal and Ami, trying to pull them close to him. As he did this he burst into tears and began to sigh, his breathing becoming heavier with each tear.

Bal and Ami held on to his arm. 'Baba, it's going to be OK soon' they said, and he turned to them and replied 'I'm so sorry that your dad's gone and that my daughter and you are grieving.'

Dee moved away from Dilly's shoulders and looked at my dad. 'I know you loved him' she said. His tears continued to fall. She then looked at me with tearful eyes and cried, saying 'I still want to see the photos of him, I just want to see them. I need to know that it's him.'

What could I say? My inner being was still shaken with the knowledge of how this daunting demand would cause an incredible pain to her. I felt this would be the straw that would break the camel's back, because my own mind was disturbed by the photos. I wished that there was a photo that could have shown Parmjit as he had been, so that she would have at least had some comfort to reassure her own mind.

As I was trying to think what to say, Bal spoke. 'I also want to see the photos of my dad, I saw Chacha when he died, and I want to see them' he said. He sat still shaking his head in utter disbelief.

Bal was desperate to see the photographs of his father. I believe he wanted this for his own peace of mind, to be reassured that it was his father. His view was absolutely right. Yet I knew it would not really give him peace of mind, rather it would haunt him, as Detective Constable Warrington had said. After seeing the photographs, I knew I felt no peace, rather more despair.

I told them what Detective Constable Warrington had said. 'At this moment I would have to agree with his position that it would not be in your best interests to see the photographs because it will cause you considerable distress' I said. It was so awful to say this, as I thought I had no right to do so. Yet I battled with the need to protect them, knowing that what I had seen was something I needed to be protected from. Their deep and agonising longing to know was understandable.

In looking at the deepness of their pain all I could say was, 'We all need to talk about this in more detail. However ultimately you will have to make the decision, in which we will support you. Yet I would be irresponsible if I didn't warn you how horrific it will be.'

Throughout the entire discussion my parents were hardly able to speak. They were rooted in their seats. My father appeared to be in a trance, staring at the floor. My mother just wept. She was speaking under her breath, holding a scarf close to her mouth. 'Why is all this happening again to us?' she asked. She turned to Dee. 'Give me all your pain' she said. Dee responded 'Mom, this is all our pain' and wept.

An hour or so had elapsed and the discussion was at an end. Words now had very little meaning, as our silence revealed the despair. Quietly we hugged each other and started to leave.

After everyone had left I felt physically drained by the entire day. Emotionally I was still contending with all the information that had been shared by Detective Constable Warrington. Combined with this was the awareness of the far-reaching effect it was all having upon my family and myself. This was evident from my family's earlier discussion, as their understandable and justifiable anger was surfacing with regard to the errors made by the police. Once the numbness and shock wore off, I felt that we would be able to see that we had been given closure - unwelcome as it was.

My tired eyes welled up again as I tried to think about the forthcoming days up until the coroner's inquest, which would officially conclude what we now knew - Parmjit was dead.

What else could be done?

The next morning I rose early to prepare myself for work, which was unusual in that I didn't usually work on Fridays. The reason I attended on this day was that I was responsible for the arrangement of a meeting which would take most of the day with regard to the adoption of two young children. This was on my mind, as were Dee and the lads, and I also knew that almost a year had elapsed since Gurjit had died. It was very difficult to embrace what they were experiencing, but it was the only way I knew of responding to them. I also knew that I needed support.

During breaks that day, I thought about Parmjit and about how my family was going to have to face the reality of death again. Overall the day went very quickly, and I certainly appreciated that.

When it was almost over I received a call on my mobile phone from Detective Constable Warrington. He said 'I've reviewed all the files again and I'm still unable to locate any details of any report filed for December 2001 or January 2002. The only report I have found was when Parmjit's wife contacted us in July 2002 asking for an update. Yet even at that stage there was no missing person report. I have to acknowledge that the fact that she had enquired about an update was an indication that she had reported Parmjit as a missing person a lot earlier.'

'My sister is so distressed about this because it is clear that she had reported Parmjit as missing a lot earlier than July 2002 and such reports went unattended to,' I replied. He responded by saying 'I have no doubt at all that she did. Unfortunately I can't find any report and I'm annoyed about this and very sorry that she has been let down. I can only imagine that this is a very difficult time for her to cope with knowing her husband has died, and on top of that we made so many blunders in following procedures in relation to a missing person.'

I sensed his frustration in not being able to assist us any further.

'Listen' he said 'I'm more than willing to continue to look into this in further detail because I want to know what went wrong in relation to the missing reports.'

'Well I'll have to speak to my sister about this and get back to you about what she feels needs to be done,' I replied.

'Once again I'm so sorry about this, because it's not good that your entire family has been let down by us and it's unacceptable. I'd more than agree if Parmjit's wife placed a formal complaint against us.'

'That will be something for my sister to consider' I said. 'Either way I'll get back to you later on today or after the weekend.'

I rang Dee. The fact that no report could be found by Detective Constable Warrington would only compound her grief. I told her what he had told me, to which she said 'I know I reported him missing in December 2001 and January 2002 and I'm just angry because it's as though they think I didn't.'

Listening to her grief was a haunting reminder of how feelings can always remain and cause severe despair when you are caught up in thinking you are somehow at fault, or could have done something to bring a different outcome. The reality was that comfort was needed. I reminded Dee that we as a family knew that she had reported Parmjit missing earlier than the police had recorded. I said 'Detective Constable Warrington has acknowledged this, but unfortunately he can't find any reports. Think what you want to do about this and we can then contact him in a few days.'

I could not stop myself from thinking about her torment and how tired she must be, battling with her emotions. I felt deeply for her, knowing that this was leading to her having to accept that the police had been unable to locate such information, or challenge the reasons why they could not. Trying to make sense of it was like being in a tug of war. Just as I thought there would be some information, it was dashed.

When I arrived home I went to see Dee. She remained distraught about the police errors. As we sat and spoke about the conversation we had had earlier she said 'I need some time to think about what I want the police to do. But I know no matter what they do now it will never change the fact that we never had the chance to give Parmjit a funeral.'

'Take your time' I responded. I felt for her having to ponder on this over the weekend, knowing that within two days it would be a year since Gurjit's death. My thoughts and prayers were for her.

CHAPTER 5

ONE YEAR ON

SUNDAY 25TH JANUARY 2004

The Sunday arrived quickly and while we were all still in the process of understanding the reality of Parmjit's death, the head-on reality that Gurjit had died one year ago to the day was staring us in the face.

Time had flown by, and it was as though we had come full circle upon ourselves. It felt very strange, because I believed we had explored the impact upon us of his death in a real way, as our love, care and concern for each other were the foundations from which we continued to build our relationships. These relationships were going to help and support us in visiting the crematorium, where a plaque had been placed in memory of Gurjit.

Baljinder was unable to come with us, as in the early hours of that morning she was going on a school trip to France. Initially she had wanted to cancel the trip when the dates had been confirmed, but she felt that no matter where she was on that day thoughts of her father would remain forever.

Before we went to the crematorium we spoke about how everything about Gurjit's death could be recalled, every word spoken, every interaction that took place and each minute corresponded with each minute of the year before. It felt as though time had been stopped to allow us all a few moments to look safely back at Gurjit's death. We talked about what the difficulties had been as well as what developments had taken place.

Chapter Five

As we arrived, an amazing sense of peace was present. It was difficult to describe, yet it was certainly calming. We approached Gurjit's plaque and placed flowers and a card, and a few minutes of silence were observed. Though it appeared that there was very little we could say, we offered each other comfort through acknowledging how difficult this was. All our tears were unified in silence as they streamed down our faces.

As we stood there I read Baljinder's and Suki's card to their father which Suki had tied to the flowers. The message was full of their dear love and longing for him.

Looking at Suki who was so moved, I thought how tough and incredibly inspirational she was. I thought how amazing it was that such a young child could face such an immense experience so well. Along with Baljinder, Bal and Ami she deserved our uttermost respect and consideration.

Looking around and seeing Dilly's face full of her everlasting love for her husband spoke volumes of hope, because I felt strength that we had responded to an entire year of contending with the pain of death and holding on to the love and faith we professed. I knew deep down that the foundations of love, faith and hope would enable us to respond to the knowledge of Parmjit's death, even though we were initially experiencing the distress of such reality.

Dee's face reflected her agony for the loss of her husband and brother. Her tears formed a stream down her face. The lads stood by her shoulder to shoulder and simultaneously looked towards the sky as their tears flowed. They then embraced their mother and Suki joined them. Their profound pain was felt, yet so was their deep well of love.

Jai and I stood close by. When we turned towards each other our eyes connected and reflected the tragedy we as a family had endured. No words could be uttered by us; rather we just embraced.

As we continued to wait, Suki spoke. It was a reminder of Gurjit in many ways as she said 'I bet you Dad misses going to the pub on Saturdays.' We all gently laughed, knowing that for Gurjit it was his one evening of peace from Dilly, as he would often tell us all.

Suki's humour was actually supportive as we all began to think of funny memories of Gurjit. This certainly made being at the crematorium a little less distressing.

After a while we left and I reflected upon what we had experienced as a family, firstly, the deepest pain caused by death and secondly, our love and longing hope within our relationships. This was cemented by the thought of the impression Parmjit and Gurjit had left in us; this I believed contributed towards sustaining us, because we had the knowledge of who they were deep in our memory. That long-standing memory also meant living with the pain of them not being with us.

With the weekend drawing to an end, speaking to Dee about what she wanted to do about the police investigation, she said 'Even though Detective Constable Warrington is willing to continue to try and find out what went wrong, I do not see what purpose it would serve, as Parmjit is not coming back. I don't think they will come out with anything different, and I don't want to keep thinking about their mistakes. It's best to let that part go.'

Gently smiling at her, I said 'What you've just said has been incredibly brave because it has been so difficult knowing all that we know. But we'll definitely write to the police after the coroner's inquest.'

Dee replied 'I don't want to think about the police, I want to think about Parmjit. I can't keep thinking about what the police did wrong because it's too much to cope with on top of knowing Parmjit has died.'

She rubbed away the tears which were slowly rolling down her face. Her body was physically shaken by the loud cries that began to surface.

'This is going to take time because we all loved him, and I know you loved him in spite of his imperfections and difficulties. That's what love does' I said, embracing her. With her head on my chest Dee's sobbing continued. I knew she was battling with the enormity of her loss. This was a time for her emotions to speak.

After about twenty minutes of silence apart from her sobs, I said 'Do you want to contact Detective Constable Warrington and tell him your views, or do you want me to?' She replied 'Can you please?' 'Of course,' I said.

The doorbell rang, and Dilly walked in. The moment she walked in she hugged Dee and they both started crying. I left them, knowing that they were consoling each other, while trying to prepare my mind to respond to such loss.

As I walked home I thought 'What a day'. Memories of Parmjit and Gurjit were pouring over me. Yet it was emotionally exhausting because tied in with such memories were thoughts of Dee and the lads and Dilly and the girls.

I woke up with the same thoughts before phoning Detective Constable Warrington and relaying Dee's position to him. I said 'As a family, and I do believe you understand, we are very annoyed by the previous police investigations which were lacking in any sort of efficiency. At the same time we appreciate that through your own investigation there have been no attempts to minimise the errors made by the police.'

'I do fully understand' he said. 'I'm very sorry for what has taken place and I'm also very concerned that the information Parmjit's wife gave wasn't recorded. Much as I'd like to find those reports, I don't think I ever will. This is unacceptable, because as Parmjit's family you deserve to know that.'

I said 'Once again, thank you for your assistance and support at this time. My sister wants to try and move away from this in order to begin to come to terms with her husband's death.'

After the call ended I felt great admiration for Dee's capacity to try to focus on Parmjit and not on the police. I felt that her strength to face such loss knowing that her relationship with Parmjit had been difficult for a number of years was a credit to her deep commitment and love for him and respect for his life.

It was now all about waiting. Within a few days the coroner's assistant, Mr Harris, contacted me - he was the same gentleman who had spoken to me when Gurjit had died. He told me that the inquest would be held at the end of April. My first thought was 'Oh no – such a long wait!' I said to him 'I appreciate the demands on your time, but is there any possibility of bringing that forward, considering how long my family have waited?' He replied 'I'll see what I can do'.

Fortunately we did not have to wait that long. A few days later he contacted me to tell me that the inquest would be held at the end of February. Even though this was nearly a month away, it was better than having to wait three months.

Thus the month was spent in continuing to explore Gurjit's death, because it was clear that even a year was not long enough to be able to fully express the pain and turmoil experienced, as well as encounter the love and hope within us. I was not going to rush this for myself, or think that such effects were no longer significant. For I knew how deep-seated the trauma was. Pretending it was not was not a sensible option. Every one of us was encouraged to realise this, so we didn't feel as though we just had to 'move on'.

The month was also spent in preparing our minds for the inquest and grappling with the reality of Parmjit's death. The main focus of discussions with Dee and the lads centred on viewing the photographs of Parmjit and dealing with the emotional effects of not having been able to arrange his funeral. This I felt would require a lot more time to come to terms with.

Ami did not want to view the photographs of his dad. He told us 'I'm struggling with the idea that this will remind me how I saw Chacha lying on the life support machine. It took me some time to get over that, and I don't want to have to experience this again by looking at pictures of my dad's body.'

Bal said 'My mind is battling, because a part of me wants to see the pictures to reassure myself that it actually is my dad, but the evidence looks clear, so I don't know how it would help me if I saw the photos.'

Dee on the other hand wanted to view the pictures, for 'peace of mind' as she wanted to make sure in her mind that it really was Parmjit. Her position was fully understandable, but Dee did not realise how graphic the photos were, and how much distress they would cause her. The images were not something that could be seen and then put out of the mind. I knew that they continued to torment me, and it was burdensome.

Of course they all had every right to see the photographs, but my heart couldn't bear the shocking pain this would, without a shadow of doubt, cause them. My conscience kept prompting me to ensure they did not have to face another profound wound. So it was good to hear Ami say to them 'Listen, I know why you want to see the photos. I had the same reason, for confirmation. I can't stop you, but please think about how it will really help, because I don't want to see you more hurt than you already are. I believe what Mama said, that the photos are horrific. I don't want to put my mind through that. I really hope you don't have to, because I know that will also affect me. Please just think about it a bit more.'

Ami's words echoed his love for his mother and brother and his desire to not see them having to face more pain.

After a lengthy discussion, Dee and Bal decided not to view the photos. However Dee did want to see one photo of Parmjit's hand which showed a distinct tattoo, and we all considered that would be appropriate.

We talked again about how we all felt knowing that Parmjit had died alone, how distressing it was to begin to accept that, and how it was made even more difficult by the fact that none of us had seen his body.

Dee said 'It's still difficult to accept that they cremated Parmjit without us. It's horrible to think about that. I wish we could turn back the clock so that we could have been there. But I know we can't change that, and this is the pain I know we are living with.'

Her face contorted as her heartfelt emotions were expressed, her eyes reflecting her deep compassion. Composing herself, she said 'We've spent over a year talking about the effects of Gurjit's death upon us all, especially supporting Dilly and the girls. This is helping me to face Parmjit's death.'

Bal interjected 'there's no real point thinking about what we could have done differently, because for me it only makes me feel anger towards the police. I don't want to feel this anger, I want to remember Dad and think about his life. I know he wasn't always there for us, but that doesn't change my love for him. All I can think about is that we honoured Chacha in preparing his body for the funeral, and that's what I also wanted to do for my dad.'

'Mom, Bal, what you've just said is what I want to say' said Ami. 'I feel good to know we can talk about this and not be afraid.'

Their words were incredibly powerful and sent shivers down my spine. They revealed tremendous resolve in the face of adverse circumstances.

CHAPTER 6

AN INQUEST WITHOUT A BODY

FRIDAY 27TH FEBRUARY 2004

The day had arrived for the Coroner's Inquest, which was held at West Bromwich Town Hall. Dee, Bal, Ami, Dilly, Jai and I attended, and when we arrived we were taken to a large room where the inquest was to be held. The room had tables set out in a box shape and I recall how cold it felt as we silently waited.

Then Detective Constable Warrington came into the room and I introduced him to everyone. He shook everyone's hand. Turning to Dee and the lads he said 'I wish to express my sincerest condolences to you as a family. I am really sorry for the errors we made and our failure to identify Parmjit earlier.'

Dee and the lads just looked at him and nodded. Understandably, they were unable to convey any message back to him. It was not a surprise, because their faces reflected an intense and deep sadness. This was their grief.

Within a few seconds of his entrance, Mr Harris, the Coroner's Assistant, walked into the room and spoke to us. He said 'The Coroner will reopen the inquest and hear evidence from the police, and then conclude the inquest, after which he will respond to the questions he knows you have for him. Can I please ask you all to rise when the coroner enters the room? This is not for the coroner, rather as a sign of respect for Parmjit as we are here for him.'

Chapter Six

During his brief speech, he maintained eye contact with Dee and the lads. I believe he was trying to convey empathy for what they were feeling in an unfamiliar setting. As he left the room we looked at each other, knowing that this was it. My throat began to go dry and my thoughts were struggling to construct a sentence in my mind as I sat inwardly trembling. This was compounded by knowing that we could feel each other's misery. My stomach was knotted with the tension and physically I felt weak with such dread.

There was total silence. Dee was shedding tears, but not outwardly crying, while Dilly and Jai were comforting her. The lads sat next to me and they kept their heads bowed and hands folded. Detective Constable Warrington also had his head bowed. I imagined it was going to be difficult for him to talk about the investigation, knowing that Dee and the lads were sitting opposite him.

As my mind was trying to focus upon the questions Dee and the lads wanted to ask, the Coroner, Mr Beaumont, entered the room and we all rose. He then bowed his head and said 'Please sit down. I will now begin these proceedings by saying that I opened an enquiry on the 11th January 2002 after an unidentified male had been discovered in a canal on the 28th December 2001. This enquiry was delayed as long as possible to enable the police to investigate his identity. As the police were unable to confirm the identity of the male the enquiry was concluded on the 9th October 2002, whereby I returned an open verdict on an unidentified male whose circumstances of death were not known. I am aware of the issues involved in the previous police investigation.' His facial expression displayed dissatisfaction.

He turned to Detective Constable Warrington. 'Can you please outline your investigation' he said. Detective Constable Warrington stood up and formally gave an oath. He spent about fifteen minutes outlining the previous police investigation, and the errors made. He then provided an overview of his investigation and the evidence that the body recovered was that of Parmjit.

Chapter Six

After giving his evidence he glanced across the table to Dee and the lads and said 'On behalf of the West Midlands Police I would like to again express my sincere and deepest apologies to Parmjit's family for all the errors that were made by our investigations.'

Dee bowed her head and started to cry in the arms of Dilly. The lads looked at him and nodded to acknowledge the apology.

The moment the evidence was given the Coroner began to draw his conclusions, saying 'The purpose of this inquiry has been to determine who has died, their particulars and how, when and where they met their death. The answers to those questions were not available at the first inquest and have become clear due to other enquiries made. I am satisfied that the person found in the canal was Mr Parmjit Singh Bal. The verdict I recorded at the first enquiry was an open verdict. This will not be altered as it cannot be concluded how Parmjit came to be in the canal.'

He then turned to me and said 'I know as a family that you would like to ask some questions and this time has been set aside for those questions.'

On behalf of Dee I said 'Parmjit's wife would like to know if his organs were also cremated', to which the Coroner said 'yes.' To many this may appear an unusual question to ask, but it was an important question for her because she needed peace of mind.

Bal asked him 'How hard was it for you as a coroner to authorise the cremation without formal identification of my father's body?'

Bal's question completely took Mr Beaumont by surprise as it seemed a role reversal; Bal was asking him how in effect he felt about the decision. He paused for a moment before saying 'I was conscious of the need to identify the body and for the family to undertake the role in all funeral arrangements. It was not an easy decision, and this is only the second time that I have had to make that decision in thirty years.'

Ami said 'Where are the clothes my father was wearing when he died?' 'I am sorry, but I do not know,' replied Mr Beaumont.

I then said 'These were the specific questions that we wanted to ask. I would like to thank you on behalf of my family.' The Coroner replied 'Thank you for attending and for your understanding.' He then stood up, as we did, and said 'the inquest has now been concluded and closed.'

A feeling of total emptiness reigned in me and I looked at Dee sobbing, while the lads were doing their best not to shed tears. However their distressed eyes spoke a million words. We were gently escorted to another room by Detective Constable Warrington, as he wanted to talk to us as well as show Jai the photographs of Parmjit.

Initially Jai and Detective Constable Warrington sat in the corner. I could tell that Jai was moved by the photographs, as he kept shaking his head, not as a sign of disbelief but as a sign of acknowledgement of how tragic Parmjit's death had been.

As this was taking place I stood next to Bal and Ami in utter silence. We needed time to think about the enormity of the reality of their father's death and the circumstances surrounding it. Dilly continued to comfort Dee as they sat huddled crying.

After Jai had seen the photos, Detective Constable Warrington then approached Dee, Bal, Ami and Dilly with the photograph that was taken of Parmjit's hand which had a tattoo of a Sikh religious symbol. The moment Dee saw it she broke down in tears, as she knew that it was Parmjit. Dilly mourned with her. Bal and Ami fought back their tears and sat holding the photograph. Bal was also shaking his head, while Ami was in a daze.

Jai came close to us and his body revealed how awful it had been to see the photographs. His eyes were filled with tears and his body was shaking as if he had just been in a battle. Indeed he had been, an emotional battle.

He spoke to Bal and Ami while I stood by and listened. 'Guys, it was right that no one else saw the photographs because they are not pleasant viewing' he said, and went to express to them how it had already affected him. 'It was difficult for me to see the photos of your dad, especially the one of him holding his hands together.'

They looked at Jai, and Ami said 'Thanks, Mama. It reinforces what I knew, which is that I'd struggle. I'm glad I made the decision not to see the photos.' Bal remained silent.

I approached Dee after she had looked at the photograph. She was crying her heart out as we comforted her. She said through a deluge of tears 'I'm glad that I did not see the rest of the photographs because I know now I would not have been able to sleep or get the images out of my head.' To which I responded 'You saw the one that mattered.'

Detective Constable Warrington, who was standing close by, then sat down by her and asked the lads to sit with him. He held Dee's hand and said 'I wish I could have turned the clock back and I wish that you could have exercised your right to have arranged Parmjit's funeral. I'm so sorry for what has happened, it should never have happened and I know this is incredibly difficult for you all.'

Bal replied 'Thank you for your honesty when you gave evidence and for acknowledging the mistakes made by the police.'

No more words could be said at that time and we rose to leave. Dilly and Ami walked on either side of Dee, holding her and comforting her as their tears fell like rain.

We travelled back home in silence, knowing Parmjit's death could now be confirmed with his family in India and immediate family, starting with my parents, Baljinder and Suki, who were waiting for us.

The moment we walked into my parents' house Baljinder and Suki clung to their aunt with tears falling, crying 'Massi, we're so sorry that Titha has gone.' Dilly began to comfort my mother. My father had his head clasped in his hands with tears running between his fingers. Baljinder and Suki embraced the lads and Bal said to them 'it's OK, we know we're in this together.' Ami said to them 'Don't worry now; we're going to get through this just as we have been.'

Jai began to summarise the coroner's inquest and the crying continued as the fullness of grief was now being expressed. Jai and I left the room, as Jai was preparing his mind to make the phone call to Parmjit's family in India, just as he had the year before when he had had to tell them that Gurjit had died.

When Jai got through he spoke to Parmjit's father and told him what had taken place, how the police were able to identify Parmjit's body and how the inquest had determined that all the evidence indicated that the body was that of Parmjit. Jai said to him 'The whole family is in shock and we want to express our condolences to you, because Parmjit was also our family and this was also our loss.' Jai repeated the information a number of times as he was also paying attention to what Parmjit's and Gurjit's father was saying.

When the call had ended, Jai turned round and said 'Parmjit's father doesn't believe that Parmjit has died. He told me he won't believe it. Parmjit's family are clearly in shock and disbelief that Parmjit and Gurjit have died in such a short time span. It's understandable to see how such pain has affected them. It's unfortunate that there is nothing we can do to provide them with any comfort at this time.'

'It's a shame, and it's hard to know that. I hope they'll find the strength and support to eventually face this' I replied.

After this we made a number of phone calls to family and friends, including our sister Patty, to inform them of the confirmation of Parmjit's death. We then went back into the lounge, where everyone continued to mourn. After a while our tears ceased, outwardly at least. Yet we continued to offer words of comfort to each other.

We moved on to talking about holding a religious memorial service for Parmjit, and Dee said 'At least this is something we can hold on to.' Once this had been explored, the discussion came to a natural ending and everyone began to leave. Jai and I remained with our parents to provide emotional support.

The rest of the day went really slowly, another emotionally exhausting day for us all. The strange feeling of knowing there was absolutely nothing we could do would immediately help to ease the pain. I began again to reflect upon Parmjit's life. Focusing upon his strengths was useful, as I began to see more about the man he had been. I wasn't ignoring his limitations, and felt that applied to us all.

It reminded me how much Parmjit had had to offer, as he had done so in the past. Though he had experienced many years of freedom from his alcohol addiction, it was unfortunate that at the time he had been unable to face the full effects on himself and his family. It was heartbreaking that he had rejected the support provided at the time that he needed it the most. Yet his alcohol addiction didn't change my love for him or my wish to see him whole and alive.

Upon further reflection I began to analyse what I could have done differently and whether I actually had done enough in the first place. I felt Dee was certainly asking herself this. I wished time could have been frozen to enable me to have responded in a way that could have brought about a different outcome for Parmjit. This was not going to happen, for I knew I did not control life.

With such thoughts going through my mind I must have fallen asleep, for when I awoke it was after 7 pm. I felt very tired as I went downstairs to see my parents. They were talking about their childhood and adult experiences of growing up in India. It was interesting to hear them, as I learned more about how they coped with loss from a very young age.

My father said 'It's always hard when someone you love dies, and it hurts so much when it's your child who goes before you. I've seen many things in my life, but nothing compares with this pain.' He began to cry. 'To see my daughters without their husbands and my grandchildren without their fathers is the worst thing I have seen in my life. I only wish I could take away the pain from their eyes' he said under a stream of tears.

My mother interjected 'No parent wants to see their child die and no child wants to see their parent die, but we will all go one day. I only wish I had gone before Parmjit and Gurjit so I didn't have to live with this pain.'

Though their faces were shrivelled with pain, their life experiences had helped them to respond to the difficulties they had endured. All I could say to them in return was 'It does hurt, and you're right about that. But you've also shown that hope does exist and this will help us all as a family to know that we will over time come to terms with their death.'

We sat there as the significance of our words began to sink in. Then I said 'I'm going to see Dee and the lads.' When I saw them, they looked remarkably calm, and not in denial; rather I sensed that they were preparing themselves to explore their loss.

I said 'How are you all feeling?' Dee responded first. 'I'm tired, but a part of me is glad that the waiting is over, because that caused so much hurt. I'm also glad that I didn't see the photos. The one I saw was enough for me to know that it was him and I know it's going to take a long time for me to deal with this.'

Her tears began to roll. 'I knew that it was Parmjit, and even though I hated what he had done because of his drinking, I knew that all I had left of him was the photo and most of my anger towards him started to disappear.'

'We now know that Dad has died and any thought of him being alive has gone' said Bal. 'We are going to have to pick ourselves up and get past this - it's like another hurdle in life which has come to test us. But I know we've had a year thinking about Chacha's death and this has helped me to start to think about Dad's death. I can't pretend it doesn't hurt because it does. I thought the police officer was compassionate and I could tell by his eyes that he was honest in his apology to us. I think that if it hadn't been for him we still wouldn't know Dad had died.'

In response I said 'Yes, it's going to take a lot of time, and we know that we will not rush this because we've been here before.'

Ami then said 'I thought the inquest was honesty summed up because we found out what we needed to know, that Dad has died, even though it's not something that is nice to find out. But I want to think about how to get through this, because at the moment my mind is battling with everything and I know this is not going to be sorted out straight away. I know we loved him and he loved us, but it was a shame that he found it hard to show that all the time. I keep thinking, if only things could have been different, but I know that won't really help me face the fact that he has died. It will just make me feel more pain.'

Bal and Ami comforted her. 'When we saw the photograph of Dad's hand we knew it was him' said Bal. 'It was hard to know that he faced death alone and it's difficult to think what his last thoughts were.'

We continued to offer words of comfort and I remained sensitive to the fact that they needed time alone to continue to explore their relationship with Parmjit. They were left contemplating the arrangements for Parmjit's memorial service.

* * * * * * * * * *

On Monday 1st March 2004 I received a phone call from Baljinder, speaking so fast that I never caught a single word. At first my heart sank, wondering what had happened. I asked her to slow down and repeat what she was saying.

'My friend saw a newspaper article about the inquest' she said. 'She doesn't know it's about us. She just told me because she said she felt sorry for whoever the family was. Mama, I couldn't tell her that he was my uncle, I felt frightened.'

I replied 'don't worry, I'll speak to Dee and let her know and hopefully we'll be able to get a copy from the publishers.' After speaking to Dee, she made enquiries about the article and the local newspaper sent her a copy. The article explained that Parmjit had been identified, though they had spelled his name incorrectly. The article also specified the failings in the identification process by the police as well as outlining the outcome of the inquest.

For the family, we would have wanted Parmjit's name to have been spelled correctly. Of course it was too late. Putting that aside, the article recorded what had caused the difficulties in identifying Parmjit due to the police investigations. This was not interpreted as a justification for us as a family, rather a confirmation about how the police and authorities were being transparent about their actions.

CHAPTER 7

PARMJIT'S MEMORIAL

SUNDAY 7TH MARCH 2004 TO
SUNDAY 14TH MARCH 2004

Dee and Jai had spoken to the Gurdwara priests with regard to arranging the Sikh religious memorial ceremony. They had explained the circumstances surrounding Parmjit's death. The priests were sensitive to this, as they knew the ceremony would be undertaken without the formal funeral process.

When the first day of the ceremony commenced, my father didn't want to attend. He told us was 'I can't bear the thought of having lost another child. It's too hard to accept this.' I felt his words revealed the emotional longing for healing against the unsearchable depths of pain we as a family had experienced.

Bal approached him and said 'Baba, we need you to be there,' to which he looked at Bal and immediately stood up and began to make his way to Parmjit's house. As it was only the immediate family at the opening ceremony, we all used this time to reflect upon Parmjit's life and reinforce our love, care and support for each other.

Considering the ceremony was going to take place over a seven-day period, all we could do was prepare our minds the best way we could for the final day. However the knowledge that Parmjit had already been cremated was a thorn in our flesh, because it was difficult to reconcile how we could say goodbye. I knew that Dee was finding this very hard to face, which was understandable, because her right to have at least held him had been taken away.

This was made very clear to me when Dilly said 'It's horrible to think what Dee's going through without seeing Parmjit's body. I don't know how I'd cope with that. When Gurjit died I didn't want to let him go at the funeral and I remember Dee holding me and reminding me that Gurjit was in my heart. I want to give her the same comfort she gave me.'

I replied to her 'You know what it means, and Dee knows that. I believe you're more than able to provide the comfort and support she needs at this time.'

Difficult and despairing as it all was, I knew deep down that we would rise up by the grace of God, for I knew this was the real and true strength that we required. Having experienced this for over a year in learning to respond to Gurjit's death, I found it more relevant.

The final day of the memorial service came and we congregated in what had been Parmjit's bedroom. My mother's cries could be heard above all, while Dee attempted to weep silently and Dilly and Mangender offered all the moral support they could muster. Jai and I remained still with our father as he struggled to cope with the deep wounds in his heart. I felt totally numb, which was a strange feeling to have as I knew Parmjit had died. My mind was trying to understand this.

When Bal, as Parmjit's eldest son, carried the religious book which was to be transported to the Gurdwara, I realised that this was the final stage of mourning. My tears for Parmjit and for Dee and the lads began to slowly trickle down my face. Dee's face became very subdued and her profound brokenness struck at the core of who she was and who we were as a family.

She crouched with her hands over her face as the ceremony was coming to an end. It felt as though she didn't want to see the role her eldest son was to perform, knowing it represented the final end of life of her husband.

My father, between Jai and me, leaned on Jai and his heavy

breathing reflected the heaviness in his heart. Ami remained with Baljinder and Suki, offering them comfort as they cried. Ami's eyes remained water-filled as he kept looking towards the ceiling as if he was searching the heavens.

The part of the ceremony within the home had ended. It was to be completed in the Gurdwara, which was only a short walk away. We waited silently for Bal to arrive. When he came through the main doors he seemed to have the weight of the world on his shoulders. He did his best to display courage, as the task he was undertaking was emotionally demanding, for he was signifying his father's life.

I sensed that Bal was trying to avoid eye contact with Dee, because only a slight glance towards her resulted in his body shaking under the reality of what was taking place.

Bal made his way into the hall and proceeded to place the religious book safely into its designated place. We followed close by. After making our way into the main hall of the Gurdwara we sat quietly as the final part of the service was being read.

Bal and Ami had a number of close friends in attendance. It was incredible to see these young men offering support and comfort to Bal and Ami as they endured their father's death. Each of their friends showed so much respect, and their presence was empathetic.

Our silence continued as the religious ceremony came to an end and we all stood to pay our final respects. In glancing at Dee, Bal and Ami, my heart bled, seeing them having to face this immeasurable grievous blow.

When the service came to an end a meal was served to everyone, representing Parmjit's final act of love, just as it had been at Gurjit's funeral. The same feeling of not wanting to eat was present, yet as before, we had to honour Parmjit, so I ate. As the day closed we spent the time reflecting upon the intense, difficult, and traumatic experiences we had faced and the love, hope and comfort we had to support each other.

Chapter Seven

In October 2004 Dee and Ami took Parmjit's ashes to India to be released, as this was the final part of the practical journey.

* * * * * * * * * *

In dealing with death the realisation soon comes that it is an extremely traumatic event and remains foremost in the mind for a long time. However it does not have to control your mind or your life. Exploring this means there has to be practical, emotional and spiritual support to help you begin to respond to the void that death creates.

For me it has been important to look at what was said, and as a result what was done, to ensure that support continues, and more importantly to identify how the long-term effects of death can be responded to. The following section seeks to outline what was discussed and what was learned in context with this and the previous chapter.

I hope your own discussions and learning in relation to the trauma of death will continue to keep you secure in your relationships.

PART 3

DISCUSSIONS FOR LEARNING & DEVELOPMENT

It may seem strange to include a section on learning and development in a book which tells a very personal story about death and bereavement. Yet the reality for my family and me was that we could no longer function in the way we had done in the past after the deaths of Parmjit and Gurjit. The traumas we experienced meant changes had already taken place, because two significant family members were no longer alive.

Through reflection on the influence this had had upon us, we needed to truthfully explore and identify what we had begun to learn, and how this had impacted upon our development as a family. Consequently we experienced a great deal which I believe many other families could learn from.

At the outset I asked, 'What could we possibly learn as a family? How would we be able to respond?' These questions could not be ignored, but needed to be embraced. Such questions, and many more, revealed that by engaging in a process we created an environment to discuss the pain. When I began to explore aspects of this in detail, this is part of what I learned:

Pain is an intense and overwhelming phenomenon which affects our emotional, rational, physical and spiritual existence because the event experienced seeks to test or erode the very foundations that are intended to sustain us. Yet the pain reveals something more powerful than itself - it will ultimately unveil love. We have to believe that.

Writing about such experiences was intended to look at the learning and development that had been gained with regard to the impact death had upon our emotions, thoughts, beliefs and relationships. Hence this is an overview of the discussions that took place within my family during 2003 and 2005. Such discussions were explored through developing a 'Family Development Support Structure' (FDSS), whereby the impact of the trauma of death that we experienced as a family was faced. The support plan was not intended to result in a complete 'recovery' from death, because we learned to understand that such issues would arise at different stages throughout our lives.

(Please refer to the Appendix Section for the full document. This can be adapted, if you consider it relevant, to your own personal circumstances).

Before writing this book I had already began to write poetry (or what I call 'reflective extracts'), not something I would ever have dreamed of doing before. At the point of writing such reflective extracts I realised that the floodgates of my emotions were being released because, it involved exploring and asking questions about:

- the despair of death;
- the pain of seeing my family's pain;
- my capacity to respond to them, let alone myself; and
- God and my belief in God.

The above had been locked inside me and it took about eighteen months to fully grasp the issues that had remained deep within me. I know writing down my thoughts and feelings was an important way of releasing the emotions and exploring my questions about separation, loss, relationships, death and God.

I believe writing such reflective extracts enabled me to take the step of writing about death, even though writing about my family's experiences was not something I had initially thought of doing. Yet there was the realisation that such an experience could possibly be captured in part by writing about the exploration of pain and hope, through knowing that support can be present.

However, to be truthful, my initial thoughts about writing this book centred upon determining:

- What is the point of writing?
- Do I know what I am actually talking about?
- Will any of this make any sense, and if so for whom?
- This then set the challenge, 'what is the real motive and purpose of writing?'
- Is it to share my experiences?
- Is it for my family?
- Is it in memory of Parmjit and Gurjit?
- Is it for my own needs?
- Is it to enable others to look at their own experiences?

The reality is that it has been a combination of all of the above. Therefore the following is my perspective of the learning that has been gained through personal experiences of death and trauma. Thus you may agree or disagree with many views, and it may or may not relate to you and your experiences, because these will be unique to you. Furthermore, it may not even make sense. The reason for this is because it has been my family's learning and I do not want to impose this on anyone. However I believe that when death takes place there will be a battle between our emotions and thoughts, which I consider will eventually lead us to face three main areas about death:

- First, our knowledge about the trauma (the event – 'what happened?')

- Second, our beliefs about our emotions and thoughts (the effects – 'What does this mean?')

- Third, our understanding about what we must do (the action – 'what do we do to respond?')

I consider that we may face similar patterns when death is explored. Therefore I will take the liberty (where appropriate) of using the important words 'we', 'us' and 'our' to represent that we can all still learn. This does not mean that I am presuming to know what others have experienced or thought. But I do believe that there are several factors which can contribute towards our development and sustain us in how to respond to life's opportunities and traumas.

I will look at such factors within this section as follows:

In Chapter 1, I will look at the impact of death in relation to the pain and despair that this caused my family.

In Chapter 2 I will look at how we can acknowledge the reality of death and the impact it has by knowing that love, relationships and support can respond to the pain experienced through ensuring that we grieve.

In Chapter 3 I will look at how important our beliefs are in understanding the truth of our own vulnerability.

Some areas will overlap, because that is the reality of our experiences; death cannot be placed in a package, nor can it be explored in isolation from all the other issues we face.

CHAPTER 1

DEATH: THE IMPACT OF DESPAIR

There is no doubt that when the death of a loved one takes place it is a shock to the system. It shakes everything up and turns it inside out.

For my family this is what death initially meant to them:

'All I wanted was to be with Gurjit, I didn't want to live without him. I just wanted someone to tell me that he hadn't died and that it was a bad dream. But every time I hoped for that, the pain in my stomach and mind wouldn't go away. I didn't want to accept he had died because it was my way of still hanging on to him.' (Dilly)

'Death really hurts you inside, it just causes so much pain and I know this is because I loved my Dad.' (Baljinder)

'I know my dad is not coming back.' (Suki)

'One day Gurjit was here and the next day God had taken him. The last time we saw him alive was the Wednesday before he died. When he was with us he just remained quiet and we had a feeling that something was not right, and when he left after dinner for the first time he never turned around to say goodbye. He just put his hand up and all we saw was the back of his head. It was as though he knew that he was not going to see us again and we wish we just called him back. The pain and hurt is so real.' (My parents)

'Even though we know he struggled with alcohol, we know he loved us a lot and did have respect for us... it hurts to know that we were not there for him when he died. We are stuck, because we do not know what we want to say besides we know that this has been very difficult for us all.' (My parents)

Chapter One

'When Gurjit died I couldn't believe it happened, I just kept thinking this isn't really happening because I didn't want him to die because I knew how much it was hurting Dilly and the girls. Deep inside it was difficult to accept he had died. When I found out that Parmjit had already died I was totally numb as I was still trying to accept that Gurjit had died. I just felt empty, but the pain really hit me hard because I knew I'd have to talk about what I was feeling, but it was so difficult because I didn't always understand what I was feeling.' (Dee)

'You've got no control, except perhaps limited control, besides prayer which may not change the event but can help you in responding.' (Bal)

'They've died and are not coming back.' (Ami)

'I felt so hurt because I knew everyone else was so hurt and I couldn't do anything straight away to help them because I couldn't believe that Gurjit had died. I couldn't really think much because the hurt was so deep and it was really hurting me. When we found out about Parmjit I felt so sad to think that we never got the chance to see him, and I felt so sorry for Dee and the lads because it was so rough.' (Jai)

Their responses revealed hurt, and that is what shock can do. This is because various emotions arise and there is very little we can do to contain them, as they become a constant feature for a considerable time. This is because the significance of our loss from the outset brings despair which appears unstoppable as we are grasping with the reality of death.

Therefore the pain becomes relevant, because the difficulty of knowing we feel we cannot get over the person's death is due to the understanding that a relationship and experience existed which is still alive - which it is, because it exists in the mind.

For my family this meant:

'There are loads of adjustment to get on with... it's bad enough we lost Dad, that was pain, but when I think about this it is more pain... but I know my dad did not leave me because he left something with me - he did not leave me, he died.' (Baljinder)

Chapter One

'If I get stopped telling people what I feel, I won't cope with it... taking support from family and friends has been a great comfort as it has helped me to talk to others and listen to what other people have had to say.' (Suki)

In talking to them further about their father's death Baljinder said: 'Our father's death will always be there, because it is part of our life and we will need to learn to cope with this. We know Dad is not coming back but we believe he would want us to get on with our life and to remember him in our hearts and minds.'

Their statements revealed how their relationship with their father was a central focus in enabling them to come to terms with his death. As Baljinder said, 'When my father passed away he came more into my life mentally.'

Thus in looking at their experiences in detail they began to recognise that their experience had been hard to understand with regard to what it meant for them. Baljinder summed this up through her reflection of the loss experienced: 'I'm not finding it difficult to talk about my dad's death; the difficult part is trying to understand my own feelings and thoughts.'

'So much of my life centred around what I did with Gurjit, so it's hard to get used to doing things on my own because when he was here I'd always have someone to talk to before making big decisions, now I have to learn to make them on my own. When days pass by I slowly learn to accept he's never coming back and no matter what I can't change that, but I can begin to take small steps to manage his death.' (Dilly)

'Because it's something you don't really think about it is very hard to cope with because when they're gone, you are left picking up the pieces to somehow trying to get on with your life. But I know it's very difficult for me and everyone else and it's going to take a long time before the pain goes away.' (Dee)

'Losing two sons is not easy to accept, because we still believe that a parent shouldn't really see a child's death. We keep thinking about them daily and keep wandering how life would be with them, but it really hurts because we know

they're not coming back to us.' (My parents)

'It's so hard to imagine how life will be without my dad and Chacha. I never thought that two people whom I loved would go so quickly, so it's hard to try and get on with life, but we've got no choice. I know there are going to be more challenges and bereavements in life, but I also know there are going to be plenty of goodness that we as a family will experience - that's the way I see it at the moment.' (Bal)

'It's difficult to try and put things into words because I know it's going to be hard to try and get used to not having my dad and Chacha here. It's also hard knowing I've got to get on with life at the same time, but it's so difficult to understand how to do that. What is important is believing we can support each other.' (Ami)

'Knowing I still have to get up every day and do all the things I have to doesn't bring me any comfort because I know Parmjit and Gurjit will no longer be part of our lives.' (Jai)

If we do not express the emotions and the thoughts that have arisen due to death, then seeking to adjust will become a difficult process as the pain will remain hidden. This pain has to be faced. Understanding the reality of this is about recognising that we will have to go into the depths of despair before we are able to talk about the despair we feel.

For my family and me, such distress involved knowing that it was Parmjit and Gurjit who faced death, while it was us as a family who had to experience the effects (distress) of death. Initially when their death took place it happened so fast it appeared to have left understanding trailing. Yet it was:

- the understanding of the relationship we had;
- the understanding of the experiences gained; and
- the understanding of the demonstration of love within us that enabled us to explore their death and our relationships.

The understanding of death we gained was about knowing that we could not control it, because we recognised death would always be there as part of our experience of life. Learning to acknowledge this was about knowing that support existed and that we were able to remember Parmjit and Gurjit without feeling afraid. We could remember because it was the life within us and around us that was the greatest influence to draw my family closer together.

Yet the drawing together was again about the realisation that our pain had to be identified, then explored and then safely expressed in a way that did not create withdrawal from each other. Therefore we asked ourselves 'what is the pain?' :

- Is it the loss of not being able to talk to Parmjit and Gurjit again?
- Is it the separation of the relationship?
- Is it about facing up to people?
- Is it about facing the details and circumstances of death?
- Is it about questioning our ability to manage and to respond to others, and our capacity to maintain future relationships?

In reality it would have been all the factors mentioned above, and many more. Just looking at the questions creates an intensity of pain in itself, because I believe our pain will always find us out. The questions that need to be answered at that point are 'What will we do?' and 'Who will we do it for?'

Thus the presenting issues centre upon:

- How can we fully understand and then acknowledge death?
- How can we learn what needs to be done and what responses are required?
- How can we identify that the loss will impact upon all interactions and relationships?

Chapter One

- How can we attend to the pain and trauma of knowing a loved one has died and is not coming back? How do we live with this truth?
- How have we considered the impact death has had upon others and ourselves?

As a result of the above it is extremely important as well as powerful and wise that when this exploring is done it is undertaken with family, friends or someone outside our support networks, eg a counsellor, rather than on our own. This is because it can help us to face the pain that the emotions and thoughts will raise.

For my family, we looked at such pain and the impact death had upon their emotions, thoughts and behaviour:

'My behaviour needed to change because I was always being moody, and felt that I needed to grow up, so I did a lot more reading, as I knew that healing would take time. My thoughts were what could I have done differently to have prevented his death, and I felt sad thinking about what Parmjit must have been thinking on his last day. Overall this has taught me to think about death and how I can grieve and I know that I can get support. I know I have had the opportunity to talk to people and need to continue when I need to.' (Dee)

'At first I told myself not to love anyone so much again in case they die. My view has changed since, because you can't stop death no matter how much you love a person. I still love Gurjit and at times have felt lost without him being here. At times some of my memory of Gurjit doesn't come quickly and this hurts because it has felt at times that he never existed.' (Dilly)

'My behaviour, thoughts and feelings have changed. I look at other family members first before I show my feelings. At first I had put my feelings to one side because I sat and felt and heard another's pain, which was hard. When I look back at the time death took place it was like being knocked for six with a cricket bat, because it was a big loss and my emotions took over straight away and it was as though my mind switched off. Now I feel more prepared and switched on and know what I have to do, because it just makes you alert not just about death but about everything else that you become involved in.' (Bal)

Chapter One

'I would say the family have been the positive influence on my behaviour, because we were in it together and we stuck together through it.' (Ami)

'My behaviour has not been affected. I was never going to let Dad's death change my behaviour at all. I wanted to remain the same person as I was before Dad's death. My feelings at first were nothing! I could not feel a thing because I was in shock, but then about a year later I started to feel more. I felt pain, a lot of pain. My thoughts after Dad's death were to be careful of those around me and to treasure precious moments, and it began to make me think about being prepared for the day Mom goes and how I would look after Suki.' (Baljinder)

'The impact on my behaviour has been very hard because, with no one telling me I tried to mature a lot faster for Mom. So I'm a lot more mature than I would have been. My thoughts are still the same but I get missing pieces, I always think 'what if they were here today?' My feelings are a lot more emotional because I always remember I've got only one parent now so I need to make sure she is OK and that nothing happens to her, because I don't know where I would be or what I would do without Mom.' (Suki)

Furthermore, with Dee, Bal and Ami we looked at the specific circumstances surrounding Parmjit's death and the pain caused by how they sought to explore it. They considered that their response to Parmjit's death would be completely different from that of Gurjit. This was because of the knowledge that their relationship with Parmjit was affected by his difficulties with alcohol misuse and his leaving the family home. As they said, 'our separation had taken place before he died.'

Asking some difficult questions was part-and-parcel of exploring what the real pain was and what their relationship was. As they engaged in this their enquiry involved asking the following:

- Was it was necessary for Parmjit to leave the family home in the first place?
- Was there another way to resolve the difficulties without him leaving?

- What were the reasons for us not giving him another chance to change?
- Were there going to be any changes in his behaviour?
- Did we care for him?
- Did we hate him?
- What causes these situations to happen and how are they dealt with?
- If we had taken him back would he still be alive?

They looked at each question, and their conclusion was that they had loved him, even though their relationship had become strained. They recognised that Parmjit leaving home, difficult as it was, needed to happen, as all attempts to implement support at that stage were being rejected by him. This caused them a lot of hurt, knowing that support was there both from the family and from professionals, yet he choose not to engage. They knew that as time passed by the questions would need to be revisited and it would require detailed examination of the evidence to support and/or refute what they felt.

In reality each question asked caused hurt, as it would have made them think about what could have been, and their final question summed up that hurt 'If we had taken him back, would he still be alive?' Yet again they realised they did not reject him or ask him to leave.

In looking at how they were managing their pain, Dee said, 'At times I thought the best way was to try and put my feelings to one side, because it was so hard to understand all the emotions that were going through my head. Slowly I've looked at my thoughts and feelings to know how Parmjit's death has affected me, but this is a difficult experience.'

Bal said 'I didn't want to talk about my dad at first because he hadn't been around as much as I felt he should have. So I thought there was no point and wanted to forget about him. But I knew deep down it wouldn't really work because every time I thought about Chacha, my mum, Ami, Massi, Billo, Suki, Nan and Baba, thoughts of my dad always came, and I knew I had no choice but to look at my relationship with him. Over time I realised I really loved him and I believe deep down that he really loved us all.'

Ami said 'I think I began to block my emotions out because I didn't want to look at the effects of Dad's death upon me. I thought I could control my thoughts about him but I found out I couldn't because the thoughts kept entering my mind every time I saw everyone else being upset. I knew I had to think about my dad in the same way I thought about Chacha's death, and crazy as it sounds I began to feel good that I could think about my dad when I remembered all the positive things about him, because at first I was really scared that all I'd feel was bad things. So I'm not trying to ignore the thoughts, but to look at them and then talk with everyone else because I know we're all in the same boat.'

My family's comments reveal that the truth of the matter is that thoughts, attitudes and emotions will surface at different stages throughout life. The important part is realising this. Therefore talking is part of the bridge building that is required in managing the emotions, thoughts and behaviours that surface.

I do not seek to underestimate the difficulties in exploring death and our experiences, because the factors that make it difficult to explore death can be the same factors that enable us to explore the death, and therefore come to terms with the reality of it.

What are such factors? There are many, but I identify three significant principle factors which when explored in depth reveal so much capacity to respond.

The factors are:

- ■ our love towards the person who died;

- the experiences we had with the person who died;
- the relationship we had developed with the person who died.

We need to recognise that because we love it is not a surprise that we experience immense and intense pain, for it is extremely difficult to let go of a relationship when it has been severed by death - this has to be acknowledged. If we seek to dismiss the pain and the helplessness caused, how do we think we are going to be able to truly support each other, and would it be safe to assume that there will be no effects upon our development?

My family knew that death caused us pain and had affected our development, yet grieving enabled us to see that the issues centred upon:

- Whether we were truly aware of what changes had taken place.
- Whether we were aware of how we had supported each other to acknowledge that death had taken place.
- Whether we were aware of how we had individually acknowledged that death had taken place.
- Whether we knew how to respond to each other in the midst of such pain.

For some of my family the pain was of unfulfilled hopes and dreams, e.g. Dilly, Baljinder and Suki with regard to Gurjit's death; for others it was the pain of expressing the ambivalence of relationships, e.g. Dee, Bal and Ami, my parents and myself with regard to Parmjit's death. Either way, the pain was locked in our experience, and this experience had to be expressed.

Hence we began to understand (at different stages) that if there was no expression of the pain experienced we would have been trapped with the tension of despair, which would have caused us to disengage from each other. Not talking and expressing only equates to more pain.

This may mean that those around us also learn from our example of silence by not seeking to raise the issue, in the belief that they or we may not be able to contain what will be released.

In particular a child or young person may seek to show that they are doing well, but just because there is not a reaction does not mean there is no turmoil within:

'Death affects you because you don't know what to feel about the person, about others or about yourself... It was as though I had no feelings, as if I blocked them out. It reminded me of going to the dentist to have a tooth out and being numb with an injection, you still know the pain is there but it takes time for the numbness to wear off.' (Baljinder)

'I just wanted to be all right so that my mum did not have to worry about me. I was afraid that she would not be there for me, so I tried to show that I was OK but I was scared.' (Suki)

'You try to pretend that everything is fine but it's not, it really does hurt when you think about it. We tried to put it to aside by thinking about others. It helped doing this for a while but we knew we would have to face this.' (Bal and Ami)

This reinforces the importance of looking at the effects of death, which I consider involves understanding that there are probably levels of separation which we as a family had to look at, namely being:

- separation from Gurjit and Parmjit when they died;
- separation from the experience of being with them;
- an emotional separation from ourselves in order to look at the pain in the first place.

However, while knowing there was a separation, there was also a parallel experience of 'joining' which took place:

- through reviewing who Gurjit and Parmjit were;
- through understanding what our experiences were with them and what beliefs sustained our relationship;

- through seeing and valuing our own contribution to our relationship with them;
- through knowing what relationships existed to support each other.

The separation and the joining can lead us to explore the key question of 'how to attend to the pain?' I believed we made joint efforts to look at the pain, and this enabled us to respond to each other. How we did this was by:

- knowing and believing in God (I appreciate that this may cause some people more pain, thinking 'how can anyone believe in God when a loved one dies?' In Chapter 3 I focus upon belief in God in more detail and hope that it may shed some light);
- knowing and believing in each another;
- ensuring that each one of us was able to talk about the experience of death and explore the pain this caused and the impact it had upon us individually and as a family;
- drawings, reading and writing (journals, diaries, poetry);
- questioning each other.

Such joint efforts meant my family shedding some insights into what they believed the reality of death meant for them after initial exploration:

'You never forget, because it will always be there, and I know it will come back in life in stages in the future and I will have to deal with it in stages and I have to ask myself how does the pain heal and know it is by identifying what it is.' (Baljinder)

'I know when I get older I will have more questions about my dad's death and about death.' (Suki)

'I've got to try and get on with life and look towards the future, but I know I've also got to look at how this has affected me at different stages when I grow. For

example when I get married and have children I'll have to explain to them about their grandfather. I've got to prepare myself at different times in my life.' (Bal)

'It is painful at times when thinking about it and I know it will always be there. I put it aside at times because it can be frightening when talking about the experience.' (Ami)

'You have to get used to death eventually, it will not be easy to cope with and will be tough to get through, but you have to live through it.' (Dilly)

'You can't pretend when death takes place because it hurts so much and every day you battle with the thoughts and emotions because they remind you of the good and difficult times.' (Dee)

'We have seen too much pain and know what the loss means, because it's about providing support, providing guidance, showing love and knowing each other's hurt and pain. At first you feel as though all your strength has gone away and that you can't talk, but it's important for us all to talk rather than keeping things locked up in our hearts, because it will affect us. We've learned that we can't really help until we know how their deaths have affected us and we know we are not alone and that we can always remember that Parmjit and Gurjit are in our hearts and this cannot be taken away.' (My parents)

In summary, the 'event of death' certainly cannot be contained and left ignored, because it creates an experience. This experience will always be influenced by the impression our loved one has left within us. Thus the importance of telling others about our own experience has to always allow for their circumstances. For there is no doubt death is painful; trying to avoid this is understandable and is not a sign of weakness, rather a sign that it is just too painful.

The reason that it is too painful is because it involves exploring our relationships, which means the embracing of pain and hope to attend to the actual experience.

The desire of longing and the desire for responding are due to bereavement being central to our identity at that point, but this does not mean that grieving has to consume our life endlessly, because we can be sustained through love.

CHAPTER 2

BEREAVEMENT:

THE LINK BETWEEN LOVE, RELATIONSHIPS, SUPPORT AND PAIN

When a traumatic event takes place our immediate focus will be on the pain; this is understandable. Yet ultimately the real pain centres upon whether we believe in love within our relationships.

Bereavement is the experience of the loss of a relationship, and grief is the expression of the loss of our relationship because of the pain that arises because of such loss. Hence bereavement is an experience of an intense crisis that immediately attacks a family structure. Therefore it will take time and a lot of energy before anyone is able to reach a stage whereby they can express the full impact of the loss.

I believe that the reason for this is because bereavement is a major life-changing event, and we will all experience this. However the manner in which we explore our grief is important. We have to be prepared to understand that our loss will take time to be explored, because the pain is so deep that it can only be released over time.

The pain of death for my family included the following:

'It felt like a big hole had been left in the family and I didn't know what to do at first. I felt exposed because it hurt so much.' (Dee)

'Never in a million years did I think I was going to become a widow at a very young age, and I always thought I would go before Gurjit. I was in shock

that my life with him ended the day he died, because the question that I asked God at that time was: 'why give me 16 years of happiness only for this to be taken away, because you should not have given me those 16 years at all for the pain, numbness and anger it caused.' (Dilly)

'What I have felt was pain because it was hard knowing that my dad and uncle should have still had a big part to play in my life. What I thought about death is that you will never know when it is going to happen, and know I can be a lot more prepared having faced it twice. When death took place it was scary, and it still can be even now as it reminds me that life is short, but it is even more difficult if you are left alone without support because that would be scary. It is also scary to think that people can think that things can be 'done and dusted' rather than looking at what needs to be talked about. Deep down it is scary to think what will happen to my loved ones that I leave behind and as a result sometimes I pray.' (Bal)

'To be honest I know death exists and it does scare me. I was one of those people who didn't think it would happen to someone close to me, now I know that one day people have to move on and if and when it happens I need to be prepared for it so I can support my family and friends. Overall it still scares me, because death can take place in an instant and I know I can't prevent it.' (Ami)

'I felt pretty much rubbish and numb when Dad died. Mom and Dad would tell me what would happen if one or both of them passed away. They told me never to blame God as God created us and gave us life. But none of this ever prepared me for losing Dad when I was 14 years old. I just never thought it was going to happen because I thought Dad would have been here throughout my life, and in a way he still is as I still feel him around me at times when I feel I need him. Death is a bad experience but also a good one. It can at first break you, but in the long run can make you stronger as you will be prepared if you experience another close death.' (Baljinder)

'I have felt like death is not just there when you are growing old because death happens to anyone at any time, but I never thought death would come this fast in my life.' (Suki)

As we begin to think about what the loss means we will experience doubt, which will make us feel there is no purpose to explore, because we will most likely:

- be at a stage of uncertainty about our self-capacity;
- be at a stage of uncertainty about how others will respond;
- be at a stage of uncertainty about our belief systems.

The reason such uncertainty will exist is purely because of the pain we have experienced. Therefore our minds will seek to act as a painkiller to what we consider the pain to be, because our minds will be battling with emotions, eg fear, anger, hatred, etc, and thoughts, eg What did I do? What could I have done? Is this really happening? Is there a reason? What will I do know?

Because of this 'battle' such emotions and thoughts will vary, and the following are a sample of what I knew took place within my family when death took place and when we began to explore the impact of death upon us:

- Anger
- Disbelief
- Despair
- Fear
- Frustration
- Guilt
- Helplessness
- Hopelessness
- Loneliness
- Numbness
- Regret
- Sadness
- Shock
- Sorrow

Chapter Two

In light of the above, pain certainly arose. The following are some of the responses that took place within my family:

Numbness and shock

When a loved one dies, numbness and shock are probably our immediate response. This is because the impact is so intense and severe that we feel lost. At the beginning, such feelings of numbness and shock tend to block out the pain. This is understandable for all, and it's one of the ways in which the mind helps us to begin to manage the emptiness created when death takes place. This was evident within my family:

'It would have been easier for me to have felt nothing and just ignored the fact that death took place, but I just didn't know what to really think or feel.' (Dilly)

'I think I just tried to blank it out because I was too afraid and was in shock because I questioned 'Why my dad?', and when I asked that I just felt numb.' (Baljinder)

'For a while we remained numb because we just didn't know what to feel and how to feel towards Dad's death, towards others and towards ourselves.' (Baljinder and Suki)

'When Gurjit died I was in so much shock, I just couldn't understand what had happened because it happened so fast. I felt so hurt because I knew Dilly and the girls were in so much pain. Yet when I found out that Parmjit had died all I felt was numbness because I couldn't really think.' (Dee)

'I kept trying to convince myself that Chacha was still alive and that he would turn up at home. I had to think this because the pain was so hard. When I found out about Dad, I didn't even want to start to think about what that meant.' (Bal)

'My mind was all over the place when I was at the hospital and I hated the fact that Chacha died because it hurt so much, I just hated it, but there was nothing I could have done, so I hated it even more. I tried to support Massi, Baljinder and Suki, and that's the only way I got through the first few days. When everyone found out about Dad, I just wanted to block everything out of my mind, I didn't

want to feel anything or think about it, I just wanted to get out of the house.' (Ami)

The reality is that the numbness and shock allow a blocking out within the first few days and weeks, and this is because the release of pain cannot be fully contended with. Hence this reinforces the reality that there needs to be a gradual release of such pain to know, believe and understand that the trauma of death has taken place.

Disbelief

The disbelief we experience takes time to overcome, because it will initially feel as though you are in a dream. This produces the constant thought 'Has this really happened?' or 'Am I going to wake up and find out it wasn't real?'

Such thoughts just add to the pain we feel, as we do not want to really believe that death has taken place so close to us. The moment we do face this it feels so daunting, because the thoughts are constant and don't look as though they will ever go away. For my family these were the emotions and thoughts that arose:

'I didn't understand why Gurjit had died, so I struggled to believe he had died, because deep, deep down I wanted to believe he had not died. It was so hard to focus on what to believe.' (Dilly)

'How could I believe that my dad had died? It was so terrible to believe, because I thought if I believed he hadn't died, then he'd come back.' (Baljinder)

'When I knew Gurjit was going to die I kept thinking it couldn't be true. Because I believed he wasn't going to die, I was too afraid to accept that he was. But with Parmjit I never saw his body, so I kept thinking he could really be alive, and it took so long before I realised he had gone.' (Dee)

'I didn't know what to believe, besides knowing I didn't want to believe that Chacha had died. Even though I felt the same when I found out about Dad, I managed my emotions a bit better.' (Baljit)

Chapter Two

'It was so hard to know what to believe when Chacha died, and then finding out Dad had also died, but I knew they had and that wasn't going to change, no matter how much I wished it could.' (Ami)

Disbelief is so real and so powerful, because it creates further pain and can prevent us from truly exploring our relationships and hindering us from working out what we truly believe about the loved one who has died, about our family and friends, about ourselves and about God. If disbelief is not looked at and challenged appropriately the pain will not fade, rather it will intensify to the point where we may not even realise the full effects it can have.

Guilt and Anger

I consider that anger and guilt generally appear together when death has taken place. Guilt will seek to challenge the legitimacy of our relationship with our loved one. But the truth of the matter is that feeling guilt is not a 'bad' thing, because it can reveal something quite powerful, and that's the love that resides within you. Anger will threaten to give a degree of control over the experience of death. I say a degree of control because I believe it really gives us some space to feel the pain without us really knowing we are feeling it, especially when we are trying to figure out to whom we should direct the anger. Hence the feelings and thoughts of guilt and anger will most likely relate to questioning our involvement surrounding the death of our loved one.

Two of the main thoughts are that we have somehow contributed to our loved one's death, or that we could have prevented it:

'I felt a lot of guilt about how Gurjit had died because I kept on thinking that if I had acted sooner things might have been different.' (Dilly)

Only when Dilly began to explore such a thought and the feelings of guilt did she come to realise that it was true feelings of love, as she understood that her actions could not have prevented Gurjit's death.

She said *'When I knew how much I loved him and that this was why I felt so bad and down, I knew I could support my daughters, because I knew they would have felt the same as me.'*

'I kept thinking that if I had stayed home with Dad instead of going to school I could have stopped it all from happening, and I felt so bad that I went to school and didn't know how ill he was. This hurt me so much. At first I was angry with mum because she sent me to school and I wanted to stay at home, and I felt so bad for a long time.' (Baljinder)

'I felt that if I had told him how much I loved him he wouldn't have died.' (Suki)

'Because I didn't know how ill Gurjit had become so quickly I felt guilty about not being able to help Dilly. I struggled with that, because I just didn't know what I could do after he had died. When Parmjit had died, I felt so much anger to think he had gone without me knowing and without me seeing him, but I knew the anger wasn't going to help me.' (Dee)

'Because I thought I couldn't help anyone when Chacha died, I felt so guilty, but afterwards I felt OK because I could help and did help my family.' (Bal)

'It was so hard to feel anything but anger, because when Chacha died I kept wondering where my dad was and kept thinking he should be here. So I was very angry that he wasn't, but I felt guilty when I found out he had also died.' (Ami)

It was very important for my family to look at such thoughts in order to see the reality of what had been experienced, because otherwise the imagination would have created havoc.

The second thought is that of not having been able to speak to the loved one before they died. Without a doubt this is a powerful drive, and so understandable. It can be very traumatic when we believe that somehow our words would have made a difference to the outcome. The truth is that they cannot, and it is unrealistic to expect in the case of a sudden death that we can have least a last conversation just moments before a person dies.

This was one of the main areas I struggled with, as it related to some of the decisions I made in the hours before Gurjit died. In particular there was the issue of my brother Jai not being at the hospital because of my advice for him to remain at home. Another was asking him to bring my cousin-sister to the hospital to see Gurjit, which prevented him from being there at the moment Gurjit died. It hurt so much, because as far as I was concerned I had failed my brother, and the guilt gnawed at me for months.

For my parents it was also very painful, as they reflected on the last moments of seeing Gurjit alive, four days before he died. They said they would never have thought that was going to be the last time they would see him alive; they had wanted him so much to hear them say they loved him.

Jai's words revealed the extent of the pain we all felt: 'I just wanted Gurjit to hear me, and I wanted to hear his voice, because I thought if he spoke he would survive.'

We all wished we could have spoken to Gurjit and Parmjit in a way that would have been comforting, but it was not to be. The way we began to move forward was with the belief that we loved them and we knew that they had known that, and that they loved us and we knew that. This certainly helped, because we began to realise that when the numbness wore off the questions truly began to take form, and that was when the reality of exploration sank in.

Hence this was something we could not be afraid of but rather needed to be aware of, so that we could help each other to acknowledge and understand our thoughts and feelings and the impact they would have on our behaviour.

The above was relevant for us all, and for Dee, Bal and Ami it became even more important when they explored Parmjit's death in further detail. This was especially so when they looked at forgiveness and how guilt and anger were factors that would impact upon this. This is what they uncovered:

Dee believed that forgiveness was important. She said 'If I didn't begin to forgive Parmjit then ultimately I would experience further pain by hanging on to his past.'

Bal considered the issue of forgiveness through asking the following: 'If I love my dad, why do I need to forgive him? How can you forgive someone if you love them?'

Ami believed 'Forgiveness is about learning to get over one's own hurt, anger and hatred and knowing that you can show love to another person.'

The above by no means suggests there was no hurt when they looked at their relationship with Parmjit. Bal identified this when he said 'I know there may be times when I'll be a bit angry about my dad's behaviour and how he died, but this doesn't mean that I haven't forgiven him, rather it means I think what a waste of a life it was not having a full opportunity to develop with him, which has been the real pain. Deep down I know he loved us but wasn't always there for us.'

Exploring their feelings and thoughts about knowing that Parmjit had been cremated without their knowledge also raised issues of guilt and anger. In Dee's case it was certainly anger. 'They had taken my rights away and I never got the opportunity to say goodbye. This has affected me.'

Similarly Bal and Ami expressed their annoyance when they said: 'We would have wanted to spend some time with our dad before the cremation. Our experiences of Chacha's and our father's deaths have been different in that it was upsetting seeing Chacha, but it just as upsetting knowing we never saw our dad when he died. This has been hard to accept.'

For Baljit and Amarjit it was poignant that they had prepared their uncle's body and said a 'proper' goodbye. It seemed like a God-given honour to these young men. They did not know that preparing their uncle's body might have given them some small consolation in the future' as they faced the knowledge that the circumstances of their own father's death meant they never saw his body.

When exploring the issues of guilt and anger, as well as many other emotions, we have to support each other to be able to express them truthfully and have the opportunity to work them through, rather than fearing the thoughts that will enter our minds.

Fear

There is no doubt that we fear having death take place in our midst, because it is so hard to imagine it happening as we go about our normal day-to-day lives. A sudden death like Gurjit's can be very difficult to acknowledge.

Furthermore the awareness that death is going to take place is just as frightening; this was also relevant in Gurjit's case. In particular I remember having to tell Baljinder and Suki in the early hours of the morning that their father was going to die. It was very difficult to prepare them for information which their minds would not have considered, and which my own mind was seeking to dismiss. Yet the reality was that fear was present.

Thus fear sought to dominate us in many ways, and our minds became hyper-sensitive. We began to wonder what was going to happen next and how we were going to be able to respond to a situation which may appear overwhelming.

An example from our own experience was when after Gurjit had died, Baljinder began to display similar symptoms that Gurjit had had. The anxiety this caused was intense, because of the fear that it would all happen again.

For Dilly this just made her feelings intensify. 'When I saw Baljinder become ill, I could see Gurjit all over again, and I panicked, thinking she was going to die, and I couldn't take that. I had to get her to the hospital, because I didn't want to think I hadn't done anything, because I was so frightened.'

We had to be mindful that an additional fear was to be preoccupied by the thought that someone else was also going to die. Such fears certainly begin to challenge the mind, and that is the reason for the importance of not being alone when facing such feelings and thoughts.

Part of the pain is contending with fears and worries that something else may happen, for example the girls were concerned that something might happen to their mother, as expressed by Baljinder: 'What worried us was thinking about what would happen if our mom died.'

For Dee, Bal and Ami, one of their main fears centred on whether the police had actually got it wrong and that Parmjit was in fact still alive, and how they would then have to manage all those emotions. Dee said: 'Every time the phone rings I get scared because I don't know whether something has happened to another family member, or whether it is going to be Parmjit telling me he is alive, or even the police saying sorry, they got it wrong. It made me feel on edge all the time.'

Likewise Bal's experience reflected what I believe most of us were experiencing, when he said 'Chacha's death was so frightening because I remember the hours before he died when he looked OK. When that changed I knew something else was happening, and because I didn't know what it was I got scared. After he died I kept wondering what I would do if someone else died. It was so scary to think about that. The only way I could try to make some sense of it was to talk about it.'

Hence we must not 'fear the fear' even though death will tend to be fearful. Rather, along with all other emotions and thoughts, we have to be truthful in acknowledging they will cause pain, yet we must believe that this does not mean that our lives will be controlled by them. This reinforces the point that it will take time, especially for children, as they will not have the language or understanding to be able to express their emotions and thoughts, and when they do, such expression will not necessarily be understood by adults. Therefore we need to be prepared to accept that emotions and thoughts will require attention at different stages throughout our life, and especially for children.

Helplessness

The experience of being helpless is real and should not be looked down upon. Along with many feelings that arise when death takes place, it is important to recognise that we will most likely feel unable to help ourselves, let alone anyone else.

Death can and will cause an intense longing within us to be whole. Yet the reality we face seeks to convince us that we will be unable to develop, and that is when the mentality of helplessness can set in and affect our entire behaviour. We begin to ask 'what is the point?' This does not mean that such a question should be feared, rather that we must recognise that we can do something for each other even when we feel we are unable to do so.

Thus in terms of the above emotions and thoughts that take place within the initial mourning due to the death of our loved one, we are then left with having to grieve and explore such emotions and thoughts in more detail. Hence I will discuss some of the issues that I consider are involved in grief.

Grief

Grieving is dealing with the internal impact of our loss, and it involves the realisation that there are many losses to manage, all occurring at the same time. It reminds us how unfair it is to think that anyone can just get on and get through such a traumatic experience. As said above, we will most likely go through various parts of grief at different periods in our lives in order to experience and learn the full impact death has had upon us.

In reality grief involves thinking about and acknowledging the pain resulting from death. Thus grief will appear frightening, because at times you understand that you are going through something but are not sure of what it is. On top of this you may also feel you do not have the ability to go through such an experience.

One way to look at this bewildering experience is to try to understand that grief produces tasks as a process of learning, rather than thinking it will produce a complete and total recovery.

As a family, grieving involved looking at how we managed some of the tasks, which included:

- talking about our relationship with Parmjit and Gurjit;
- supporting each other in expressing our feelings and emotions;
- examining our own thoughts and behaviour as adults in order to look at what examples we were setting;
- learning more about our family roles and responsibilities;
- having an awareness of long term hope.

By looking at the above, questions had to be considered to determine whether grief was in fact surfacing. Some of the questions were:

- How do we accept the reality of death?
- In what ways are we trying to show everyone that we are coming to terms with our loss? How is this dealing with our pain?
- Are we giving each other permission to express our pain for the loss?
- Are we prepared to recognise that this will involve expressing feelings and thoughts which may frighten us and therefore make us not want to talk, because we are afraid how others will respond to us?

The above shows the importance of understanding that grief is a process of responding to the trauma of death - and one of the strengths that exist in enabling us to go through this exploration is the mark or impression left within us by our loved one who died.

Another significant mark is made by those who are alive, in this case family and friends who can motivate us simply by their presence. When the intensity of despair rises, it is the thoughts of those close to us that can make us stand and psychologically fight the despair. For the resource within family and friends is incredible, especially:

- when we believe in each other;
- when we love each other;
- when we have a knowledge and understanding of each other's pain and relationships.

Thus, for us, looking at grief was important, to begin to learn that it was OK to feel uncertainty about the pain, because this was part of what we had experienced. The time spent talking with each other was necessary to recognise that we were not alone and would have to look at this together. I believe this provided the 'foundation' from which we began to explore our experiences:

'What has been painful is knowing that if I don't talk about what I feel and think, more pain is going to happen, so I've learned to grieve because I know I loved Gurjit.' (Dilly)

'It's helped me so much to talk with those close to me. At times the pain can make me think I'm not really talking about what's happened, but I know we'll all get through this.' (Dee)

'I've learned that people cope in different ways and that other people just expect you to get over the death, but that is probably because they are unable to show their pain. I know the separation is physical, but the hurt is emotional.' (Baljinder)

'I thought that people were going to forget and move on, but you realise other people's pain and know the hurdles that face you. I know what work has to be done to help each other grow and learn, and this can take place through listening to each other and understanding how we feel.' (Bal)

'I know other people are around me, I know them and I know they will be

there for me. With my dad I've questioned what went wrong. It hurt how his life ended, it happened so fast and left me thinking I've got no understanding. But I know my pain is there and I'm learning to know what has to be done to look at it.' (Ami)

Their comments revealed in many ways that there would be some uncomfortable thoughts they would have to look at, and these would most likely centre upon:

- how to revisit our experiences;
- how to express truth about our past and current relationships;
- how to relate to each other.

The above is uncomfortable, because that's what pain creates, yet grief can dismantle what is uncomfortable by showing that deep underneath the pain is love. That sounds very uncomfortable, yet I believe that's what we'll find if we are willing to explore. Yet this love and care can still reside within the midst of the chaos and pain we experience.

For Dilly this reality was relevant as she considered that the initial difficulties in her emotional acceptance of Gurjit's death centred upon:

- her feelings of anger and self-doubt;
- her uncertainty about her own confidence and ability to respond to the future.

Furthermore she informed me that she found exploring Gurjit's death very difficult. I considered her response was positive, as she did not seek to pretend in order to 'appease' people. This was important for her to reflect upon. She said 'I didn't want to just think that I was coping, I needed to know that I was. I could only know by thinking about my relationship with Gurjit and looking at the effects of his death upon me, even though at first it was very difficult to think about his death.'

Overall she felt: 'This has not been easy, and that is why I can only do it a bit at a time to build my confidence that I can respond to this hurt. I know crying helped me to release many of my emotions. After such crying I started to learn more about what the emotions were and how they was affecting me. Yet the biggest thing I learned was that it was OK to grieve for my love of my husband.'

Hence in order to support us, shared grief is a major positive strength that can enable a child, young person or adult to express grief through:

- Asking as well as answering unanswered questions. It is important to promote our capacity to ask questions, as this is one of the major routes of learning and can prevent us being locked in fear of exploring. Furthermore adults have to understand that when a child or young person asks questions it is positive, and this has to be embraced rather than shunned, even when we may not have the answers as well as when such questions cause us pain.

- Providing each other moral support.

- Revealing that love and care are still present to meet our developmental needs and support us in our own identity and belief systems, which can aid us in developing positive physical, psychological, emotional and spiritual health.

- Addressing the worries, concerns and fears we have about death, separation from our relationship with the deceased and uncertainties about future relationships. Through expression we can develop the capacity to think through making such emotions less overwhelming.

- Facilitating more discussion and accessing reading material can enable us to get more information and a clearer understanding of what is involved in grief and how this impacts upon our experiences. For children and young people this will need to take into account their developmental age and understanding.

Thus in terms of the above, grief needs to be faced head on by truth, which means it will be a challenge. Yet the challenge cannot take place unless there are meaningful relationships established to explore the impact death has upon us. Hence the need for strong and secure relationships becomes very important to begin to attend to some of the emotions and thoughts that arise while we are grieving, and I will comment upon this next.

Relationships

I recognise that though there is no manual for facing death, I believe our relationships are this manual. Relationships have structure, and that structure is love, for it is the love that enables our development to take place. This development will consist of many factors that can enable us to make appropriate decisions in how we explore our experiences and understand the pain we feel.

We will already know that the loss of a relationship impacts upon us because our loved one formed an essential part in our life. Therefore it is important that we are supported in maintaining a bond or connection with the deceased without fearing the trauma we have experienced.

Hence I believe that even though pain will surface, this is because the connection can only truly take place through reviewing our relationships.

For Bal, Ami, Baljinder and Suki, part of their exploration meant understanding the significance of their relationship with their respective fathers. The purpose of this was to enable them to maintain an 'emotional connection' with what the relationship was. Hence it was important for this to be discussed in order for them to be able to realise that it was good to be able to think about their father without having to fear or worry:

'It is hard to share experiences with somebody who has not gone through it

because they don't know what you are talking about. I needed to share it with others who have experienced death.' (Baljinder)

'My dad will always be part of my life. Just because he died doesn't mean that I can't think about him.' (Suki)

'I know that the good and bad memories will be in me for a while but I think it is good to look at them both because I know I loved my dad.' (Bal)

'It is difficult to try and think about someone who was in your life one day and gone the next, but I remember them because I respected them and did love them so badly.' (Ami)

When we looked at our relationship with Parmjit and Gurjit as well as our current relationships, these are some of the questions we explored:

- How would we describe our relationships with Parmjit and Gurjit?
- How did our relationships develop?
- How would we view our involvement in such relationships?
- What were the strengths and limitations of our relationships?
- What is it that we miss most about them?
- The experience of separation leaves us with what feelings and thoughts?
- What worries us the most?
- What are we finding difficult to accept and manage?
- Are we really able to talk freely about our feelings about death with family/friends?
- How important is it for us to make sense of what has happened and what is happening?

Looking at the above certainly created some uncertainty and despair on top of what we were already feeling about our loss. I can describe the experience like this: 'sometimes to get to the light of understanding there needs to be an experience of walking in the dark.'

To explore this 'walking in the dark' we needed to identify what we felt, thought and believed when considering what the questions meant. This helped us to begin to express what we had felt unable to express about the pain and hurt. For what really hurts is not being able to express the hurt and knowing that there cannot be a return to the place we long for.

In terms of 'what kind of relationship we had?' and 'what were the most important aspects of the relationship?', we all had different types of relationships with Parmjit and Gurjit, as identified below.

Dilly told me that exploring her relationship with Gurjit through questioning what the relationship was, what the relationship meant to her and what the relationship produced was beneficial, as it helped her to understand that she could respond to her circumstances. She said 'I was able to explore the kind of relationship I had with Gurjit and what the most important parts of the relationship were. From this I knew what I missed about him and what made me feel afraid and angry about him dying. I also began to look hard at what I was finding difficult to cope with. But I know that talking and thinking about Gurjit does not hurt as much as it used to, because I look at what we achieved together. I know I will have questions in my head and they will be there in the years to come, which will cause some hurt.'

For Dee, she believed there were many aspects to her relationship with Parmjit that she needed to think about in order to help her make sense of his death. As she said: 'Getting married at a young age was nerve racking, but we managed to support each other. That was what he did for a very long time until he got involved with the wrong crowd and began to drink heavily. At first I just thought he would grow out of it, but then I realised it was causing a lot of strain upon our marriage. As time passed by I began to see how much he meant to me, even when his drinking problems affected our relationship, but he was still my husband and I loved him so much and just wanted him to be free from such problems. I tried so hard to help him and get him help, but he didn't accept it until his behaviour became really problematic, and by that time it was too late. However I remember all the good things about him before alcohol took over his life, because he was really generous, loving and caring and I can't forget that part of him. He was also very funny and very knowledgeable about his culture, and this helps me to know that he was a good person and that he did love me as much as I loved him. There are days when I've been angry thinking about the loss of the relationship and the opportunities we had to grow together, and then there are days when I look at my sons and am grateful for having known Parmjit.'

With regard to Baljinder's and Suki's relationship with their father, they said: 'He was a kind and caring person and we admired him for putting up with mum's 'moaning' and he always put other people first. Our memory of our dad has been a good way to cope with his death, even though at times when we think about him we feel lost because there was so much that we would have liked to have experienced with him.'

For Bal and Ami, their relationship with their father contained positives and limitations, as they recognised: 'We know he loved us, but his drinking problems came to the point where he wasn't able to show that to us. We remember growing up when he used to be there and play with us, and take us on trips as a family, and we saw the kind and gentle side to him. We also knew that whenever anyone became ill in the family he would worry. It was a shame that alcohol got the better of him, but deep down we loved him as our father and we know that we'll have to keep looking at our relationship with him as we grow older. Also we've had to learn that we did all we could for him, even though we would have liked to have seen him with us. When he was not around we'd always look up to our Baba, Chacha and Mamas as they filled that father-figure gap for us and that helped us a lot. He will always be our father and we'll never forget him because we love him.'

Their comments reveal to me how relationships are the core of our identity, because we belong to each other and this takes place through the development of:

- Appropriate attachments, to ensure we demonstrate consideration, care, and compassion.
- Acceptance of each other's strengths, limitations and vulnerabilities, to ensure we continue to face reality.
- Awareness of each other's needs, to ensure that we promote and safeguard each other's welfare.

Through such development we can truly protect each other within our relationships from further pain, the pain of isolation, by ensuring we continue to share information appropriately and for each other's benefit so that we can continue to:

- make effective and informed decisions.
- respond to each other and meet the short-term needs, as well as plan for our long-term needs.
- believe in each other, and this belief should not be about assuming we will be all right, rather it needs to be a belief that we can continue to love in the midst of the difficulties through valuing each other and recognising each other's pain.
- to explore and express our emotions and thoughts together.

Thus in terms of the above, a relationship cannot exist in isolation and any attempt to believe that it is possible will only lead to pain being ignored. Hence as a result the importance of support work cannot be underestimated

Support for children and young people, as well as adults

When looking at support when death has taken place it is important to look at:

Chapter Two

- What support is required
- Who requires the immediate support
- Who can provide the support.

Upon reflection of my family's experiences I felt that during the initial days and weeks after Gurjit's and Parmjit's death the level of anxiety and uncertainty was at its highest, yet the intensity of support was able to match such pain. The reason was that we ensured none of us were left alone at that stage to face the experience of separation and loss.

This did not ignore the reality that the experience was painful. We certainly knew that we did not have all the answers, nor were we able to respond perfectly considering we were sitting with each other's pain. Thus the immediate way of providing support was to be present to hear each other tell our stories by trusting each other.

Hence time spent creating a secure place in which we feel safe enough to talk about the unsafe thoughts and feelings we are experiencing is likely to prevent further problems in the long run.

For us, as we continued to hear each other and help each other express our emotions, we began to truly look at our relationships, knowing that we would have to continue to learn, by understanding we could not address every single issue that we had experienced.

Dee, Dilly, Bal, Ami, Baljinder and Suki looked at how they had been able to talk about their experiences:

'I can talk to certain people about the loss of my husband, but outside the family I do not go into details of the death. I can talk about it when the subject comes up or when people ask me about my husband and I am able to talk without feeling frightened or being isolated anymore.' (Dee)

'I have been able to talk about my experiences to family members and friends. Sometimes I find it hard to talk about certain things, because it was Gurjit I would tell, and know I talk to God about certain things.' (Dilly)

'When I have spoken about my experiences I have felt a lot better and more comfortable, but I will only speak to people who I feel will listen and hear, as well as people who have experienced death.' (Bal)

'I can talk about my experiences to people I know have had people close to them pass away, so I tell them how I felt and how I am dealing with it over time and what I had to do.' (Ami)

'In the first few months after Dad passed away I found it easy to talk about it to those around me. A very close childhood friend had lost both her parents, so I found it good to talk to her. But as I got older I started to feel it was a hard subject to talk about as I met new people, because it's not a conversation that you can just spark up. I find Dad's death easier to talk about when I've got to know the person and have a good friendship with them, but sometimes I can't even remember bits about Dad's death as I was so young and you tend to look at things differently as the years have gone on.' (Baljinder)

'It's been easy to talk about what we went through from the day of death to now. It's easy talking about it with my family, but when it comes to talking about my experiences to friends and outsiders I keep parts blocked off because it's hard to talk about them.' (Suki)

Hence, talking about our experiences means realising the importance of building upon the positive fact that such exploring will be difficult, just as it is important to recognise that the timing has to be right in order to enable each other to face grief.

The knowledge that this has to be faced has to remain, because until the pain is faced there will be no managing of the loss experienced. However rushing in due to the fear that if the exploration has not commenced a person will break down is just as damaging, if the person truly is not in a position to be able to explore and if the support networks are not in place.

For my family, how they believed they began to respond was important for them to see how they had actually begun to look at their pain:

Chapter Two

'I am coping in the best way I can in losing my life partner who I thought I was going to grow old with. It was very hard because finding out almost two years after his death was difficult and I miss him a lot even with what happened in our marriage. Also it was difficult knowing that there was 13 months between Parmjit and Gurjit dying. I first began to learn to cope by switching things to the back of my mind, and then I began to learn to share my own experiences with others. Also reading books on bereavement has helped me to identify how others have dealt with the effects of death.' (Dee)

'I've coped with God's strength and the support given by my family. Also I know I cannot dwell on this tragedy forever because it can ruin you.' (Dilly)

'I have coped and managed by learning about what has happened to me and my family and talking about this and hearing different thoughts from people mainly within the family. The other way I have coped and managed is by meeting Indy. When I speak to her, she listens to what I have to say and then she puts her point across from what she has experienced. I have also coped by focusing on tasks and aims in my life and setting targets and looking at my own attitude in how I respond to people.' (Bal)

'I think I have coped well with both deaths. I still need to do some reading so I can be more prepared for the future. I know I kept myself occupied with my own stuff and realised that I shut out most of my experiences, but I know I can't ignore it, and have been able to talk but need to go into depth about my loss. Yet I know I have spoken to other people about my experiences of death when they have faced bereavement and realised that this has helped me cope.' (Ami)

'I have coped and managed with Dad's death by talking about it and coming to terms with the fact that he is not coming back and that I have to adapt to a new life without him. I know my dad would have wanted me to carry on with my life and to make the most of it.' (Baljinder)

'I have coped by having my loving family around me, because every one of them has done something to help me through and helped me cope with our loss.' (Suki)

Chapter Two

Because of my nieces and nephews I will comment specifically about support work for children and young people. Firstly, I believe it is extremely important to consider how children and young people are supported when bereavement has taken place. The reason for this is that it takes a lot of energy, commitment, and preparation to begin to enable a child or young person to face the full effects of the loss of a relationship.

Secondly, I consider that children and young people will experience many worries, anxieties and uncertainties, and as adults we have to sensitively ensure that such anxieties can be expressed, through:

- Supporting them to understand what they are feeling;
- Supporting them to talk openly about their pain;
- Supporting them in their relationships within and outside of the family.

Thus supporting them in opportunities to express their loss and help them to heal is crucial, because they will most likely move in and out of their experiences and emotions in stages until they are able to respond to such reflections and exploration as part of a continual cycle.

Therefore this should not be entered into lightly. As adults we need to be responsible for ensuring that a child or young person is offered consistency in the midst of the experience of pain. Hence we should not be embarrassed or ashamed to seek support from outside our family and social networks for a child or young person who is experiencing bereavement. It can be very unfair to try to provide a child or young person with the opportunity to explore, and then as adults be unable to see this through. We need to recognise that as adults known to the child or young person we hold a vital role in providing support. However this should also mean being prepared to allow other people to engage with the child or young person because their welfare and development has to be central to all decisions we make as adults.

Therefore as a family system we need to understand that our responses will either mediate or amplify the effects of death. For us this meant we needed to demonstrate security, stability and affection to enable them to develop their self-confidence and belief.

This support is about preventing a child or young person having to experience isolation, because we should not underestimate their distress. While at the same time it is important for them to experience the grief because we should not also underestimate their capacity to respond.

Hence as adults it is vital that a child's level of distress is identified and responded to, while also paying attention to our own level of distress. Hence patience is important because it is about ensuring the child is able to break down their pain in parts, otherwise, if attempts to rush this are undertaken, their pain could potentially break them down. It is important to remember that long-term support work is required, because there is no short fix in responding to death.

Therefore it is important to be truthful with a child, and to ensure that our conversations are appropriate for their development. I believe it will be very difficult for a child to respond if he/she thinks we as adults do not want to engage. It is pointless trying to guess, rather as adults we need to know what the child thinks and feels by asking questions, commencing discussions and observing them and maintaining focus upon meeting their needs.

Hence it is important to support them in understanding death, as their knowledge will enhance over time because support needs to be matched to a child's age and level of understanding and development, because to support them in the expression of their pain, serious attention is required to meet their needs:

'I know I have to get on with life, but can't exactly do it easily because there are loads of adjustments to get on with. I have to carry on knowing this will always be missing. I can't understand the pain until I accept it exists. For me the pain at times has been the loss of hope and belief.' (Baljinder)

'I tried to hide my feelings but it doesn't help. It is good to cry... The pain is not being able to talk to him and being away from him.' (Suki)

'My numbness is all that I felt, the memories reminded me of having to face the pain.' (Bal)

'I've had to look at my experience of pain and how I've been stuck in the middle of the pain.' (Ami)

Thus providing information is vital to support them to understand what has happened, as well as begin to explain some of the effects death has had upon them. This is about providing them with some reassurance that what they are feeling, thinking, believing etc will in the main be similar to what those around them are also feeling, thinking and believing. It is important to ensure that they do not feel further burdened by thinking they have to go through such a process immediately, and quickly, and certainly not alone.

Therefore:

- As adults we need to be prepared as best as we can be to hear what is said, even though it may appear uncomfortable. For we need to sit there with our children and listen to them and hear their inner turmoil without seeking to relay our own knowledge and experience. They need to be heard, which means identifying their fears, uncertainties, beliefs, hopes and strengths. Once heard they need to be supported in how this reveals their love for the deceased and for those living. Our knowledge and experience becomes useful once they have had the opportunity to express their pain through telling their story.

- As adults we need to recognise that a child or young person will experience distress due to the event of death, but also if they feel no resolution is coming. Thus they may reveal that they are 'doing well' because they do not want to look at the pain, because others are not either looking at their own pain, as well as not asking them about such experiences. It is very easy, but very irresponsible, for us as adults to presume a child or young person is coping so that we do not have to face the knowledge of the reality that he or she might not be.

■ As adults we need to appreciate that they need time to look at what has taken place and how they make sense of this is important for their long term adaptation.

In summary the provision of support for children and young people's needs should:

■ be age appropriate.

■ contain information which is clear and truthful, and a realisation that this will need to be repeated several times over the years to come.

■ consider and listen to their views and feelings in order to hear their thoughts and understand their experiences.

■ ensure that they are comfortable in expressing their emotions and thoughts to explore their loss.

■ gently challenge distorted views and beliefs, eg blaming oneself.

■ ensure that appropriate support networks are available for them.

■ enable them to look at how they may want to answer questions asked of them by others, eg their friends.

■ develop their identity through focusing on how they are valued within and outside the family.

■ maintain focus on boundaries and routines.

■ ensure that as adults we demonstrate our own grief appropriately.

Summary

Bereavement, without a doubt, will impact upon us in many ways, whether we choose to accept it or not. Thus as adults we have to take the responsibility of ensuring that we continue to respond to each other without fearing our own vulnerabilities.

Hence, even though everything appears bleak, we actually have the opportunity when we grieve to truly explore and develop in the midst of the pain and heartache. This development is not about obtaining perfection or assuming everything is going to be fine, because neither can be achieved. Rather we have to be open to the reality that our vulnerabilities will ultimately reveal the hope of strength which is also in our midst.

Thus, how we explore our grief is through our relationships. One of the reasons that the exploration has to take place within our relationships is because within such relationships we are contending with the effects of death. Therefore there is a need to recognise that when we think about the loss due to death it will create further pain. It is through such thinking that the relationship is reviewed and a response built, however the process of development takes time to manage the changes experienced. A reason for this is that learning does not automatically reveal itself immediately.

As we grieve, we need support. For my family this support existed within and outside the family, because it was important for us to be able to approach people who we felt comfortable to talk to. Thus it cannot be over-emphasised that support needs to be available for children and young people. We must also remember there is no shame in seeking support from professional agencies, because the most important and central focus is the needs of the child or young person. Experiencing death at a relatively young age will need to be worked out over a lifetime, but this does not mean that it has to control their life. As a family this meant recognising that not everyone was able to explore their experience at once or at the same time, because everything has a time and a season.

CHAPTER 3

THE DEPENDENCY OF VULNERABILITY

What we face must not be feared and what we face must not be ignored, for what we face is our vulnerability with the truth and belief that life resides within.

The feelings and thoughts associated with experiencing the death of my two brothers were overwhelming, because many questions arose which revealed the pain, namely:

- How could this happen to my family?
- How did we never see any of this taking place?
- Was there anything we could have done to prevent their deaths?
- How can I respond?
- How can I provide any support?
- How is this going to affect my family and me?
- How am I going to be able to talk about this?

Such questions only served to push me into action, as for some apparent reason I did not focus too much attention to my feelings at that stage. Though I knew it was important to identify and acknowledge such emotions, I knew it was just as important for me at that stage not to be 'governed' by those emotions. My only way to manage the pain at that stage was to respond through action.

Therefore for me, acknowledging that death had taken place when it did became immediate - on an intellectual level. However the emotional acceptance which had to be embraced was a different matter and one which I began to realise would pose the greatest challenge. The reason for this was that overall I knew that this experience of trauma required expression, and this expression involved looking deep within in order to reach out by knowing that until I reached out I could not reach within.

Yet in spite of knowing that, I realised it was so easy to hide in my professional role of thinking my purpose was to offer support, and that was what I initially did. Only by looking back did I realise how I had initially begun to shut down in order to respond. This appeared somewhat contradictory and even confusing for me when I knew that I also had to express my emotions to support family members in expressing their emotions, and vice versa. Therefore it took time to begin to actually look at the effects of loss and talk about this, as I was too preoccupied in ensuring that everyone else was developing.

My mistake was that I did not open up as much as I should have. Hence I learned and know that I am still learning to understand that development can only really take place in a shared experience. This is because responding to the grief of bereavement can be very draining, and without ensuring appropriate support being in place emotions, thoughts and behaviour will always be open to further pain - the pain of closure of oneself from others.

I believe this because I consider that being opened up is to stop oneself from being closed down. If we seek to block out an experience which is not really blocked it becomes split, because:

- it gets broken down into smaller, more manageable explorations which are productive; or
- it can totally overwhelm a person by remaining hidden.

In other words, if talking about our loss is undertaken with the intention of truly exploring, it will open us up to see and realise that existence still remains. However not talking about the loss will most likely result in the loss of self to relate to another, because there will be:

■ a turning within (i.e. closure to the experience); or

■ a turning against (i.e. anger and guilt).

What is needed is a turning towards the acceptance that death has occurred and exploration of this will reveal life through the sharing of our own vulnerabilities.

The above has been a continuous experience for my family, because there has been so much to respond to. This was very important for us to remember as it pointed towards how we were learning to respond to the impact of death. Such learning was in the midst of the vulnerabilities and for Dee, Dilly, Bal, Ami, Baljinder and Suki their statements certainly captured this:

What do you think you have learned?

'I know I have to do a lot of reading. This will help me to help others with different experiences of death. Also to talk about the things Parmjit did, whether they were good or bad, and talk with family members - this sometimes helps to be open where you can. But sometimes it is hard to talk to my sons about their dad. I've learned to be open to a degree to any question asked of me about my experiences, yet there are many parts of my relationship that I am unable to talk about openly with others, as they are personal to me. I've learned to be grateful and to ensure I spend time with those I love, and I feel a much stronger person in myself and I've learned not to go into a discussion by arguing, and I've learned that reading helps me to understand how I can help others with similar experiences.' (Dee)

'I've learned that death can come unexpectedly and turn your life upside down, but it is up to you if you want it to rule your own life or get on with life with those who are with you, and it is important to treasure them because as the saying goes 'you never know what you've got until you lose it.' Therefore I am grateful with what I have got and my daughters are a reminder of Gurjit to me in many ways.' (Dilly)

Chapter Three

'I am learning to listen and hear others before I make any statement as well as having the evidence to back up what I am saying. I've also learned to understand what I need to do to respond to what is in front of me which is building relationships and talking about my experiences.' (Bal)

'I have learned how to take on bigger responsibilities and that whatever I do I need to make sure I know what benefit or consequence it brings to my family. I have also learned to listen to other people's experiences and views, but I still have a lot to learn.' (Ami)

'I have learned that death is part of life and is unavoidable. I have also learned that it is good to talk about death and about the person who has passed away in order for you to cope with it, no matter how much it makes you cry or upset because it will open you up a bit more.' (Baljinder)

'I have learned so much in the past five years. I have learned not to hate God for death because it is going to happen. I've learned that moving on isn't a bad thing, but this does not mean I have forgotten my past because that will always be there. I have learned that my family are the key to helping me through and that we can fight or get angry but we are still there for each other and love each other. I've also learned that thinking about our experiences and memories isn't a bad thing, it's good to think about all our happy times together and even though Dad and Tithia have moved on they are there looking down on us watching what we have become.' (Suki)

What difficulties do you think remain ahead for you and the family?

'I think it can be difficult to be open to address the difficulties of certain parts of my relationship with Parmjit and to come to terms with that. But it is important for me to remember the relationship I had and the love in that relationship. I know there will be obstacles along the way when I look at my relationship with him.' (Dee)

'I know that some family members have had difficulty talking about Gurjit's death, but I know Gurjit left a mark in our life. He was gifted and I am glad we had the pleasure of his company. There are going to be difficulties in our life ahead, especially when there are events such as weddings. But I believe we can get through them with God's and the family's help.' (Dilly)

Chapter Three

'I cannot see any alternative to telling the truth. The only thing is if we stop getting together and being around one another. I know everyone is moving on with their life and I know we will face difficult times, but I know we will be standing there for one another. I also know that if I don't know God then I know I will have difficulties in responding to others.' (Bal)

'I don't know what difficulties are ahead, but as a family we will take these difficulties and challenges together.' (Ami)

'I can't think of many difficulties except special occasions such as birthdays, which are hard as Dad was always there and the first person to wish me happy birthday. I think the most difficult thing for me will be the day I get married, as dads usually give their daughters away and I won't have my dad there, so that will be very hard for me, and also starting a family, as kids will ask questions about their granddad. I think I would find it difficult to explain to them how Dad passed away, but I won't find it difficult in describing what a great person he was.' (Baljinder)

'For me it will be difficult when we get married or go to university or if there are other children born into the family, because my dad and Tithia won't be here to see us move on with chapters of our life and share in our life as we can't share that with them.' (Suki)

Their views present the reality of their experiences and the truth of knowing that their exploration will still take time, and such words speak to my heart. I hope they will reveal to you that love, faith and hope can still arise in the midst of our pain and despair and that while we don't have all the answers to life's challenges, that's OK because we can gain strength through knowing our vulnerabilities.

As time goes by each of my family members will take on new knowledge which will in return influence how they understand their experience of facing the death of our loved ones. Again this is not a difficulty if there is awareness that this will take place. For it is important not to rush issues for the sake of hoping that once they have been raised they do not need to be explored at any other stage. The reason is because there needs to be an awareness that there has not been total restoration, rather a realisation that there is more exploring to be done.

This exploration brings me to an area of great importance, because it can either be seen as the greatest source of strength or the greatest cause of despair; belief in God.

The purpose of talking about God centres upon my belief in God. This belief is from my personal experience of learning gained through over twenty years of knowing, believing and understanding as much as I can about who God is. Yet the truth is I have still got so much to learn and understand.

Thus for me, my belief in God was (and still is) the most important factor that enabled me to respond to my family. While a belief in each other was also important it could not sustain development on its own.

Therefore I seek to inform readers that this has been my personal experience. This for me is evidence that God is real, because we are all different and God takes time to reveal to us who He is. The question is whether we take the time to hear and then respond.

However I fully appreciate and am sensitive to the fact that individual pain and hurt is deep and seems as though it will never fade, and that the thought of God can create further despair, because either your faith has been challenged or you have never thought of believing in God in the first place. Furthermore I appreciate that thinking about God's existence at such time can be difficult when we are enduring such pain.

Hence my prayer is that we remain open to those around us, and learn what it means to believe in God in spite of the tragedies we experience and as a result develop the relationships we have. Again I do not seek to minimise others' experience of bereavement and hope that as you read on you will find the strength to continue to respond to your loved ones, as I know that as a family we are always learning that this is a continuous experience.

Therefore I would hope that what is written does not cause you discomfort, rather I would hope that it can reveal that the pain experienced means that we will need to search for the meaning of life. For me, the meaning of life only exists in the knowledge, belief and understanding of who God is. Furthermore you may not believe that God exists or you may believe that somehow He has abandoned you because death took place. I would hope that you will take the courage to read on, because I know I do not have all the answers to life.

Furthermore I hope that what is written at least enables a discussion for you and others as my intention is not to 'promote' God, because God is not dependent upon me.

Yet I do sincerely believe that God does exist and that what is required, in the midst of our pain, is a willingness and a desire to search for God and learn how to respond to those around us who are also enduring the emotional and psychological scars that bereavement has created.

Therefore for me, belief in God is simply about belief in God, in spite of the circumstances. This does not mean that it is a belief that does not question, explore and challenge what the belief is. Rather it is about having faith to trust and having knowledge and understanding to examine. Because for me, belief in God has to determine :

- Do I believe in God, or do I believe in what I ask of God?
- Is evidence of God's existence dependent upon change to my circumstances?

For me this means that God remains in the midst of all that takes place in our lives and circumstances. Such involvement enables faith to develop within us and produces hope that we can continue to know, believe and understand who God is. I consider that this experience:

- is intended to sustain us when life's challenges and traumas arise;
- is intended to sustain us to continue to respond to meet the needs of others through the development of relationships which are central to God.

Hence believing in God and having faith in God can enable and support us through experiencing a traumatic event. While at the same time such faith and belief can be a point of despair and despondency when we think that everything should be fine and that nothing can or should go wrong in our lives or the lives of our loved ones.

In terms of my experience, it has all been about finding out more about who God is. Because there is no doubt that the pain of death, separation and trauma will create questions about belief and faith in Him. Thus it is important to reflect upon what faith is and what meaning death has for us because the loss will confront the reality of what we believe and our faith.

For Dee, Dilly, Bal, Ami, Baljinder and Suki it was important for them to look at belief in God:

'I know that God does intervene when loved ones die because God is here for anyone that lets him into their life.' (Dee)

'I didn't hate God through my ordeal and I still don't, because I know he had a reason why Gurjit was taken, and God didn't leave us in our ordeal, he was in the midst of our pain. I also know 100% that Gurjit is with Him. One day God will reveal when we are ready to hear the answer. I still love God. Without him we are lost.' (Dilly)

'Even though I know God is there no matter what, I have felt distant from Him. I've asked God about what happened to my dad and uncle and there are no clear answers but then I know nothing happens overnight. Overall my belief is not that strong towards God.' (Bal)

Chapter Three

'To be honest I don't know, as I have felt that I am a lost sheep when it comes to God, because I feel I have drifted away. I've just wondered and don't know any more about God, and I'm just struggling to believe because things have changed.' (Ami)

'I have never really been a religious person, but I have always believed in God and that God does things for a reason. I look at it like this: God created this world and the people in this world. He brings people into this world everyday but also has the power to take out people every day. People cannot live forever and God needs the people he takes to fulfil other things. I could never blame or hate God for Dad's death. Instead I thank him for giving me such an amazing dad and making my time with my dad memorable.' (Baljinder)

'My belief in God has always been the same; I know he is up there. I don't hate him for taking Dad because it's not just us who he takes people from. I am always praying to God because I know he is there to listen, and because of death I have prayed a lot more than I would of done.' (Suki)

I consider these views reveal their willingness to look at parts of their pain and not fear thinking about God or questioning what has taken place.

For me it highlights that rather than fearing the thought of death, the greatest fears relate to what the faith means, who is God and where is God in the midst of the reality of such pain. This is the real challenge that is set before us - finding and encountering God while still living with and enduring pain and still responding to and meeting the needs of others who are also in pain.

This does not mean that we distance ourselves from exploring the challenges because we think the challenge will undo and dismantle the faith we hold. The challenge cannot undo the faith, though it can undo our willingness to trust God and believe that God can be known and understood.

Furthermore this does not mean that we ignore the questions, rather we ask them knowing that an answer may not arise. Yet the question is an intention of seeking understanding, not seeking blame or even resolution, because the reality is that with death there is no human resolution, only an eternal one.

Chapter Three

Therefore to consider that God can help us respond to life's challenges is a good belief to have, while having awareness that a resolution or change may not take place does not mean that our faith and belief is ineffective or that God does not exist. If this is not looked at, it can result in us not dealing with the doubts that we have, about ourselves, others and more importantly about God. Because to actually explore, and be still in the midst of such uncertainty is difficult, especially when there are opposing concepts that enter our minds such as:

- having faith while contending with doubt;
- having hope while living in despair;
- seeking to demonstrate love while consumed with anger and apathy;
- longing for relationships, yet fearing what the true connection means for us.

However if this challenge is not seen as an opportunity to develop, it may prevent any true and purposeful exploration of our experiences. In looking at the above it is important to ask ourselves:

- Do we think that if we identify and explore our vulnerabilities, fears and doubts that it will shake the foundation of our faith and our relationships?
- Or do we recognise that such exploring is about a realisation of how much we need God?

If it is about God, then are we prepared to understand what we may be truly reluctant to explore in the first place?

- Does God really exist?
- Who is God?
- What is the purpose of our experiences and where is God in this?
- What are my doubts about God and how have they come about?

Chapter Three

■ And a vital question to at least ask is : Where am I in all of this?

When we and those around us have experienced a trauma then some of the above questions will arise. Many of the questions will require reconciliation in our minds, while other questions may remain, and yet new questions may bring additional learning. The questions may include:

■ Can we identify, even when there has been a traumatic event, that God's love still abounds?

■ Does the knowledge that God's love is sufficient to sustain us support us, or is it too difficult to comprehend?

■ Do we think that God owes us a response and a guarantee of success and achievement and a life of total comfort?

By asking such questions we can realise that belief in God is not about having a provision it is about eternity, therefore:

■ Can we identify God in the midst of all difficulties experienced?

■ Or do we want relief from the despair, and clarity before responding?

As we explore this we have to realise that difficulties will continue, and faith has always been about knowing the hope that resides within us, therefore :

■ Do we want our character developed and built to know God, or do we want healing of all that what we consider we have suffered and endured?

■ Are we at peace to know that not all healing will be complete in this life, and yet be prepared to demonstrate love, kindness, compassion, sensitivity etc to people?

Thus overall we have to be prepared and willing to discuss and explore areas that will cause distress and despair, and reveal a level of vulnerability that we have not known and which will be at times bewildering.

The reason for this is because faith is not faith until it is challenged and perseveres, and it only does so when we respond to what is severe because our response to death will not only be immediate but long-term, thus our response to God will also be long-term.

However the beauty of life is that God does understand that people need time in order to explore the emotions and thoughts as a result of trauma. This is because God knows that we are 'vulnerable' and we will most likely try everything to hide and minimise the vulnerability because this pain will test the belief and faith. For me I had to question the significance of this and what truth existed in my faith that would enable me to face that pain and trauma. If I tried to ignore the impact of the experience upon me it would be due to fear, because true faith is not affected by an experience; it is independent of my experience.

Thus the real question that I needed to ask was, how has my faith impacted upon the circumstance, others and me? This pain tested my relationship with God and others in terms of whether I was still be able to respond and be willing to continue to input into another's life, as well as receive from another person.

Thus for me, belief has been about engaging in the reality of the experiences that have been within me and around me. From this I've learned that there cannot be any engagement without openness to the vulnerability that exists, and there is no intimacy without submitting to one another through love.

This understanding of love for me has been about an awareness that loss will take place and hurt will arise. However, knowing that we love is a powerful demonstration that suffering does not have to control us.

To understand love, it is important to recognise that it cannot be separated from God, because God is love. Thus seeking to love is about knowing this is about seeking God. Yet we have to determine: What are we turning to God for? Is it to find a solution, resolution and comfort for our pain? Or is our search to learn to understand who God is, and as a result who we are and what we can actually do for others?

If the only focus is on pain, it will ultimately lead us to withdraw from God. Because to know God does not mean that pain will disappear; rather, it will most likely remain. Because to remain broken is not a limitation, rather it is true strength and courage to continue despite the circumstances endured.

As a result an additional challenge to our belief and faith in God is: what do we think about God's silence at the trauma that others and we experience? For there is no doubt that God's silence appears to compound the tragedy we endure and that at such time God again appears distant from us. At such a time it is easy to use our understanding of such silence as equating to justifying our doubts and inability to trust God.

For me this has meant looking at faith by asking more questions such as :

- In the midst of trauma and pain, where anger, hatred and inner rage are also present, does love surface and become manifest in what we do?
- Does this love stand up to testing against the doubts that we have about who God is?

When you look at your circumstances, do you see beyond what is around you? This 'searching, seeking and seeing' involves identifying that which will be positive as well as frightening. Yet it is that which causes us to be frightened which we try so hard to ignore. To face that which appears insurmountable is not an easy task to manage, especially when we also lack confidence, belief and trust in God and others.

It is no surprise that we rely upon developing and implementing a plan, because it provides us with some reassurance to respond to and attend to whatever the issue or difficulty is, and it also makes us feel a sense of control over an uncontrollable situation. This does not mean that having a strategy to bring about improvements for people's lives is wrong, rather we need to realise that when a traumatic event has taken place this would indicate that all sense of planning is not about exploration, rather about containment.

Again there is nothing wrong with seeking immediate containment, because we cannot always and immediately express the uncertainty we face. So how do we seek God with all our mind, heart and soul, when our mind, heart and soul is consumed with intense pain?

The answer for me reverts back to questioning what do I know, believe and understand about God. I know this belief, knowledge and understanding will always require review, challenge, analysis and further knowledge to believe and understand. This also requires the capacity to review how I relate to others and the influence and impact I have upon their lives, and recognising the influence and impact they have on my life.

Through doing this we can importantly look at how we actually perceive God and how we express our hurt, pain, agony and emotional torment. Such expression will include admitting to ourselves how it has affected our relationship with God and others. This is a way forward and a necessary one, otherwise there is a danger that we can easily ignore and minimise the difficulties that arise and not face reality, which is not a wise move, or we can become so consumed in our difficulties that we pay limited attention to anyone else.

Seeking to focus all our attention on restoration and resolution as the basis of then responding to others - eg 'I have to sort my own difficulties out before I can support another' - is not based upon reality but on insecurity and fear.

The reality is very simple: we won't be able to, because if we could we would have no insight into another person's pain and turmoil and no foresight into God's love and grace.

Chapter Three

Summary

Though the deaths of my brothers have been a traumatic experience, the trauma has not changed my belief, knowledge and understanding of who God is. Rather my belief has continued to develop, while being tested and explored. This is because my belief in God incorporates the belief in hope - the hope being that God loves and does care, and that His strength resides in us.

Thus for me, seeking God is about remaining connected to people through relationships that seek to enable development. Parts of our pain will remain, yet if we look deeper we will see the love, joy and affection God has implanted in us. This is more than capable of reaching out and above the despair we experience. Hence we need to learn who God is before we can recognise such capacity, and then come to an understanding of who we are.

Therefore overall we have to realise that our response reveals our mind, heart and soul. This means we must not ignore the present with all its issues and difficulties, while we must also not lose focus of the future and all that God has implemented. This is because doubt seeks to cause the most severe trauma to us, and to hinder us from seeking God. If doubt achieves that, then we cannot truly be there for each other, because doubt will have impacted upon our capacity to remain open to receive God's Love as well as express our Love to God and each other.

The hardest truth is to face that which challenges us in the midst of trauma, and that is: God is the greatest source of support we can give to each other, because with belief in who God is we can endure for each other, for God's love is living and active and is in our midst.

I would hope that when you explore your experience and your relationships, that you'll see the love residing within you which can enable you to respond.

APPENDICES:

FAMILY DEVELOPMENT SUPPORT STRUCTURE (FDSS)

As part of my role as a social worker, I had already began to research and explore issues on bereavement and trauma before Gurjit's and Parmjit's death. The reason for this was due to working with children and young people who had experienced various traumas in life.

Therefore in developing this support plan (like many who work in an arena of trauma) I was already exposed to working in difficult circumstances. This does not mean that I knew how to respond all the time to the various circumstances experienced. However I believe that by having some insights into loss enabled me to transfer this learning within my own family. Again this did not mean that everything would be fine, because it would have been unwise for me to have assumed that such guidance would resolve all the issues.

The following support plan was developed to enable us to explore the trauma of bereavement. The plan was never intended to resolve all the issues experienced, rather it was intended to guide us in exploring.

For my family and me, it took two to three years to begin to make sense of many of the issues contained within such documents. Furthermore we knew many parts would be revisited, especially for my young nieces and nephews.

Each document was adjusted for the adults, children and young people within my family. Even though what is presented appears more in tune with an adult audience, it can be translated appropriately when talking to children and young people by further reading around support work for them people as well as simply 'being there' for them. As an example, when we applied Document A, my nieces always explored to the extent they wanted to. They found the section on relationships the most positive, because it enabled them to express their deep love for their father and the deep pain they had experienced due to his death.

The fact that it took one year to get through the first document revealed that there were many areas to discuss. Yet this was a positive feature, because we knew we were not going to rush this and that we would explore issues not even contained within the documents.

With regards to a time-line, our discussions took place as follows:

In 2003:

- Weekly discussions with Dilly for six months and then fortnightly for a further six months. (Baljinder and Suki were involved in some joint support work with their mother).
- Fortnightly discussions with Baljinder and Suki for 12 months.
- Fortnightly discussions with Dee, Bal and Ami for 12 months.
- Family discussions monthly.

The first year was very important because it began to set the foundations from which further exploration could take place in the future. In 2004 I held:

- Monthly discussions with Dilly for six months.
- Monthly discussions with Dee for six months.
- Fortnightly discussions with Bal, Ami, Baljinder and Suki for six months, and then monthly discussions for six months.
- Family discussions monthly.

The second year was just as important, because we were able to look in further detail at the changes that had taken place and thus prepare to respond to this. We used some of the learning gained when exploring the effects of Parmjit's death.

In 2005 I held family discussions monthly for 6 months, and then bi-monthly for six months.

The third year was about looking at our overall learning about the loss we had experienced. The support plan was split into three specific sections:

1. Death (FDSS Document A)

This document focuses briefly on death in terms of mourning and grief, and the impact on our relationships. As a family it took one year (2003 to 2004) to get through this document as we looked at our feelings and the impact of death.

2. Grief (FDSS Document B)

This document focuses upon exploring grief in more detail by considering the potential issues that we are likely to experience and possible ways to develop our responses to others. As a family it took about one and a half years (between 2004 to 2006) to get through this document as we built upon our learning gained to further understand the effects of death and the impact upon our relationships.

3. Bereavement (FDSS Document C)

This document was intended to provide an overall exploration of our experiences so that we could look at what we had learned in detail and what areas we would have to still explore within the future. It was not looked at on this basis because it was meant for future exploration once we had truly examined the effects of death.

Thus the support plan may be applied where appropriate to your own experiences as you determine. My hope is that it will enable you in exploring your loss and your continual development, and reveal that a concerted effort can support us to respond to the traumas we experience.

FAMILY DEVELOPMENT
SUPPORT STRUCTURE

DOCUMENT A: DEATH

SECTION 1: DEATH

The factors that can cause us to experience difficulties with regard to getting over the death of Gurjit and Parmjit can be seen to be the same factors that can enable us to begin to acknowledge and come to terms with their death. The experience we had of being with them which was cemented by the love we demonstrated to them and them to us, which formed our relationship through intimacy.

There is no doubt that our loss will be hard to understand. However this can be made even more difficult through:

- not exploring their death;
- not exploring the relationship we had;
- not exploring our current relationships.

Therefore identifying that there will be a longing for interactions reinforces the pain, yet it is also such longing which reinforces the reality that death has taken place. Thus to experience our loss we will need to face the reality of the intense emotions and thoughts which will arise, such as:

- Anger
- Anxiety
- Disbelief

- Fear
- Guilt
- Numbness
- Regret
- Sadness
- Shock

It is no surprise that we may find it difficult to identify or understand our emotions and make sense of what has been experienced. The importance of being able to share such emotions and thoughts is to help each other face and attend to the pain caused.

Therefore support is required because some emotions and thoughts may appear so overwhelming that we think that to reveal them highlights instability, whereas in fact it reveals a pain which requires redress. Being prepared to listen to each other and hear the deepest fears, anxieties, doubts and sorrow, as well as the innermost desire for hope and restoration, is necessary in order to begin to learn to adapt and respond. Yet resolution cannot be explored until the pain is heard.

This means clear messages have to be given to each other for us to know, believe and understand that it is safe to express the harrowing thoughts caused by trauma, which in effect are an additional trauma to respond to. Without opportunities to talk we set each other up for future unresolved pain, which will surface at different times in different ways, and we will struggle to make sense of what is taking place.

SECTION 2: MOURNING

Death has meant a 'separation' from Gurjit and Parmjit. Therefore when we mourn we are recognising that there is no longer a physical relationship with them, even though our emotional relationship remains. Thus mourning enables us to commence experiencing the emotional pain of our loss. The following can assist us in looking at how we are mourning:

- What is our understanding of their death?
- Has this assisted us in understanding that their death is irreversible?
- What does the reality of such loss mean to us?
- How has this supported us in being able to mourn their death?
- What involvement have we had together in mourning their deaths?
- How are we focusing upon the relationships we had with them?
- Has the mourning process supported us in understanding each other's emotional distress and responses?

The above will raise immediate and intense emotions and thoughts associated with their deaths, because it reinforces the fact that separation has taken place. Two main emotions that generally arise are anger and guilt. We may feel angry because we feel guilt, so the anger being expressed can be seen as a way in which guilt is being questioned. The following questions may assist us in looking and thinking about anger and guilt:

- Do we believe that what we thought or did had an effect upon their deaths?
- What are we angry about with regard to their deaths?
- Are we afraid to express such anger?
- Is our anger related to our beliefs not materialising?
- How have we been able to express any anger related to their deaths?

- Do we feel any guilt about their deaths?
- Do we think that our anger and feelings of guilt reveal how much we loved and cared for them?

SECTION 3: GRIEF

Grief is the internal acknowledgement of the love we demonstrated to Gurjit and Parmjit. Thus the love can help us respond to the magnitude of our loss. This is not intended to sound simplistic. Rather, when reflecting upon the love given and received and the closeness of our relationships, grieving can be embraced as part of the demonstration of the love we have for them.

However, grieving can be hard to identify, understand and express, because it will consist of many tasks. The tasks are not about seeking an achievement, rather they are an acknowledgement that the hurt is deep. For grief is the tool that enables us to explore the painful emotions and thoughts we have experienced. Hence this will include determining the following:

- In what ways do we seek to respond to the reality of their deaths? Does this deal with the emotional pain?
- How do we acknowledge the expression of our loss?
- Are we prepared to acknowledge that expressing our pain will involve thoughts which may frighten us?

As a result of the above, grief will reveal the impact of death upon our emotions and thoughts, whereby fear and despair can be seen, but grief also raises awareness that determination and hope can also exist. Therefore it is important to recognise that expressing grief will take some time, as it requires truth to explore and hope to believe that emotions and thoughts and experiences due to death do not have to dictate and control our life. At the same time we must realise that it is important not to dismiss the emotions and thoughts in the hope that it will not impact upon us.

Thus grief is intended to move us to the acceptance of loss and identifying the need for adjustment to the loss. The readjustment can take place by asking questions such as:

- What strength have we gained from sharing our experiences of our relationship with Parmjit and Gurjit?
- What influence did they have upon our lives, and how has that supported us and helped us to begin to face the reality of their deaths?

SECTION 4: INTERPERSONAL RELATIONSHIPS

Exploring the relationship we had with Gurjit and Parmjit is necessary because it holds a central position of the grief process. There can be no progression without this. Thus the time undertaken in looking at this, painful as it will be, can certainly assist us in the overall adjustments that we will need to make. Such exploring can take place through various means, such as:

- Talking about the importance of the relationship to us and the experiences within the relationship.
- Talking about the impact the relationship had upon us.
- Talking about the impact of the loss of relationship.
- Writing about how we have began to review the relationship.
- Writing about how we have began to review the loss of relationship.

- Writing about how we have explored our current relationships, and our roles and responsibilities within those relationships.
- Responding to our own as well as other people's questions about the relationship and experience.
- Creative expressions e.g. drawing, writing a letter, poetry, writing a song.

Thus asking questions about our relationships can assist us in looking at our pain and support us in recognising that hope still exists when we explore:

- How did we show our love for Gurjit and Parmjit?
- How did they show their love for us?
- How would we describe the relationship we had with Gurjit and Parmjit?
- What were the strengths and limitations of the relationship?
- What did we value about them?
- What do you think they valued about us?
- How would we describe their character, personality, successes and limitations?
- How would they have described our character, personality, successes and limitations?
- What do we miss about them?
- What hurts in thinking and talking about them?
- What are we finding difficult to accept about our loss?
- Do we believe that they knew how much we loved them?
- Are we able to talk freely about our emotions and thoughts about them with each other and our friends?

DOCUMENT B: GRIEF

It can be seen that grief is based upon the principle of love, because we are grieving the loss of love. Thus if we ignore the grief we will have difficulty in understanding the love. As a result this can impact upon our capacity to respond to each other.

- Do we think we have withdrawn love from others, or has our love for them grown?
- Are we experiencing difficulties in expressing our love towards others?
- How does love enable us to respond to the loss experienced?

Thus grief involves the combination of:

- Reviewing the past;
- Managing the present;
- Considering the future.

If our response is an acknowledgement that we were frightened, then it is a good starting place, because it means we are grieving and not dismissing. Seeking to face the future (which appears to be distant), cannot be considered until the past has been reviewed. Only then can we truly begin to manage the present uncertainties.

Not engaging in the process of grief will only add to our emotional pain, and this will hold us back. There is no doubt that being alone or wanting to be left alone for some time to reflect is just as important to implement. However this has to be carefully observed, as invisibility needs to be monitored so that we do not hide from connecting with our current relationships.

Therefore it is no surprise that grief will take some time, because it deals with love and the intensity of relationship we had. To respond to the overwhelming emotions, the disbelief and the pain created, we need to explore this before parts of healing can commence:

- What emotions and thoughts do we have about Parmjit's and Gurjit's deaths?
- What do we believe and disbelieve about their deaths?
- Has the acknowledgement of loss resulted in us experiencing further emotional pain?
- How can this emotional pain resurface in our lives, and does this frighten us?
- In what ways do we think we are adapting to our experiences and circumstances?
- What do we think healing means?

When we look at the above it is important that we recognise the need to be patient to enable each other to express our grief through sharing, as well as challenging any unwillingness to explore reality and let go of grieving. Furthermore we also need to recognise that if we choose to reject the acceptance of loss and not to fully explore the experience of loss, it will impact upon our capacity to come to terms with our loss:

- In what ways do we think we have had difficulty in identifying and understanding our own responses to the loss?

- In what ways have we attempted to separate ourselves from our pain in order to respond to others?
- What do we think may be the difficulties if we think we can avoid exploring the pain caused?
- What do we think may be the difficulties if we focus purely on the pain caused?
- In what ways have we been able to express and understand our feelings and hence convey our emotional pain?
- In what ways do we believe we and others are still able to develop relationships and respond within these relationships?
- In what ways do we feel that others understand us? Likewise, how informed is our understanding of others?
- Is the loss of our relationship still difficult to fully accept? If not, what evidence do we rely upon to support our view? If so, how is this affecting our current relationships and development?
- Is our attitude about future relationships and development positive and realistic or fearful and uncertain?

Hence looking back after the first year, second year, third year and so on after Gurjit's and Parmjit's deaths will bring back emotions and thoughts which we will have explored. This should not be feared as thinking we have not looked at the effects of death. Rather it reveals that we may be more ready to look at such effects in further detail. Reviewing will require a willingness to face the emotional pain caused by such a void:

- Does such reflection reawaken painful emotions and thoughts for us?
- Does it confirm to us that we have begun to move towards adapting? If so, what has changed?

■ Are we able to talk freely about such reflection with each other and friends?

■ Are we able to think through the issues and difficulties by having hope of being able to meet the challenges that arise in life?

FAMILY DEVELOPMENT
SUPPORT STRUCTURE

DOCUMENT C: BEREAVEMENT

SECTION 1: LOSS

Phases of bereavement can consist of:

- Disbelief and shock, which can involve the refusal to accept the truth of what has happened.
- Exploring our emotions and thoughts, which can lead to the gradual realisation and acknowledgement of what has happened.
- Adaptation, which is the full acceptance of what has happened and acceptance of working through the pain of what has happened.

Looking at such phases reinforces the reality that bereavement has to be worked through by:

- Recognition of the irreversible effects and impact of death.
- Recognition that the disruptive effects do not always show themselves immediately.
- Recognition that the quality of relationships that exist can sustain attachment and consistency.
- Recognition that we have to accept each other's emotional pain.

Therefore bereavement will reveal:

- Our capacity to explore our pain.

- Our capacity to plan.
- Our capacity to build and develop relationships.
- Our awareness of how our relationship with Parmjit and Gurjit influenced our lives.

When we look at this, our emotions will need to be understood, because they can enable us to continue to understand that they play an important role in exploring the relationships we had. The following questions may assist us to again review our emotions and identify how through continual support we can express them safely:

- What emotions arise when we think about the significance of our loss?
- How do our emotions and thoughts of bereavement impact upon our behaviour now?
- What are the challenges we face in seeking to express our emotions and thoughts?
- What are the potential difficulties that could arise if we do not review our emotions and explore our experience?
- What can enable us to review our experiences, and conversely what would prevent us from exploring our experiences?
- Upon reflection, how would we assess our capacity in looking at the trauma experienced?

Remember that when emotions are expressed they do not come out in a neat package. Therefore relying upon the trust that exists in our current relationships should support us, as well as enable us to respond in love to each other.

Through looking at the above we can ask further questions to review how we are responding to our loss, as well as how we are responding to our relationships, such as:

- How can the memory of Gurjit and Parmjit be a strength in attending to our loss?
- How can this enable us to look at the grief of our loss and the grief of those around us, as well as the changes made?
- What have we learned from the bereavement experience?
- What strength have we found in responding to our experience of bereavement?
- What changes have taken place? What developments have been made in our relationships?

SECTION 2: NEEDS & DECISION-MAKING

Needs arise because they have always existed. Thus the impact of death upon needs will be present. Yet it takes time for the needs to actually materialise, because there is no longer a physical relationship with Parmjit and Gurjit. Therefore many needs may remain unmet and as a result may impact upon our emotions and thoughts. Such needs have to be identified to consider the significance they have for each of us.

The following questions may assist us in looking at how each other's needs are intertwined:

- What main needs were met when we were in a relationship with Gurjit and Parmjit before their deaths?
- What do we now consider to be our main needs? In what ways are these needs being met? In what ways are these needs not being met?
- In what ways have our experiences of loss left us with unmet needs?
- How do we respond to our own needs?
- How do we respond to the needs of others?

- Does unmet need make us withdraw from each other or does it cause us to explore relationships and seek support?
- How do we demonstrate our concerns to ensure each other's needs are not overlooked?

The demonstration of how our needs are met within relationships centres upon how decisions are made. Thus decision-making will not go away, as it is part of the whole process of grieving. The amount, nature and seriousness of decisions to be made will certainly influence our emotions and thoughts. The key of support is vital to enable us to make decisions, yet it is important not to rush into decisions which will have a long-lasting effect.

The recognition of this can assist us in knowing that a plan will be required, and the purpose of the plan is to consider as many of the options available to us as possible with regard to whatever the topic area is. Therefore the following questions may assist us in looking at our decision making:

- What decisions do we need to continue to make? Which of these decisions are short term and which long term? How are these decisions challenging us?
- What is the likely impact of the decisions to be made upon us all?
- When making decisions, how do we consider all options and implement a plan?
- In what ways are we managing the challenges of such decision making (ie What factors are enabling us to respond?)

SECTION 3: BELIEF SYSTEMS

There is no doubt that the question of our beliefs did arise when Gurjit's and Parmjit's death took place, for our beliefs influenced, motivated and impacted upon us all. Furthermore there is no doubt that death will seek to challenge our beliefs about our family, friends, social networks, ourselves, our loved ones, and God.

The following questions may assist us to continue to identify the strengths that remain within us and each other and hence reveal the source of our belief:.

What did we believe before Gurjit and Parmjit died about:

- each other?
- our friends?
- Gurjit and Parmjit?
- Ourselves?
- Death?
- God?

What do we now believe about the above?

- How do we think our beliefs have been tested and challenged?
- What concerns us about how our experiences have tested and challenged our beliefs and faith?
- What strengths do we think our beliefs have developed within us?

SECTION 4: ADAPTATION, RESILIENCE & REFLECTION

Adaptation will involve having to contend with the experience of emotional pain that has been caused through death. It means caring about the loss experienced and not avoiding the emotions and thoughts it raises. Without the exploration we will need to seriously question whether we are truly able to plan ahead, if we have not looked at the painful emotional and psychological effects upon us.

Thus adapting to this intense experience requires awareness that healing can take place. The healing with regard to adaptation does not necessarily mean a total restoration, because that would be unrealistic. Rather the healing is about:

- developing an understanding of the pain of loss and the difficulties caused through such loss.
- developing an understanding of each other's needs.
- developing an understanding that the love that we had for Gurjit and Parmjit will never change in spite of the irreversible separation.
- developing an understanding that the love that we have for each other can continue to grow.

Are we acknowledging the emotions and thoughts we have due to our experiences? If yes, what is the evidence to support our view of such exploration? If no, what do we think are the blocks preventing us from coming to terms with the reality of our loss and experiences?

Upon looking at the issue of adaptation, it takes place through the development of resilience. Hence resilience is a combination of many factors, such as family support, belief systems etc, that have been built up over time to respond to the many traumas that impact upon us.

When death has taken place, upon review it seems somewhat vain and futile to even consider what our strengths are. Yet it is such resilience within us and around us that will enable us to appreciate how we have contributed to each other's life and development.

Questions to explore with regard to our resilience include:

- What factors do we think exist within us and around us that are contributing to our resilience to explore death and our relationships?

■ In what ways can we continue to develop this resilience?

Thus when we seek to adapt and develop our resilience in order to respond we will always need to understand the importance of reflection. For reflection will be about re-questioning what we have explored with regard to:

■ our experiences;
■ our relationships;
■ our responses to death;
■ our current development.

The following questions can enable us to look at how we do reflect upon our experiences:

■ What has such exploration taught us about each other?
■ In what ways do we think we can respond in the present and in the future with the trauma that has taken place?

www.ingramcontent.com/pod-product-compliance
Lightning Source LLC
Chambersburg PA
CBHW062157270326
41930CB00009B/1566